PRAISE FOR
CUSTOMER SHARE
MARKETING

"Careful! This is powerful stuff. Hands on, practical, honest, and rational—exactly what you need to push your marketing program forward. Tom Osenton just bulldozed the profession (if you can call it that!) several years forward."

Seth Godin, *author of* Survival Is Not Enough *and* Permission Marketing

"Here at last, a practical guide for tapping into the marketing power and intimacy of the Web. Osenton shows us how to create highly profitable, enduring online customer relationships ... today, not five years from now!"

Chuck Fruit, *Vice President & Marketing Chief of Staff,*
The Coca-Cola Company

"Invaluable insight into utilizing the Web to grow profitability. Osenton's book is one of the few that mixes theory, with a strong does of reality, to give an outcome of real-world practical applications. An innovative, thought-provoking read for any industry."

Jeff Rotsch, *President, Sales, General Mills*

"With this book, Tom Osenton shifts the entire marketing paradigm and ushers in a revolutionary new era. This book defines the future of marketing and will change our key beliefs and foundations. *Customer Share Marketing* forces us to re-think how we manage our brands and businesses. The book describes a system for corporate growth across one's entire brand portfolio."

Bruce Miller, President, Market Data Corporation

"The Internet is here to stay and will be one of the most remarkable devices for marketers of every type of product in the world. Tom Osenton knows more about marketing and the Internet than anyone I know. When he puts the two worlds together in this book, the information and advice is priceless."

Bob Dowling, President & Editor-In-Chief, The Hollywood Reporter

"Today's customer cannot be taken for granted. Focused, constant, personal, and relevant marketing messages are a must to maintain their loyalty. All of us need to be smarter and use the new technology tools to achieve our objectives. This book stimulates new thinking."

Tony Ponturo, Vice President, Corporate Media & Sports Marketing, Anheuser-Busch, Inc.

"This book is about nothing less than the next giant step in marketing theory and practice. Osenton's mix of context, vision, actionable strategies, and proven tactics is dead on."

Tom Stein, President, Stein Rogan + Partners

"Osenton's book is practical advice for marketers who embrace a broader view than the old model of 'we advertise, the customer buys.' The new world requires understanding of multiple disciplines which work in harmony."

Richard Edelman, President & CEO, Edelman Public Relations Worldwide

"Customer Share Marketing is a concept whose time has come and one that was lost on so many Internet entrepreneurs in the late '90s. Osenton has identified and articulated the next important marketing discipline for successful 21st century businesses."

Ken Magill, Editor, iMarketing News

CUSTOMER SHARE MARKETING

ISBN 0-13-067167-3

90000

9 780130 671677

FINANCIAL TIMES PRENTICE HALL BOOKS

For more information, please go to www.ft-ph.com

Deirdre Breakenridge
Cyberbranding: Brand Building in the Digital Economy

William C. Byham, Audrey B. Smith, and Matthew J. Paese
Grow Your Own Leaders: How to Identify, Develop, and Retain Leadership Talent

Jonathan Cagan and Craig M. Vogel
Creating Breakthrough Products: Innovation from Product Planning to Program Approval

Subir Chowdhury
The Talent Era: Achieving a High Return on Talent

Sherry Cooper
Ride the Wave: Taking Control in a Turbulent Financial Age

James W. Cortada
21st Century Business: Managing and Working in the New Digital Economy

James W. Cortada
Making the Information Society: Experience, Consequences, and Possibilities

Aswath Damodaran
The Dark Side of Valuation: Valuing Old Tech, New Tech, and New Economy Companies

Sarvanan Devaraj and Rajiv Kohli
The IT Payoff: Measuring the Business Value of Information Technology Investments

Jaime Ellertson and Charles W. Ogilvie
Frontiers of Financial Services: Turning Customer Interactions Into Profits

Nicholas D. Evans
Business Agility: Strategies for Gaining Competitive Advantage through Mobile Business Solutions

FINANCIAL TIMES

Prentice Hall

In an increasingly competitive world, it is quality
of thinking that gives an edge—an idea that opens new
doors, a technique that solves a problem, or an insight
that simply helps make sense of it all.

We work with leading authors in the various arenas
of business and finance to bring cutting-edge thinking
and best learning practice to a global market.

It is our goal to create world-class print publications
and electronic products that give readers
knowledge and understanding which can then be
applied, whether studying or at work.

To find out more about our business
products, you can visit us at www.ft-ph.com

Pearson
Education

CUSTOMER SHARE MARKETING

HOW THE WORLD'S GREAT MARKETERS UNLOCK PROFITS FROM CUSTOMER LOYALTY

Tom Osenton

FINANCIAL TIMES
Prentice Hall

An Imprint of PEARSON EDUCATION
London • New York • San Francisco • Toronto • Sydney
Tokyo • Singapore • Hong Kong • Cape Town • Madrid •
Paris • Milan • Munich • Amsterdam

Library of Congress Cataloging-in-Publication Data

A CIP catalog record for this book can be obtained from the Library of Congress.

Editorial/Production Supervision: *Joan L. McNamara*
Compositor: *Pine Tree Composition*
Acquisitions Editor: *Tim Moore*
Editorial Assistant: *Allyson Kloss*
Marketing Manager: *Bryan Gambrel*
Buyer: *Maura Zaldivar*
Cover Designer: *Talar Agasyan-Boorujy*
Cover Design Director: *Jerry Votta*
Interior Designer: *Gail Cocker-Bogusz*
Project Coordinator: *Anne R. Garcia*

© 2002 by Prentice Hall PTR
Prentice-Hall, Inc.
Upper Saddle River, New Jersey 07458

Customer Share Marketing is a trademark of the Customer Share Group LLC.

Prentice Hall books are widely used by corporations and government agencies for training, marketing, and resale.

The publisher offers discounts on this book when ordered in bulk quantities. For more information, contact:
Corporate Sales Department
Prentice Hall PTR
One Lake Street
Upper Saddle River, NJ 07458
Phone: 800-382-3419; Fax: 201-236-7141; Email (Internet): corpsales@prenhall.com

All product names mentioned herein are the trademarks of their respective owners.

Printed in the United States of America
10 9 8 7 6 5 4 3 2 1

ISBN: 0-13-067167-3

Pearson Education LTD.
Pearson Education Australia PTY, Limited
Pearson Education Singapore, Pte. Ltd
Pearson Education North Asia Ltd
Pearson Education Canada, Ltd.
Pearson Educación de Mexico, S.A. de C.V.
Pearson Education—Japan
Pearson Education Malaysia, Pte. Ltd

To Mary-Ellen, Curran, and Matt—my family.

CONTENTS

ACKNOWLEDGMENTS

There are so many people who had a hand in making this book possible, but there are a special few whom I would like to thank here.

My greatest thanks of all to my wife Mary-Ellen, who read every word of this book as I wrote it. Thank you for putting up with that, and with me. Thank you also for believing that I can do anything and for being my greatest champion in this life.

To my daughter Curran, who indulged me in conversation on the way to the kitchen about the impact that the Web will have on all of us. *Merci beaucoup, cher Curran. Je suis si fier que vous soyez ma fille.* To my son Matt, who often serenaded me, as I wrote, with *Mozart's Sonata in A Major*. Thanks for inspiring me, Matt.

To Tim Moore, my acquisitions editor at *Financial Times/Prentice Hall,* for seeing something worthwhile in my original book proposal and for helping me create a much better book than the one I proposed.

To my agent Dianne Littwin, who had faith early on and helped transfer that faith to the best possible publisher for this book.

To Russ Hall, who helped me every step of the way with encouragement and professional advice out of the Lone Star state. To Stephen Mendonca for his honesty and insights, and to Michelle Darraugh for helping me greatly sharpen the focus of the book.

Endless thanks to my business partner Susan Duncan, whose outstanding feedback helped make for a much better book. To my other business partner, Bruce Miller, who continuously delights and amazes me.

I've been extremely fortunate to have two mentors in my life. Don Murray, the Pulitzer-Prize winning writer, was my first mentor at the University of New Hampshire. At 76, Don is still going strong and has several books in the works, as well as his enormously popular column in the *Boston Globe*. To Don I will be eternally grateful for helping me learn the craft. *Nulla dies sine linea.*

My second mentor is Bob Dowling, the president and editor-in-chief of *The Hollywood Reporter*. Bob is a true publishing visionary and sees things that most others don't or can't. He taught me everything I know about publishing and most of what I know about marketing. To Bob, my most sincere thanks for sharing your wisdom with me.

To Billy Perkins for lending his professional expertise in marketing and advertising to provide big-picture insights. To *PriceWaterhouseCoopers'* Tim Ryan for connecting the dots and supporting the vision. Sincere thanks to the *Tuesday Group*—the Boston-based *Think Tank*—the best group of advisors and friends any author could ever have.

To Hank Close, vice president of sales & marketing at *Comedy Central*—Hank is one of the few people who would listen to me from the very beginning, even if I didn't make any sense. To my favorite newspaper/magazine editor in the world, John Rawlings of *The Sporting News,* who taught me everything that I know about hockey. To Tom Stein, president of Stein Rogan + Partners, one of the most brilliant and creative new economy marketers out there, for always helping to condense my stream of consciousness ramblings into consumable and coherent bites. To Jackie Thomas, director of the Class of '45 Library at *Phillips Exeter Academy*, and Tad Nishimura for their great support. To Paul Belliveau for all of his important help. Thanks also to Kela Kexel for her help from Mad City, and to Michael Dowling for his insights from Tinseltown.

I would be remiss if I didn't acknowledge our family dog Dakota, who sat beside my chair and kept me company while I wrote at 4:30 a.m.

Finally, my sincere thanks to Allyson Kloss, Tim Moore's assistant at *FT/PH*, who helped generate a replacement advance check for this book after the first one flew out the window of my car on the way to the bank. It's now somewhere on I-95 between Portsmouth, New Hampshire, and Boston.

S. D. G.

FOREWORD

WARNING! This book could radically change the way you do business! This is not about the next marketing buzzword, (though it could create some buzz) or some software that promises to deepen customer relationships. It's about common-sense marketing principles that work. Tom Osenton gives us a new set of marketing principles that, if executed properly and with a long-term commitment, can help any company capture more of its customers' business and keep those customers for life.

The concept of customer share marketing can help any company that runs up against a market share wall. We've applied many of these same marketing principles for many years at Wells Fargo to help us achieve our vision of satisfying customers' financial needs and helping them succeed financially.

At Wells Fargo, we believe our single biggest market share growth opportunity is right in front of our own eyes: our own 21 million customers. Every day, on average, they give three-fourths of their business to our competitors. Every day they're just waiting for us to listen to their needs, ask them the right questions, and offer them the products and services they need to save time and money. We still have a long way to go. Ninety-five percent of them buy insurance from our competitors. Eighty-six percent of our customers who have a mortgage have it with our competitors. Ninety-five percent of our banking customers have no brokerage relationship with us.

Several years ago we asked ourselves a critical question: *What industry are we in?* We started out as a bank 150 years ago, but banking as a stand-alone industry now is dead. It has become a part of an industry that is *seven times larger than banking* and growing much faster: the financial services industry. We believe it's the largest, fastest growing, most fragmented industry in the world.

The traditional measure of a bank's market share—deposits—now is archaic. Deposit-taking is a stagnant business. Our market share of banking deposits in some of our states is as high as 30 percent—but our share of total household financial assets in those states is as low as 3 percent. Deposit-taking is a pond. Financial services is the Pacific Ocean. Where would you rather fish? That's where our market share growth opportunity is. The average American household has about 15 financial services products. The average Wells Fargo banking household or commercial customer has only about four products with us. By redefining the industry we're competing in, Wells Fargo intuitively has been practicing what Tom clearly articulates in this book.

The concept of customer share marketing is simple: We all have loyal customers who can buy more from us if we give them relevant and compelling reasons to do so. This type of sales and marketing focus makes so much sense, yet many companies spend millions trying to buy more new customers—just for the sake of getting bigger. Why do we spend so little time *retaining* and *growing* business from loyal customers who said *yes* to us a long time ago?

Keeping customers gets lip service from many companies. But, as Tom points out, the clock is ticking if you don't move now to earn more of your customers' business. If you don't, your competitors will. Losing a customer's revenue or assets, and trying to replace that customer through expensive acquisition efforts can be a significant obstacle to increasing profits. At Wells Fargo, it costs us *five times* as much to *acquire* one new customer as it does to *retain* one. By focusing on needs-based selling and service quality improvements, we've been able to reduce the percent of customers we're losing every year from 20 percent down to about 15 percent. If we were able to retain half the customers we lose each year, we'd increase our net income by at least 10 percent. There are also efficiencies associated with customer share marketing—every two percent of customers that we retain would be equal to cutting costs by 10 percent.

Retaining customers is just the first step of customer share marketing. The second step is earning more business from loyal customers. Another one of our objectives is to grow revenue each and every year at a double-digit rate. To do that, we believe we must sell *one more product to every customer every year,* and the more products they buy, the better the deal they should get. For example, when a customer buys a mortgage from us, they should also buy title insurance, a home equity line, a checking account, a savings account, a credit card, and a debit card. Right now only 21 percent of our customers have a credit card with us.

If we can sell our customers eight financial services products that can save them time and money, we will certainly be the first financial services company to grow market share by growing customer share. Growth by growing customer share is a priority focus for us at Wells Fargo, and it is the forward-thinking strategy that Tom articulates.

We focus not so much on selling products, but more on our customers' needs. Our job is not to sell mortgages. It is to help our customers buy homes. Our job is not to sell mutual funds or annuities or 401(k) plans. It is to help our customers save for retirement, pay for their children's college education, or start a new business.

When we help a customer get a mortgage to buy a home, our mortgage company pays for the cost of collecting a very comprehensive financial snapshot of that customer. The rest of our enterprise uses that customer intelligence to help serve the customer better and cross-sell more products. This deepens the relationship and bond we already have with our customers, and it means more of our customers will think of us when they want to buy their next financial product.

The Web certainly plays a vital role in our customer share marketing strategy. *Wellsfargo.com* is our fastest growing sales channel and allows our customers to save time and money by managing all their financial services from one single location on the Web.

The Web is also an important outbound marketing tool for us and allows us to communicate one-to-one with millions of customers. We use the technology not only to capture key customer intelligence, but also to personalize our one-to-one marketing efforts. We can predict the types of products our customers are most likely to buy, based on transaction history, as well as their preference for using our stores, ATMs, phone banks, or *wellsfargo.com*.

The battle for market share continues. Smart companies will make market share gains in a more intimate way, based largely on the private, one-to-one conversations that they have with their loyal customers.

I believe the principles in this book can be practiced by successful businesses worldwide, especially those businesses that have worked long and hard to acquire customers, build brands, and grow a business. These are the businesses that are sitting on an untapped company asset—customer loyalty.

Now, the challenge is to mine the asset.

Dick Kovacevich
Chairman & CEO
Wells Fargo & Company

INTRODUCTION

Every Saturday morning, I fill up the family car with gas at the local *Mobil* station. The routine is generally the same, week in and week out, and usually costs anywhere from $23 to $27, depending on the price of gas and exactly how much of it we've consumed over the past week. *Lift the handle, select the grade, reset to $00.00, fill the tank, and pay the attendant.* A week later, I'm back at the pump: *lifting the handle, selecting the grade, resetting to $00.00, filling the tank, and paying the attendant.* At this point, I could perform the task in my sleep, consistently contributing, on average, about $25 per week to the station's business.

Until one Saturday, while I was paying the attendant for gas, I also bought a dozen donuts and a cup of coffee. It was the first time that I ever spent more than $30 during one visit to the *Mobil* and it caused me to realize something about gas—that it was basically like toothpaste or shampoo. I realized that no matter what the folks at *Mobil* did to entice me to buy more gas, I would only buy more when I ran out.

I also realized something about the business of selling gas—it's all about *market share*. It's about selling gas to more people as opposed to selling more gas to the same people. In marketing terms, growth for a gas station is all about acquiring new customers.

As for the returning loyal customers—like me—the only way to generate more money from *retained customers* is to sell them something else along with the gas—like donuts and coffee. Unlike an acquisition strategy that primarily relies on new customers to grow *market share*, a retention strategy gives marketers the opportunity to grow *customer share* by selling more to the customers they already have.

MARKET SHARE MARKETING: THE ART OF ACQUIRING CUSTOMERS

Over the last half-century, the leading marketers, advertisers, and agencies in the United States perfected the art of acquiring customers and growing *market share*. In fact, it's very unlikely that we will ever witness such a run on customer acquisition as we did during the decades immediately following World War II, when consumers began to establish brand preference across dozens of products. It's difficult to imagine any group of marketers better at developing and successfully executing wholesale customer acquisition strategies since 1950 than U.S. marketers and their agencies.

But with market share levels largely established, it has become very difficult and very expensive for marketers to grow sales by growing market share.

Ask most nationally branded packaged goods manufacturers today who buys their soap or their beer, and they'll tell you 29- to 49-year-old women or 21- to 49-year old men. On the other hand, ask *L.L. Bean* who buys its outdoor gear, and the company produces a printout of the names and addresses of individual customers, along with their purchasing histories, that would fill a room. Direct marketers such as *L.L. Bean* have always known who their customers were—literally and figuratively. For mass marketers that primarily promote to enormous groups of people based largely on demographics, a list of consumers who buy their products once, twice, or two dozen times a year, for the most part, simply doesn't exist.

So why should this be important to mass marketers now?

HITTING THE MARKET SHARE WALL

After a company has sold to virtually every man, woman, and child on the planet, how does it profitably grow sales? When a company with an established and loyal customer base is unable to grow by adding new customers, that company has "hit the market share wall." Look at *Procter & Gamble,* for example: an enormously successful company that was launched by two immigrants in 1837 when the population of the United States was less than 16 million.

Now, more than 160 years later, *P & G* proudly boasts in its 2000 Annual Report that it successfully *markets more than 300 products to more than 5 billion consumers in 140 countries.* Think of that—five *billion* consumers. If the world's population is 6 billion and the remaining 1 billion are either too young, or too poor, or have no access to *P & G* products, how do companies such as *P & G* proactively impact sales growth? Significant growth for such companies, more often than not, has come from acquiring competitors, launching line extensions to existing brands, or making the case to consumers, through costly advertising and promotion, to switch brands.

But now the Web enables a new and powerful fourth alternative: a three-pronged strategy that (1) uses the power of mass marketing to both sell products and acquire permission to communicate with prospects and customers directly by future email, (2) uses email to create one-to-one permission-granted, relationship-enhancing conversations with existing loyal customers, and (3) uses the Web as a sales facilitator at the center of promotions that encourage and drive repeat sales online or offline.

CUSTOMER SHARE MARKETING: GETTING MORE FROM EXISTING CUSTOMERS

Though it is difficult to measure, the value of brand loyalty as a *P & G* asset across its stable of products worldwide is significant and powerful. Consider the impact on company sales if *P & G* more aggressively employed cross-selling strategies to leverage the loyalty that a customer has for one *P & G* product to buy another.

There is a significant amount of stored brand equity associated with the products and services of thousands of companies. That stored brand equity, or brand loyalty, can be leveraged to help sell customers more of the same product or more products within a family of brands. For example, offering combination discounts on compatible *P & G* household care products, such as *Bounty* paper towels, *Mr. Clean* multipurpose cleaner, or *Cascade* dishwashing detergent, with multiple purchases of *Joy* dishwashing liquid could move the sales needle for a host of *P & G* brands.

In many ways, *P & G* is like the local gas station. It markets and sells *fixed consumption products* such as laundry detergent—products that are typically purchased only when the consumer runs out. Selling more *Tide* to consumers who already have a box is difficult at best. But create a customer loyalty program that rewards loyal *Tide* users with the opportunity to receive electronically delivered coupons with discounts on *Downy Fabric Softener* or a package of *Pringles*—both *P & G* brands—and you have the makings of a customer share marketing program that proactively markets more of what a company has to sell on a one-to-one basis.

MASS MARKETING AND DIRECT MARKETING

This book is not about mass marketing *or* direct marketing. It's about mass marketing *and* direct marketing working together to sell more to existing customers. It is also about how the Web makes it possible, practical, and profitable to do both. Historically, we have treated these important and disparate marketing initiatives as mutually exclusive activities, with *mass marketing* ad man David Ogilvy on one end of Madison Avenue and *direct marketing* guru Lester Wunderman on the other.

But the Web is beginning to change that as more and more established brands are realizing that the interactive nature of the Web can be an effective and affordable means of enhancing customer relationships as well as growing customer share.

BEST PRACTICES FROM THE WORLD'S LEADING MARKETERS

The marketing principles discussed in this book can be applied to the marketing initiatives at companies of all shapes and sizes—both B2C and B2B. It doesn't matter what you're selling or to whom or how many customers you have. Whether you're a company with 50 customers or 5,000,000, the objectives are the same—*to generate increased sales and profits.*

You'll be able to learn how the world's leading marketers, such as *Frito-Lay, Coca-Cola,* and *Johnson & Johnson* are applying customer share marketing strategies to generate more sales from loyal customers. *Best practice* examples are presented in two separate chapters:

Chapter 11, *"Acquiring Customers and Permission,"* is a collection of *best practice* acquisition examples from leading marketers such as *American Express, Frito-Lay, and BMW,* which detail how companies such as these are using the Web to acquire both sales *and* permission for the purpose of building an inhouse permission-granted database of prospects and customers.

Chapter 13, *"Retaining Customers and Growing Customer Share,"* is a collection of *best practice* retention and customer share growth examples from companies such as *Campbell Soup, Kellogg's,* and the *Coca-Cola Company,* which illustrate the effective use of the permission-granted list to convert prospects to customers, customers to repeat customers, and repeat customers to loyal customers for life. You will learn how companies are using customer *share marketing* strategies to increase the amount of business from the loyal customers they have invested millions to acquire.

Best practice examples are presented as formatted mini-case studies that cover a breadth of marketing disciplines—from online and offline advertising to acquisition email marketing to customer promotions—and make it easy to understand the elements, strategy, and in many cases, the results of the effort.

There are also a few important words and phrases that are used frequently throughout the book and require a clear definition to avoid confusion:

Prospects and *Customers*: *Prospects* are defined as potential customers. Until they actually purchase something, they remain *prospects*. *Customers* are the folks who have purchased something from you—trading their money for your product. This may seem obvious, but many people categorize prospects that sign up for promotions or enewsletters as customers. For our purposes, they are not.

Opt-in and *Permission:* There is considerable debate over what is permission and what is not, and whether opt-in is the same as permission. For our purposes, *opt-in* names represent a list of prospects that are rented from a third-party broker. Even though permission may have been granted to a third-party, the names in your permission-granted database should be names of either prospects or customers who have granted permission directly to you, not through a third party. If permission is not granted directly to the marketer, then the name is neither permission-granted nor owned by the marketer. Third-party opt-in names can be a very valuable source of pre-qualified leads, but until those leads say yes to you, they are considered opt-in names.

GETTING SERIOUS

One hundred years from now, when the book that chronicles 21st century marketing strategies is written, it will no doubt describe the work of marketers who were successful at practicing both market share *and* customer share strategies as part of a truly integrated marketing strategy. The book will also show how mass marketers made the shift to embracing direct marketing as an important complementary initiative in order to successfully manage 21st century customer relationships.

This shift is rapidly gaining momentum as marketers of all sizes are getting serious about how they can best use the Web and email to more effectively manage their best customers. The innovators have already begun to make use of the Web to more effectively manage and grow their customer relationships. Regardless of whether you are a Web marketing innovator or just starting to integrate the power of the Web into your marketing plans, this book is designed to help you keep moving forward—maximizing the Web as a tool to unlock profits from loyal customers you already have.

I

THE BATTLE FOR MARKET SHARE

As the end of the 20th century approached, many of the companies that owed their existence to mass marketing were, for the first time, questioning its effectiveness. With scores of industries maturing and market share levels stabilizing, the issue of future organic growth was a real one for many companies. To complicate matters even further, the World Wide Web appeared in the mid-1990s with enormous promise for all businesses, but with little to show for it by century's end.

As the new century dawned, the ongoing battle for slivers of the market share pie continued. The challenges facing marketers worldwide became clear: how to generate profitable growth from ongoing operations and whether or not the Web would play a role in making that happen.

CHAPTER 1

THE WEB WEIGHS IN

In many ways, the Web is really a modern-day miracle. It was not created for commercial use. It is not owned by anyone and can't be acquired by anyone. It has no board of directors and is not traded on the NASDAQ. It reports to no one, is neither Democrat nor Republican, and has no zip code. But there is little debate as to whether or not this network of computers and servers that circles the globe will profoundly impact every business on the planet. It's just a matter of how and when, and whether or not a company takes control of its Web destiny and proactively uses the Web as a marketing weapon or if it reactively follows the pack because it feels it has to.

The Web has to be the most democratic medium of all time. Any person on the planet with a computer, talent, and training can be a programmer, a producer, a director, a writer, or an artist. The Internet was birthed as a communication channel—a kind of online emergency broadcast system. For years, groups of dedicated men and women labored to engineer it, breathe life into it, and provide the momentum necessary to perpetuate it. From the perspective of the worlds outside of Palo Alto and Cambridge, the Web pretty much appeared out of nowhere, delivered to the front doors of marketers and consumers with no strings attached.

The Web was really a wonderful gift to all of us, consumers and marketers alike. If you don't think so, ask any major book publisher what effect the Web had on its sales for the last five years of the 20th century. More than a few publishing house bonuses were earned because the Web appeared, and innovators outside of the book industry figured out how to use it to sell more books.

Now, the rest of the human race has to figure out what to do with the Web. Intuitively, marketers realize that the Web holds a greater upside potential for their business. But that path is often not a simple one, especially since most of the first 5 or 6 years of the Web's existence was focused on e-commerce—enabling transactions online. That certainly works if you're Land's End or Nordstrom. But if you're Coca-Cola or Kellogg, it's still about brick-and-mortar sales and motivating consumers to make more trips to Safeway to buy soft drinks and cereal.

For the overwhelming majority of businesses worldwide, the bottom line is *still* this: How can the Web help me sell shoes, insurance, music, soda pop, cars, potato chips, movies, gum, hotel rooms, entertainment, clothes, news, weather, sports, religion, politics, or food?

A NEW CHANNEL, A NEW DYNAMIC

Unlike existing channels at the time of its birth, the Web allowed the user greater control of the interaction and more input on determining where to go and when to go there. This interactive dynamic was not at all like television, which was designed to do something *to* the user, such as inform or entertain them. The Web, on the other hand, doesn't do anything *to* or *for* the user until the user does something to it.

With the Web, users inform or entertain themselves. No one watches the Web—not yet anyway. The Web is a medium that requires the user to interact with it, such as *surf, search,* and *download*—all action verbs. Consumers take online communication personally and have little patience with blatant, company-centric attempts at commercialism.

Though they have grown accustomed to being bombarded with commercial messages through other media on a daily basis, consumers view one-to-one messages that are addressed to them and delivered inside of the home to their email inbox as invasive unless requested by them. This dynamic requires marketers to completely rethink the manner in which they communicate with consumers, especially in the online environment.

MR. WATSON, YOU'VE GOT MAIL!

Table 1.1 chronicles the history of communication, the medium used to communicate, and if the communication is one-way or two-way.

Incredibly, the Web is the first two-way communication and sales channel since the invention of the telephone by Alexander Graham Bell in 1876. Over the last 125+ years, we've seen the invention of radio (1895) and television (1939), not to mention the explosion of thousands of popular magazines and newspapers—all huge boons to the growth of U.S. economy.

But the Web is a rare breed, with an interactive element that allows for both one-to-one and mass communication in one medium. As marketers began to flock to the Web like prospectors looking to stake a claim, it wasn't the one-to-one communication capability that first interested them. The overwhelming number of marketers spent the entire 20th century communicating to customers primarily through mass

TABLE 1.1 One-Way, Two-Way, Mass, or Direct Marketing

Channel	Introduced	1-Way or 2-Way Communication	1-to-1 or 1-to Many Communication	Direct or Mass Communication
Letters	500 BC	2-way	1-to-1	Direct
Books	1453 AD	1-way	1-to-many	Mass
Newspapers	1689 AD	1-way	1-to-many	Mass
Magazines	1741 AD	1-way	1-to-many	Mass
Telegraph	1861 AD	2-way	1-to-1	Direct
Telephone	1876 AD	2-way	1-to-1	Direct
Radio	1894 AD	1-way	1-to-many	Mass
Television	1939 AD	1-way	1-to-many	Mass
Web/email	1994 AD	1-way	1-to-many	Mass
		2-way	1-to-1	Direct

© 2001 Customer Share Group LLC

marketing vehicles. So naturally, marketers first gravitated to the Web to market as they had always marketed—sending *one* broad message *to many* consumers, as opposed to sending *many* specific messages directly to *one* consumer at a time.

A NEEDLE IN A WEB FULL OF HAYSTACKS

After the Web began to gain visibility in 1994, the existing offline interruption-advertising model began to make a move over to the Web. Print ads became banner ads, and technology enabled sound and motion as well as the dynamic of interactivity to advertising online. However, advertising on the Web was sadly overestimated in terms of both volume and effectiveness.

The Web is a very different medium than either print or broadcast television or radio. It's a very personal tool for consumers, whose use is most often triggered by a personal need or desire to answer a question, solve a problem, or communicate in two directions—to find and purchase a favorite pair of wool socks or to read and send email. To this extent, the dynamic of Web use—at least at this point in the channel's technological adolescence—much more resembles the utility of the Yellow Pages as a source of data and as a solution-provider for consumer-specific problems or needs, such as researching a movie fact or planning the family vacation.

The dynamics of the Web have greatly shifted the control of the medium to the user, and this creates a real challenge for marketers. Seth Godin, best-selling author of *Permission Marketing,* introduced the concept of asking for permission before sending a commercial message to someone. This concept has, for the most part, not been practiced in the offline world of traditional advertising. The notion of asking people for permission to send them commercial messages about mascara or mufflers is not something that Madison Avenue has historically done. Commercial messages have been broadcast like an SOS in a tropical storm with the hope that someone will hear it and act on it.

Selling by yelling was the preferred method of generating sales in the 20th century. But as Generation Y ages and become more independent consumers, it's unlikely that they will simply follow previous generations into the predictable crosshairs of advertisers that have products to sell by age, gender and income. Where will the generation of consumers born between 1980 and 1999 be congregating a decade from now? How will the generation that has never known a world without the Web and email be informed and entertained when they become mainstream consumers?

The marketing landscape has already greatly changed. The Web allows so many people access to so much, it creates a very new and very real challenge for marketers everywhere. It's frankly harder to sell to an informed consumer. There's no doubt that marketers will continue to generate their *sender-perspective* advertising messages. But because the Web is a two-way medium, there are dozens of ways for consumers to learn about the products and services marketers have to sell.

Beyond a marketer's own hype, consumers are increasingly relying on other consumers for detailed information through public postings and chat rooms where they can ask questions and receive unbiased reviews from actual users of products they might be thinking of buying.

Though the dust has settled from the dotcom debacle in the late 1990s, there was a time when the excitement and promise of the channel reigned and caused a great deal of confusion around the Web's purpose as well as its relevant and sensible business applications.

WEBMANIA

I was once recruited for the CEO spot at a Web startup at the height of the dotcom frenzy in 1999. The company was well funded, had been in business for over 2 years, had a staff of over 50 people, incredibly posh office space, and absolutely no revenue—no ads, no subs, no fees, no e-commerce, no income. Period.

When I spoke with one of the founders about the opportunity, I asked him, "What are your revenue streams?"

He looked at me and chuckled and said: "That's why we're looking for a CEO."

Here was a company that had already raised tens of millions of dollars from venture capitalists, but didn't have a clue as to how dollar one would be raised from either consumers or advertisers. I knew at that moment that the Web was like a drug, intoxicating business people into thinking that the rules simply didn't matter, or at least didn't apply to them.

THE FIVE MYTHS OF THE EARLY WEB

For many, the Web was this magical mystery land where anyone with a computer could generate extra income by simply hanging out a shingle—a land where the rules of business were suspended, revenue was only a concept, and costs were someone else's problem.

But as it turns out, those were all myths. Traditional business rules *do* apply to the Web, and those that ignored those tenets ultimately paid the price—literally and figuratively.

My favorite quote that came out of the Web's honeymoon period appeared in a 1998 press release from a company that was hoping to go public later in the year. The company's CFO provided some creative damage control when he reported that "the company is currently in a pre-revenue generation phase." Needless to say, the IPO never happened.

The Web is another communication channel, just like the telephone or a catalog or television or radio, through which businesses can communicate with and sell to their prospects and customers. Even though the Web is a kind of super channel, essentially combining the qualities of all other channels, the rules are the same. The business disciplines, objectives, and financial expectations still apply to all businesses—online or offline.

For a while there, not everyone agreed with that statement, and instead believed the myth that rules of business were changing. Confusing the changing manner in which business was conducted with a change in the absolute rules that dictate business success or failure was a fatal mistake for many businesses. Here's a list of the five most popular myths that influenced many during the early days of this new channel:

1. *Anyone can run a successful business on the web.* Talent, hard work, and good luck are not enough. Running a business isn't like playing for the Cincinnati Reds. Successful businesses have to deliver on three imperatives, not just two out of three:

   • Provide a product or service that people want or need
   • Find customers willing to pay for it.
   • Produce revenue that outpaces costs to deliver a profit

   Many businesses burned through tens of millions of dollars in the late 1990's because their talent, hard work, and good luck were chasing bad business ideas or businesses that were simply unable to differentiate themselves from the many competitors that already existed. We didn't, and still don't, need more businesses that copied existing models without delivering any new benefits. Did we really need another sporting goods store online? You had to feel for Michael Jordan, Wayne Gretzky, and John Elway when someone convinced them that the world needed MVP.com. It clearly did not.

2. *Now it's just a matter of monetizing the eyeballs.* The wholesale aggregation of eyeballs for the purpose of selling them to advertisers was a popular early Web revenue strategy. But many sites didn't count on the eyeballs glazing over as online ad measurement metrics consistently slid southward. Web sites found that advertising as the sole revenue stream was a very difficult model to sustain, with over 80 percent of available inventory Web-wide going unsold.

3. *It was either a bad business plan or a poorly executed one.* How about, it was a bad business idea with no chance of ever generating enough revenue to outpace costs? Not all ideas are good ones, and not all businesses will succeed, even with an unlimited amount of time and money. Some companies never asked and answered the tough question: Can this business ever deliver on the three imperatives of successful businesses? Poor judgment rather than lack of stellar execution was more often the case when greenlighting many startup dotcoms. *Not even a great business plan can help a bad business idea succeed.*

4. *Technology drives the Web.* This is like saying that studio cameras drive television, or that printing presses drive the magazine industry. It's *content* that drives the Web, and the Web—like a telephone network—is made up of wires and hardware and software. All by itself, the Web is like an empty city. But populate it with people of all kinds, from all over the world, and it becomes a vibrant community where people read and write, talk and listen, buy and sell,

work and play. The Web is just a shell, like an operating system, inside of which wonderful things can happen. Microsoft Word may organize John Grisham's next novel, but it can't write it for him. *Not even great technology can help a bad business idea succeed.*

5. *Business models on the Web are evolving.* This phrase simply added to the confusion around the Web. You can say new products are evolving. You can say that the Web is saving companies millions by eliminating costs in their value chains. What is a business model but revenue for a product or service from a customer and costs associated with successfully delivering that product or service. The business model that works best is the one that delivers mutual satisfaction for customer and company, and that model is not evolving.

There's no denying it: Making money is still the yardstick for businesses, especially public ones. Not even the Web can change that. Fidelity's Peter Lynch put it best when he said, "Wall Street rewards earnings." From this perspective, the dotcom crash was inevitable, especially for new companies that were trying to establish a loyal customer base for the very first time.

TECHNOLOGY ALONE WAS NOT ENOUGH

There was also an infatuation with technology. To be sure, without the enabling technology, the Web wouldn't exist. But technology alone is not enough to sustain most businesses and can't solve all of the Web's problems. It may seem logical that most Chicago Cub fans live within the city limits of the Windy City, or at least in the state of Illinois. But it's through human interaction that you would learn that nearly 75 percent of Cub fans live outside of Illinois. So if marketing to Cub fans is a priority for you, and your software tells you that they probably all live in zip codes starting with the number 6, then it's likely that you are overlooking three-quarters of your target audience.

The best technology makes the online experience easier and more pleasant for the consumer and is usually invisible to them. For the business, technology should, among other things, provide insights into the online behavior and habits of consumers—intelligence that can be used in tandem with human judgment to adjust and refine marketing efforts.

Back in the 1960s, supermarkets installed very cool electronic doors at the entrances to their stores. Just step on the little rubber mat and swoosh, the door swings open, making it possible for shoppers to enter and exit with ease, especially if they are pushing a cart or carrying an armload of groceries. But no one goes to the supermarket because of the electronic doors. It's much more about location, selection, service, and price—all issues of marketing. It's no different on the Web.

Though it may help them get in the door more easily, it's the art of using the science that builds loyalty and keeps consumers coming back for more.

All by itself, no matter how cool it is, technology is simply not enough to satisfy the needs and desires of consumers. There have been scores of very cool devices from splash pages to autoresponders that can help (or sometimes hinder) communication or selling. Imagine walking through a very cool electronic door into a supermarket that was poorly organized, was low on inventory, had no customer service people to help you, and sold at the same price as the competition just down the street. How quickly do you walk back out through that very cool electronic door?

So What Is the Web and How Can It Help Impact Sales?

Let's take a closer look at the Web from an application standpoint. The Web is a multipurpose channel with unique characteristics, unlike any other existing channel. The Web is:

■ *An information channel.* A boundless resource that is controlled by the user. Unlike television or radio, the end-user determines what content he or she will access when. To this point, while television and radio requires little of the end-user for him or her to be informed and entertained, the Web requires the end-user to be greatly involved with the medium. There's no sitting back watching or listening to the Web. It must be worked by end-users to achieve satisfaction.

■ *A two-way communication channel.* The first two-way communication channel since the telephone was invented over 125 years ago. A way for consumers to send and receive messages with other consumers or with companies through email. A way for companies to communicate with their employees, and employees with their companies, through email and intranets.

■ *A mass-marketing channel.* A way for marketers to promote indirectly to consumers through advertising or sponsorships. Because most marketers and their agencies were practitioners of this art offline, they moved it to the online space in the form of banners, tiles, buttons, interstitials, superstitials, pop-ups, pop-unders, and other forms of advertising.

■ *A direct marketing channel.* A way for marketers to promote directly to addressable individuals—either B2B (business-to-business) or B2C (business-to-consumer)—through email. The most inexpensive and targeted advertising method since the Persians made letter-writing popular in 500 B.C.:

• Paper: $0
• Postage: $0
• Cost Per Thousand (CPM): $0

If companies send messages to their own list of prospects and customers, the cost of those names is $0.

■ *A direct sales channel.* For some companies, such as catalogers, selling and distributing directly to customers has been a long-time practice. But for many manufacturers, such as Timberland, the move to the Web opened up a new sales channel as well as the need to get a whole lot closer to their customer base by accepting and fulfilling individual orders directly. The Web has enabled many manufacturers the opportunity to become retailers themselves.

■ *A self-contained sales environment that's open 24/7/365.* Prior to the Web, consumers had basically three ways to buy products and services: (1) by walking into a brick-and-mortar retail store, (2) by calling a toll-free number and connecting with a company's call center, and (3) by mail order. The Web allows a consumer to accomplish a variety of steps without ever leaving the keyboard. For example, a customer can:

• Receive and read promotion about the product
• View and read about the product at its Web site
• Comparison shop with regard to the product
• Read what other consumers have to say about the product
• Ask questions about the product through online chat
• Purchase the product
• Be part of the online research/focus groups that help shape the product

The Web has enabled a unique sales and marketing environment—one that can deliver all elements of the buying experience without ever taking your finger off of the mouse. This is a dynamic that marketers will find increasingly important as they become more proficient at the art and science of online marketing.

■ *A procurement channel.* A way for businesses to link directly with their suppliers to simplify and maximize the procurement process as a way to save money and generate revenue. The Web helps enable a procurement process that achieves important benefits, such as increased process efficiencies to reduce operating costs and accelerated speed-to-market to maximize revenue opportunities.

The Web is really quite a unique medium. One might say that it captures the best of all media: the depth of information found in books, the local/regional coverage of newspapers, the analytics of magazines, the immediacy of radio, the sound, color, motion, and mass reach of television, the two-way communication capability of the telephone, the pinpoint targeting ability of direct mail, and the ability for the end-user to control the entire experience through the interactive nature of the Web itself. One of the few things that the Web doesn't do today is compete on par with the entertainment value of movies and television. But that's only a matter of time and technology.

From a commercial standpoint, businesses have explored a number of different models since 1994, with half a dozen providing the basis for most online businesses today.

HOW THE WEB IS USED: SEVEN BUSINESS MODELS

There are all kinds of companies—an estimated 75,000,000 worldwide—that now have some type of presence on the Web. Some are simply tooting their own horns, while others are busy transacting sales and shipping orders. Some, such as *llbean.com* sell their own products while others, such as *amazon.com* primarily sell somebody else's products. Some only promote online and close sales offline, as does much of the service sector. Companies are also beginning to use the Web to conduct their own research. It's fast, it's affordable, and as you develop your permission-granted email list, you have direct access to a potential pool of qualitative or quantitative research participants.

For the most part, whatever the business or industry, it probably falls into one of these seven basic business models that are designed to help businesses build brand, grow sales, or both:

1. *Brochureware model.* Designed to inform end-users and to promote offline sales. Not every company can use the Web to actually transact or close sales in an online environment. Some, like the service sector, primarily use the Web to generate leads, still relying on in-person or over-the-telephone follow-up to close the sale. However, the service sector is also beginning to use the Internet and Web to more proactively communicate with their clients using the Web and permission-granted email. Brochureware is most often utilized by service-based companies but is also used by corporations as a way to communicate the corporate message through annual reports, press releases, and other postings. Examples of leading companies that use the brochureware model:

   - *www.century21.com* (real estate)
   - *www.allstate.com* (insurance)
   - *www.mckinsey.com* (management consulting)

2. *Advertising-based model.* Designed to generate ad revenue based on the delivery of eyeballs, impressions, click-throughs, or conversions. Often used by news and information sites. This was one of the first models to migrate to the Web from the offline world. But with it came a higher level of accountability because the Web was able to closely track the exact number of individuals that viewed a page, clicked through an ad, and, ultimately, whether or not the clicks were converted into a sale. Examples of leading companies that use the advertising-based model:

   - *www.espn.com* (sports)
   - *www.cnn.com* (news)
   - *www.weather.com* (weather)

3. *E-commerce model.* Designed to sell products or services directly to end-users. For B2C companies, the transaction and exchange of money from buyer to seller occurs online. For B2B companies, the transaction usually occurs online through the electronic placement of a purchase order (e-procurement), while

the actual exchange of money from buyer to seller might occur offline. Examples of leading companies that use the B2C e-commerce model:

- *www.landsend.com* (clothes)
- *www.bally.com* (shoes)
- *www.amazon.com* (books, etc.)

Examples of leading companies that use the B2B e-commerce model:

- *www.microsoft.com* (software)
- *www.ibm.com* (computers, servers)
- *www.dell.com* (computers, servers)

4. *Sales facilitation model.* Designed to help facilitate and promote offline sales. Most often used in major promotions to coordinate the trapping of names, email addresses, permission, and other consumer data. Also used to input unique codes for the purpose of earning credits toward the purchase or awarding of prizes. Encourages repeat purchases at retail for packaged goods companies such as the potato chip and soft drink categories. Examples of leading companies that use the sales facilitation model:

- *www.sprite.com* (soft drink)
- *www.frito-lay.com* (snacks)
- *www.mgd.com* (beer, Miller Genuine Draft)

5. *Fee-based model.* Designed to generate revenue based on transactions. It's important to distinguish between fees and subscriptions. Fees represent a revenue stream to a company based on its involvement in enabling a transaction like buying or selling stock or buying or selling products or services marketed through an auction site, for example. Examples of leading companies that use the fee-based model:

- *www.ebay.com* (auctions)
- *www.schwab.com* (stock trades)
- *www.etrade.com* (stock trades)

6. *Subscription-based model.* Designed to generate revenue based on subscription access to proprietary

information or expertise. This model closely resembles the newsletter publishing model in the offline world, where subscribers usually pay a healthy price for the privilege of receiving specific and unique intelligence. Examples of leading companies that use the subscription-based model:

- *www.consumerreports.org* (product information)
- *www.wsj.com* (business news)
- *www.variety.com* (Hollywood news)

7. *Mall or portal model.* Designed to generate revenue based on a number of streams due to the enormous traffic generated through the doors of a site. Sites such as the major portals can generate revenue from advertising and sponsorships, e-commerce, subscription access, transactional fees, and other innovative partnerships. Examples of leading companies that use the mall or portal model:

- *www.yahoo.com*
- *www.aol.com*
- *www.altavista.com*

WHAT ARE THE OBJECTIVES OF YOUR WEB SITE?

Many think of the Web as a place for companies to sell products through an online catalog and e-commerce transactions. Some view the Web as a place to promote offline sales, as in many service-based businesses. Others see the Web and email as an effective communication combination with which they can promote directly with prospects and customers through permission-granted email.

How is your business using the Web? Are you actively using the Web to acquire and retain customers or to grow customer share, and in the process, grow market share? What is the purpose of your Web site, and can it do more? Does or could your Web site:

1. Inform?
2. Build brand?
3. Generate offline leads?
4. Transact business online through e-commerce?
5. Facilitate offline sales through promotions?
6. Reduce costs by eliminating steps in the value chain?
7. All of the above?

In any of the above examples, the opportunity to inexpensively communicate in a direct and outbound way through permission-granted email is often overlooked. Whether you are a global conglomerate or the local wine merchant, you can use the Web to help strengthen and grow customer relationships. The opportunity to have a requested, relevant, and respectful conversation with 50 B2B customers or 500,000 B2C customers is there. It's an inexpensive and productive way to have a quiet conversation with your best prospects and customers on the way to selling them more of what you have to sell.

THE CENTURY OF MARKET SHARE

Selling more to loyal customers was not a specific focus for marketers in the 20th century. It was much more about acquiring customers and establishing market share. That marketing strategy received an enormous boost when, at mid-century, the greatest mass-marketing vehicle ever created debuted and helped to reinforce a market share business philosophy that sought to sell products and services to as many people as possible.

What followed was the most successful period in history of matching new customers with new brands or companies. It created unprecedented wealth for two and half generations, rewarding company leadership based on their ability to acquire. This practice only served to perpetuate the pursuit of market share as the de facto prescription for business success in the 20th century—the Century of Market Share.

2

THE CENTURY OF MARKET SHARE

The customer can have any color he wants,
so long as it's black.

—Henry Ford, on the color options available for his
immensely popular Model T

Henry Ford's vision for the 20th century was a good one. Create as many cars as possible and sell them to as many people as possible—and it worked. Ford sold 1,700 cars over the first 15 months of the company's existence and emerged as the leader of the second Industrial Revolution.

In 1908, Ford introduced what would be the best-selling car during his lifetime—the Model T. At $825, the Model T was the hottest car on wheels. Americans liked what they saw and began to show up in record numbers for the chance to own a piece of the open road. But production of the popular Model T simply took too long. So Ford went back to the drawing board in order to improve productivity and simply build cars faster and cheaper.

Ford's innovative moving assembly line allowed for significantly greater productivity and helped reduce chassis assembly from a little over 12 hours to just an hour and a half. The whole car could be put together in less than 3 hours, and this meant that Ford could now meet the demands of the masses. By the end of 1913, Ford owned a 50 percent share of the automobile market in the United States.

OWNING THE MARKET

Ford's vision signaled an enormous change for American business and helped raise the standard of living for Americans. The increase in productivity helped to make cars affordable for millions of Americans, and by the time the Model T was discontinued in 1927, Ford had produced and sold over 15 million cars.

His innovative productivity model was copied and improved by many and allowed for the mass manufacturing of thousands of different products through two world wars and a depression.

Ford had started a trend that would certainly continue long after his death and would be fueled by a nation just returning from war. As veterans returned and rejoined the workforce, the country was poised for consumption. Ford's mass manufacturing model was there in many forms to oblige.

THE MASTER-SLAVE PARADIGM

Out of this one-size-fits-all manufacturing model grew a company-centric, or master-slave, relationship between company and customer as depicted in Table 2.1. In such a relationship, where the master is the company and the slave is the customer, the master speaks and the slave listens. The master builds and the slave buys.

TABLE 2.1   Company-Centric or Customer-Centric?

	Market Share Strategy	Customer Share Strategy	Marketing Focus
Master	Speaks	Listens	Company-Centric
Slave	Listens	Speaks	Customer-Centric

© 2001 Customer Share Group LLC

The company-centric model that employs mass-marketing tactics to sell as many products to as many people as possible supports a growth strategy that relies on increasing sales by increasing market share. Ironically, it was the 18th- and 19th-century general storekeeper whose universe of customers was limited to those nearby who pioneered the customer share approach to marketing.

In these entrepreneurial businesses of the day, the storekeeper reversed roles with the customer and became the listener while the customer became the speaker. The storekeeper was generally rewarded for paying attention to the wants and desires of customers, making sure that he was stocked with all the preferred products when customers went to market on their appointed shopping day. The result: large orders fulfilling as close to, if not exactly, 100 percent of the weekly needs of customers and their families.

It was Henry Ford's inability to respond to customers who were demanding new car models each and every year that led to the erosion of his market share. Ford the master had spoken, unable to make the mind-shift required to take on a customer-centric marketing focus—where the *master listens* and the *slave speaks*. Essentially, he told his customers that they could buy what he had to sell.

His competition, of course, was only too happy to respond to consumers and quickly established the tradition of introducing new car models every year. Ford, the man who had earned the title Father of Market Share, was forced to watch his own company's market share drop precipitously after he discontinued manufacturing of the Model T in 1927.

MARKETING IN THE 20TH CENTURY

As the 20th century began, the overwhelming means of advertising products and services was print in newspapers and magazines. If you had a product that was distributed nationally, the only realistic advertising option for the first 20 years of the 20th century was magazine advertising.

Table 2.2 demonstrates that approximately every 20 years during the 20th century, a new means or channel of advertising to consumers was introduced. For the first 20 years of the century, the primary means of reaching national audiences was through magazines such as *Redbook, Cosmopolitan,* and *The Saturday Evening Post.* During this same period, catalogers such as Orvis and L.L. Bean primarily used direct mail to reach their customers one by one.

Table 2.2   Primary Advertising Channels in the 20th Century

1900–1920	1921–1940	1941–1960	1961–1980	1981–2000
Print	Print	Print	Print	Print
Direct Mail	Direct Mail	Direct Mail	Direct Mail	Direct Mail
	Radio	Radio	Radio	Radio
		Television	Television	Television
			Toll Free #s	Toll Free #s
				Internet/
				Web/
				Email

© *2001 Customer Share Group LLC*

Commercial network radio was added to the mix in the mid-1920s, and for the first time, advertisers were able to promote their products in association with live radio broadcasts. At the outset, the broadcast model for advertising did not take the form of 30- or 60-second commercials. Instead, a single sponsor most often underwrote the cost of a radio broadcast such as when the Eveready Company developed the *Eveready Hour* in 1924.

THE GOLDEN AGE OF RADIO

The so-called Golden Age of Radio began in 1930 when Americans huddled by their sets in the evening for entertainment. Listening to live radio broadcasts was the new and exciting entertainment form of the day. Orson Wells demonstrated the medium's enormous power of persuasion with his infamous reading of *War of the Worlds* on *Mercury Theater of the Air* in 1938. The realistic nature of the live broadcast caused widespread panic among listeners, who actually thought that Martians were invading Earth.

Launched in 1926, the National Broadcasting Company (NBC) was owned by the Radio Corporation of America (RCA), a major manufacturer of radios at the time. RCA therefore had a vested interest in seeing the new medium succeed. In fact, NBC created two networks—the Red and the Blue—and recruited the top radio talent of the day for its broadcasts on both networks. The Red and Blue networks became hugely successful, and profits were invested in the development of a brand new broadcast technology—television.

The Columbia Broadcasting System (CBS) went on the air in 1927 as the Columbia Phonograph Broadcasting Company. Within two years, William Paley, who promoted his family's cigar business on radio, bought the upstart network for $400,000. The 22-affiliate network was renamed Columbia Broadcasting System and focused on the development of programming as its primary objective, unlike NBC, which was more interested in using radio to sell radios.

But in the early 1940s the Federal Communications Commission (FCC) intervened to investigate NBC's monopolistic practices as the owner of two radio networks. As a result of the investigation, RCA was forced to divest itself of one of the networks, and sold the Blue Network to the American Broadcasting System on October 12, 1943 for $8 million. Thus, the American Broadcasting Companies (ABC) was born, acquired by Edward J. Noble, who had made his fortune selling Life Savers.

The novelty of sounds being broadcast over the airwaves by radio technology lasted a relatively short time, with a new communication technology just on the horizon. From the same roots that gave birth to network radio came the most powerful mass marketing vehicle of all time. Television not only served as free in-home entertainment of the type of programming that before was available only in movie theaters, but it also served as a way to introduce consumers to a seemingly endless array of new products and services. This concurrent combination made television a lethal weapon in establishing brand loyalty for the very first time for many consumers.

TELEVISION, THE MARKET MAKER

The same advertising sponsorship model that fueled radio programming also carried over to television during its early days. The drama, comedy, and variety shows were actually produced by the sponsors, while news and sports programming was left to the network to produce. NBC shows such as *The Kraft TV Theater* and the *Philco/Goodyear Playhouse* were typical of how advertisers promoted their products over the airwaves. It was definitely a soft sell.

But when NBC pioneered what they called the magazine advertising concept for television in the early 1950s by inserting the commercials within the show, essentially interrupting the entertainment, television advertising changed forever. The harder sell commercial insertions annoyed many viewers, right from the start. But this was the price to be paid if broadcast television was to remain a free, over-the-air provider of information and entertainment.

For much of the 20th century, we were bludgeoned with what Godin calls interruption marketing—messages that interrupt us while we are watching our favorite TV show, listening to our favorite radio station, reading our favorite magazine or newspaper, and even while we're sitting in a movie theater patiently waiting for the feature presentation to start.

Bob Dowling, president and editor-in-chief of *The Hollywood Reporter,* is a master of developing content that hits the mark for recipients. He has developed dozens of successful ad-supported magazines that deliver what the recipient wants or needs. Dowling offers another perspective on interruption marketing:

> The vast majority of advertising messages have been designed to interrupt recipients from the flow of what they were doing in the first place. Most commercial messages are still written from the perspective of the sender, not the recipient. The message is about my product, not necessarily your interests. By definition, the message is self-serving to the sender and can only mildly anticipate the wants, needs, desires of the recipient.

ONE-WAY, OUTBOUND MESSAGES

Interestingly, both television and radio were designed to transmit only and not receive. Neither medium required, encouraged, or was technically able to receive signals back from the people who received them. If fact, there was no way of knowing exactly who received the signals. Both were designed to communicate in one direction—out to consumers—with no practical or immediate way to respond.

The control over programming was largely out of the consumers' hands. The networks determined what information and entertainment would be delivered and when it would be delivered, with no regard to the needs, desires, or schedules of consumers. But times and schedules were simpler then. More often than not, Mom was a homemaker and Dad worked for the same company for 40 years. Television offered three programming options, and sports stars spent their entire careers with one team. Target audiences were captive and rarely moved around, making it a whole lot easier for marketers to reach and influence them over and over again.

THE WAR FOR MARKET SHARE

As more and more Americans established their brand preferences throughout the 1950s and 1960s, the fight for market share became intense. Once advertisers realized and witnessed the persuasive power of advertising on television, they rushed to the medium with the hope of grabbing a larger share of their own markets. During the first 20 years of commercial network television, advertisers battled for the wholesale acquisition of customers whose brand loyalty across dozens of products was up for grabs.

But once the first significant generation of brand loyalists established their preferences and began to pass along those preferences to their children, market share increases usually came at the expense of the other guy by getting people to switch brands.

Coca-Cola and Pepsi battled every day to wrestle 1 percent share of market away from the other. They still battle for share, but the stakes are a little higher today than they were half a century ago. A 1 percent move in market share from one company to the other could represent over $1 billion worldwide across all product lines.

For decades we have seen more than our fair share of taste test commercials. Those ads are designed to convince 1 percent of Coke drinkers to become Pepsi drinkers, or vice versa. This type of marketing strategy is fueled by mass-marketing initiatives like ads on the Super Bowl or even product placement in major motion pictures. The objective: Get more people to drink Coke over Pepsi or Pepsi over Coke.

GLOBAL GROWTH:
ACQUIRING EVEN MORE CUSTOMERS

The battle for market share grew even more intense after millions of consumers had settled on a brand to handle the daily and weekly needs and desires—from washing clothes to drinking soda pop. So, marketers sought growth in the same way that they had always sought growth—by acquiring more customers—but this time the stakes were higher, and so was the cost, as marketers began to woo new customers in more than 200 countries around the globe.

The battle moved out beyond the boundaries of the United States and North America to untapped territories all over the world. For some, the global acquisition of new customers ultimately approached saturation, with marketing efforts on all continents, in dozens of languages, and reaching nearly every human on the earth.

WHILE THE PIE GETS BIGGER, THE SLICES GET SMALLER

Concurrently, growth for some brands also came in the form of the development and distribution of line extensions to existing brands by creating a real or perceived benefit, such as tartar control or mint-flavored options. Even though creating more than 30 different options for one brand of toothpaste was an expensive proposition, it nonetheless became a legitimate means of growing a brand.

The micro-marketing of an explosion of line extensions helped some brands capture new customers with a new or improved benefit in the battle for market share, but represented another extraordinarily expensive way to grow sales.

IF YOU CAN'T BEAT 'EM, BUY 'EM

With distribution of hundreds of products in nearly every country in the world, global marketers ultimately looked to their competition for customer acquisition and sales growth by acquiring entire companies. Consolidation across many industries helped temporarily improve both the top and bottom lines for many companies. But after the efficiencies are taken and the acquired sales are absorbed, the issue ultimately comes back to the same fundamental question: How can a company—any company—create meaningful growth from the customers it already has?

THE CHANGING FACE OF ADVERTISING

When you take the informational power and reach of the Web and add to it the ability to communicate directly with individuals on relevant topics for pennies, you have a very powerful marketing tool that needs to be understood. Add to the equation the ability to accurately measure recipients' responses to commercial messages as well as their browsing habits relative to their site visits, what do you have? You have a marketing medium that is:

- An informational storehouse with the ability to answer almost any question
- Targeted to individuals by name
- Relevant to those individuals' needs and desires
- Accountable in terms of its effectiveness

You also have the makings of a paradigm shift that could change the face of advertising as we know it. As challenging as the retail channel has become for resellers, it's nothing compared to the challenge facing advertisers and their agencies that are charged with getting the attention of targets whose senses are being attacked everywhere they surf, change channels, turn pages, ride elevators, or even stroll down the street.

Naturally curious consumers are using the Web to educate themselves, and educated consumers need to be treated differently than the ones who passively *watch*, especially if marketers hope to build a relationship based on trust and an opportunity to capture the consumer's next five sales.

The challenge, though, isn't for consumers. Consumers have figured out how to use the Web. Though most businesses have some type of presence on the Web, the real challenge now is for them to figure out how they can effectively use the Web to move the needle on sales.

3

MARKETING THROUGH THE CHAOS

When David Ogilvy started his ad agency back in 1948, the world was the ad agency's oyster. Ogilvy, a consummate copywriter himself, helped elevate the creation of advertising to an art form. One of the world's most successful ad agencies of the second half of the 20th century, Ogilvy & Mather helped build some of America's most prominent brands—American Express, Maxwell House, and Pepperidge Farms, to name a few.

But the agency that became famous for creating the phrase *Don't Leave Home Without It* has seen better days. Now part of global conglomerate WPP Group PLC, Ogilvy & Mather Worldwide is one of several agencies that has been called out on the carpet by one of its biggest clients, Unilever, to discuss a pay-for-performance method of compensation—until recently, unheard of for agencies like Ogilvy.

With annual spending of about $3.5 billion to market its products, Unilever wants more effective advertising, especially when it is spending annually what amounts to $14 for every man, woman, and child in the United States.

MAY I HAVE YOUR ATTENTION, PLEASE?

Getting the attention of consumers today is no easy task, and getting them to take action can be next to impossible. There are just so many external as well as internal distractions. After some time, consumers simply adapt to the noise and, to a great degree, tune it out.

Traditional advertising, as we know it, was born in a simpler time—a time when people had the time to listen, when two-parent households were more the norm, with one parent typically home all day. Watching television after work was a habit. Reading the newsweekly or the monthly house and garden magazine was a habit. But habits have changed, and so have priorities. Now, getting home in time to kiss the kiddies good night is a more of a realistic objective for working parents than watching a sitcom.

Advertisers and their agencies are struggling with these issues, and the solutions are not all that simple. The objective of 20th century advertisers was reach. Even when targeting a specific group, delivering one message to the maximum number of 29- to 49-year-old women was, and still is, the objective. Ads went out, and sales were expected to happen. If sales were lackluster, the remedy from the agencies creating and being compensated for placing the advertising was historically chanted like a mantra: frequency, frequency, frequency. Though frequency probably did help break through the noise barriers, there's no doubt that agencies also benefited from the frequency model.

Direct, one-to-one messages and ongoing conversations with prospects and customers are not what Madison Avenue historically created. But that may be changing, especially if agencies want to keep the media piece. In response, most major agencies now have their own interactive shops that handle the online initiatives. But more often than not, these shops are hanging onto their cool names and independent identities, which can sometimes get in the way of creating truly seamless and integrated marketing initiatives. This probably grew out the fact that Madison Avenue did not move all that quickly to embrace the Web, and all it had to offer as a powerful marketing weapon. Instead, the large agencies typically acquired their interactive competencies by buying an upstart group of online creative types from the Valley (Silicon) or the Alley (New York). These actions indicated that the agencies knew that they had to add these services. Their biggest clients were demanding them—building Web sites and creating banner ads.

But even today, Madison Avenue is not totally comfortable with the notion that it might also be in the business of creating campaigns that communicate with customers one at a time as a way to cut through the noise and build customer relationships.

THE FRAGMENTATION FACTOR

In fairness to agency world executives, is it really their fault that advertising has had to work harder and harder to get the audience's attention? Are ads any less creative than in the days of David Ogilvy? Is it the writing? The graphics? The production quality?

So what's changed? Why are advertisers increasingly examining the effectiveness of their commercial messages? There are seven important factors to consider:

1. *Unprecedented audience fragmentation.* With hundreds of television programming options, thousands of newspaper, magazine, and book options, and millions·of Web site options, it's simply harder to get someone's attention today. When Ogilvy started his agency in 1948,

there weren't any network television options to carry advertising. That didn't happen until 1949, when ABC, CBS, and NBC went on the air for the first time as national networks. Cable was still more than 25 years away, and Fox was just a movie studio. In this hundred-channel, VCR, DVD, MP3 world, the three networks' share of audience has dramatically decreased.

2. *Consumer product saturation.* David Ogilvy was in the right place at the right time. The time to be in the advertising business was immediately following World War II, when Madison Avenue was fueled by the most active period of new product launches in U.S. history. A country that was hungry to buy helped feed several decades of new product consumption during the Golden Age of advertising. The challenge to convince 100 million extraordinarily busy and distracted Americans to switch brands of toothpaste in the 21st century will be a daunting one. For many consumer products, the upside to switching after making a brand selection years ago is just not that compelling. Add to this the fact that the local Rite Aid or CVS carries over 100 variations of toothpaste—more than 30 iterations of the Crest brand alone—slicing the market share pie into infinitesimal slices that result in waging a very expensive battle for a market share point or two.

3. *More media-savvy consumers.* Consumers are simply more jaded than they were during the post-war years. From Viet Nam to Watergate to Ralph Nader to Bill Clinton, consumers are much more cynical, much more aware, and much less naïve than they were a generation ago.

4. *Less in-home time.* More parents are working outside of the home today, and those at home are busy shuttling kids to and from all sorts of activities. Once parents do come home after commuting both ways to work, a typical pattern today might look like this: (a) check the answering machine; (b) open the mail; (c) check email; (d) cook dinner or order out; (e) eat

dinner; (f) make sure the kids do their homework; (g) help the kids do their homework. At this point in the evening, watching TV has about the same odds as going to bed. If your advertising runs during the fringe prime-time period (6:00 p.m. to 8:00 p.m.), many in your target audience are busy trying to figure out fractions with their fifth-grader. How does an advertiser get through to this person?

5. *Explosion in personal, two-way communication.* Between cell phones, email, and live chat, an entire generation of consumers are spending a disproportionate percentage of their free time communicating in a one-to-one environment. Time that was formerly devoted to more traditional forms of ad-supported information and entertainment such as TV, radio, magazines, and newspapers are now being replaced with non-ad supported options. This can't be a good thing for advertisers who must figure out how to reach these members of Generation Y when they become full-fledged consumers.

6. *Explosion in non-advertising-supported entertainment forms.* Offline and online video games, movie rentals, and cable television channels have all siphoned eyeballs away from traditional ad-supported media. There are even some gaming Web sites that offer premium subscribers a version of their site that eliminates the ads altogether.

7. *Web as a measurable medium.* Because of its interactive and measurable nature, the Web has actually raised the level of awareness around the effectiveness of all advertising. Advertisers have moved into a medium that allows them to measure the results of their efforts from two perspectives: (a) *Web ads,* which enable advertisers to measure the action taken by consumers from click-through to conversion, and (b) *email,* which enables advertisers to measure the action taken by consumers that receive individually addressed, permission-granted messages.

All of these factors combine to make communication more difficult and getting someone's attention next to impossible. So advertisers and the media that carry their messages have put their heads together to come up with mass-marketing "band-aids" to stop a bleeding jugular.

OTHER SYMPTOMS
OF AN AILING PATIENT

There have been numerous other attempts to make ads work better over the last quarter century. In television, the number of commercial minutes-per-hour has steadily grown. In print, the separation of church and state has become an antiquated rule of conservative journalists. The very word *advertorial* suggests complicity and that the two are now combined in a blur of text and images and logos, creating the *integration* of church and state.

On the Web, marketers are using technology to create new, more invasive forms of interruption marketing. The interstitial ad that pops up when you click onto a site may be the all-time most invasive form of advertising. Then there are the winking, blinking, and nodding ads that are crammed onto the home pages of Web sites, attempting to say all and sell all on page one. Like a walk through Times Square on New Year's Eve, there's so much noise, neon, and nonsense that it overloads our senses. We can focus on nothing, and we therefore see and hear nothing.

Now, the latest solution to help improve underperformance of advertising on the Web: bigger ads. Bigger ads, louder ads, more ads, longer ads, pop-up ads, pop-under ads, rich media ads. The search for the Holy Grail continues while Americans rush through life, spending less and less time in places where the advertiser is trying to get their attention by using text, images, sound, and motion.

The technology sword can cut both ways for advertisers. Consumers have access to ad-blocking software that allows them to filter out interstitials, banners, cookies, and more. Companies marketing the software say that their software will soon come loaded onto new PCs, making it easier for consumers to use. Internet Service Providers (ISPs) are also expected to offer ad-blocking options as a way to entice consumers to sign up for Web access.

BLAME AND PUNISHMENT

We witnessed a sea change in the agency world over the last 25 years of the 20th century, including unprecedented consolidation, shrinking agency staffs, the constant hiring and firing of agencies, changes in methods of compensation, and lots of finger-pointing. But none of these actions is the answer. The world of mass marketing is not changing—it already has changed. There are way too many people talking and too few people listening for mass marketing to work as it once did. Gone are the days when two-thirds of the country watched *I Love Lucy* on a single night. Gone are the days when great advertising was enough.

The effectiveness of mass marketing has diminished, but the expectations that some have of its performance has not. Our expectations relative to the objectives of mass marketing must be adjusted. For advertisers truly interested in creating relationships with their customers, mass marketing alone is not enough to cut through the volume of noise to hit an overworked, sleep-deprived target that barely has the time to talk to his or her kids.

ONE-TO-ONE MEDIA

The practice of sending addressable one-to-one media has been around for a very long time. Prior to the nation's birth, printing presses reached the colonies from England in the mid 1600s, and soon thereafter, the first newspapers rolled.

After the United States Postal Service was established, newspapers and magazines were delivered to individuals through the mail in what could be viewed as the very first forms of direct marketing. Prior to this, newspapers and magazines were sold randomly for a penny apiece on street corners.

Then Orvis, the manufacturer of travel, fly fishing, and hunting gear, sent out its first catalog in 1856 and a purer form of commercial direct marketing was born, in which the entire purpose of the mailing was to sell product. The Direct Marketing Association (DMA), the trade association for direct marketers, considers the Orvis catalog as the true beginning of the practice of formal direct marketing in the United States.

Table 3.1 chronicles the history of commercial media—vehicles that all receive some level of support from advertisers. But, that wasn't always the case. Ironically, both newspapers and magazines started out purely as sources of information and were primarily supported by newsstand and subscriber revenues during the early years. But, once the 20th century began, advertising in print—and later in radio—became an increasingly important revenue stream.

Long before the advent of the advertising agency, printed media carried advertisers' messages directly to individuals at an address. The practice was targeted and usually requested, and was part of the early beginnings of some great brands, such as jewelry giant Tiffany & Co. and outdoor gear baron L.L. Bean, that are still going strong today.

TABLE 3.1 Chronology of Commercial Media

Medium	Introduced	Identity of Recipients	Elements of Communication
Newspapers	1689	Known	Text & Images
Magazines	1741	Known	Text & Images
Catalogs	1856	Known	Text & Images
Radio	1894	Unknown	Sound
Television	1939	Unknown	Text, Images, Sound, & Motion
Web/Email	1994	Known	Text, Images, Sound, Motion, & Interactivity

© 2001 Customer Share Group LLC

Ironically, the next two significant advances in commercial media—radio in 1894 and television in 1939—were broadcast media, sending signals out over the air to whoever owned a radio or television. Even though the media types were eventually able to define more specifically the demographics of their audiences through research, the names and addresses of the recipients were still unknown to the advertisers and to most media.

Exactly 100 years after the invention of radio, a new commercial communication channel was introduced. When the Web emerged in 1994 with its interactive capabilities, it had all of the characteristics of those early communication channels with the added ability to send and receive messages to and from known recipients on a one-to-one basis.

From this perspective, the Web is a direct marketing channel with the interactive capability of identifying individuals through purchases and promotional sign-ups. It is also a world that allows for the display of traditional advertising in the form of banner and other types of ads. These display ads have the interactive capability that allows prospects to click through and even divulge their identities (email address). This interactive nature of display ads—where individual prospects can identify themselves by granting permission to receive future commercial messages—represents the collision of two forms of marketing: the art of advertising and the science of direct marketing.

Historically, some have viewed advertising as a higher form of marketing, while direct marketing has been viewed as the purview of marketers that create junk mail. To some extent, this same view carries over to the new channel as well, where advertisers largely view email as an insignificant marketing event relative to the more traditional forms of advertising.

But the advent of permission has changed all of that and helps marketers to begin to identify, capture, and store their most loyal customers in a permission-granted email database. Some of the most loyal customers that a brand has are happily identifying themselves, by name and email address, to the brand owners as the very center of the core target. It is for this reason that all advertising campaigns should start with email as the first element in building any advertising campaign, not the last.

THINKING THROUGH COMMUNICATION FROM THE INSIDE OUT

More than 2,000 years ago, when there was no Web, no television, no newspapers, no mass communication of any kind, the means of spreading the word or promoting an idea was by word of mouth. People would gather to hear a message, then after hearing it, they would write it down and send it by courier to places far away to spread the word. This is how most religions started thousands of years ago.

During the summer of 2001, Sony Pictures developed a campaign around the release of one of its movies, from the inside out. Sony started the process by asking this two-part question: Who is at the center of the core audience, and how can we communicate with them directly to kick-start the type of word-of-mouth buzz that helps sell tickets during the first weekend? Sony was promoting the release of *Baby Boy,* the story of a young, troubled African American man living in South-Central Los Angeles, written by Academy-Award nominee John Singleton.

Sony started its campaign by sending an email from Singleton to more than 1.3 million African Americans. Sony then ran banner ads on Web sites frequented by African Americans, such as *www.bet.com,* and finally ran broader newspaper and television advertising.

Sony started this campaign with individual conversations, moved to niche media, and then to mass media. This was a campaign designed from the inside out—starting with direct marketing and moving out to mass marketing—and this is the way that advertisers and their agencies need to be thinking in the Information Economy—from the inside out.

This is the type of thinking that ad agencies should be presenting to Unilever.

The Evolution of Email

Email has largely been viewed as a means to deliver simple text. But that's certainly changing, especially as it relates to the commercial use of email. In many ways, email is following the same evolutionary path as other forms of communication. First, email contained only text. Then text and images. Then text, images, and sound. And finally, text, images, sound, and motion.

Prior to Gutenberg's invention of the printing press, text came in the form of handwritten letters. Then text took the form of books. Images were added to books, newspapers, and magazines. Then came the capture and transmission of sound over wire, and then over the airwaves, until Thomas Edison paved the way for the capture and delivery of motion with the invention of the kinescope in 1892.

Email was named email because early on it was electronically delivered mail or text through a wire. As the capacity of delivering data electronically improves, email will become a medium that enables the delivery of all the elements of communication—from two lines of text to 30-minute infomercials, and ultimately crossing over to the delivery of full-length movies. As this evolution continues, will we even call it email anymore?

Technology will continue to assist in the evolution of the delivery of digitized matter. *Push email* delivers updates directly to the email software that help people manage the sending and receiving of email, such as Microsoft Outlook. *Push email* obviates the need for an advertiser to send a new email each time a message is sent to a prospect or customer. Instead, the recipient just clicks on an email that sits in the inbox and is updated whenever new information is available.

Chatting with Your Buddy

With the popularity of instant messaging (IM) rivaling that of email, advertisers appeared to be blocked from entering the sacred space of traditional (if a one-year-old technology can be called that) IM such as on AOL. But along came the buddy bot—an automated agent that sits on the buddy list of IM enthusiasts and allows users to communicate either with a computer or with other users.

The new media heads at Capitol Records used the IM technology to help alternative rock band Radiohead debut their June 2001 release of *Amnesiac* as well as to push the album's hit single *Kid A* straight to No. 1 on *Billboard's* Hot 100 during the first week of release. The label also incorporated a viral element that allowed users to email the entire album to friends two weeks prior to the album's release. Fans could then listen to the album via streaming technology, and more than 250,000 Radiohead fans did just that. This technology combines two powerful elements that make commercial messages even more powerful: (1) word-of-mouth endorsements from friends and (2) permission. The only way to utilize the offering is to download the simple software. This action essentially constitutes the granting of permission.

News travels quickly over the Web, and soon excitement surrounding both the new album and the new technology swept across chat rooms, news groups, and clubs worldwide, and Capitol had itself a cyber-marketing hit as well as an excellent example of how a company can use the Web, email, and other electronic communication technologies to sell music.

THE WORLD IS A STAGE OF ADVERTAINMENT

The excitement of sound and motion delivered over the Web or through email will provide new challenges and opportunities for advertisers and their agencies. Will the delivery of multimedia messages over the Internet be labeled something completely different? Is the advertiser-sponsored film short, such as BMW has produced with top Hollywood directors such as Guy Ritchie, a step toward a whole new form of advertising and entertainment? Could these new marketing messages be considered *Advertainments?*

Marketers need to view email as a means of exciting a customer who has given permission to receive commercial messages. Perhaps the email links to *www.bmwfilms.com* and streams a film short that shows the product in action. Or maybe the email delivers the entire message itself without streaming. The point is that email can deliver or link to messages that are every bit as creative as any advertising on TV, and companies such as BMW continue to push the envelope on the delivery of exceptional commercial messages in the online environment. The difference, though, is that these messages will be invited into the consumer's computer—permission-granted messages that are *requested, relevant,* and *respectful.* Table 3.2 details the four major elements of communication and the chronological order in which they were introduced. Interestingly, the very same elements migrated to the Internet, and then to the Web, in the very same chronological order—first text, then images, then sound, and motion.

TABLE 3.2 The Elements of Communication

Element	Introduced	Technology
Text	1453	Movable Type
Images	1829	Photography
Sound	1876/1877	Telephone/Phonograph
Motion	1892	Kinescope
© 2001 Customer Share Group LLC		

As the capacity of technology improves, email will be a medium that will enable the delivery of all elements of communication—from two lines of text to 30-minute infomercials. Email is a medium that will ultimately allow us to send anything digitizable of any size. Once this happens, the dynamic of the Web will add to it the ability to entertain and inform users, just as television and movies do today. When that happens, consumers will, for the first time, watch the Web as well as interact with it. It is likely that the Web will evolve and progress through many stages of appealing to the senses of seeing and hearing before breaking through the sensory frontier of appealing to the other three senses: smell, touch, and taste.

THE MEDIUM IS THE MESSAGE

The cultural theorist Marshall McLuhan once said that the environment that the technology creates or enables is what changes us, not the technology itself. The Web creates an extraordinarily rare environment where:

1. Advertisers identify themselves and their products to prospects as they can and do in more traditional mass-marketing media;
2. Prospects identify themselves to advertisers as interested in the product not only by purchasing products, but often by signing up for sweepstakes or e-newsletters;
3. Advertisers begin one-to-one conversations with prospects and customers for the purpose of building a relationship through a medium that costs pennies to send (email);
4. Prospects and customers engage in two-way, one-to-one conversations, asking questions and buying products and services.

The combination of text, images, sound, and motion is a very powerful combination. Just look at the impact that television had on the marketing of products and services after it was widely introduced in the late 1940s. The Web's potential is even greater than that of television. Like TV, it combines all elements of communication in one medium. It is widely available to the masses. But, unlike TV, it is an interactive medium, allowing for two-way communication—from prospect to advertiser and advertiser to prospect—and an opportunity for advertisers to begin one-to-one, permission-granted conversations using all elements of communication.

THE THREE LEVELS
OF PROSPECT INVOLVEMENT

The Web has not only compressed time for advertisers and their customers, but has also allowed for a prospect to experience all three levels of interaction with many advertisers' messages, without leaving the online environment. Whether it's a banner ad or an email, prospects are able to (1) *view* an ad or read an email promoting a product, essentially creating an impression; (2) *take action* by clicking through either the ad or the email, linking to a Web site for more information about the product; and (3) *purchase* the product in those cases where e-commerce is enabled. See Table 3.3.

TABLE 3.3   Three Levels of Prospect Involvement

Level of Involvement	Type of Involvement	Online Ad or Email	Offline Ad
Level 1	View	Impression	Impression
Level 2	Action	Click-Through	Walk-In or Call
Level 3	Purchase	Conversion at Web Site	Conversion at Retail or Through Call Center

© 2001 Customer Share Group LLC

In the online environment, a prospect can quickly move from level 1 to level 3 in a matter of minutes or even seconds. The prospect only needs to click through the ad or the email to move to the next level in an online environment, but in the offline environment is required to physically go to the retailer, or at least to a telephone, in order to take action.

Capturing a prospect's identity and permission at level 2 represents the marketing intersection where mass marketing and direct marketing meet. It is at this level that an ongoing, extremely efficient and relevant permission-granted relationship can begin—one that can uniquely complement the work that mass marketing must continue to do in launching new products, in helping to build brand equity, and in motivating prospects and customers to take action.

THE WORLDS OF DAVID OGILVY
AND LESTER WUNDERMAN COLLIDE
ON THE WEB

Even though the practice of direct marketing preceded him by at least 75 years, it was Lester Wunderman who helped professionalize the science. Considered the father of direct marketing, in 1958 Wunderman started his own agency in New York, Wunderman Ricotta & Kline, that later became the world's largest direct marketing agency before being acquired by Young & Rubicam in 1973. Wunderman's agency was adept at selling everything from books to records by sending individually addressed messages to consumers.

David Ogilvy was considered by many to be the father of modern day advertising. As the creator of great advertising, Ogilvy was really thought of as an artist. The art of Ogilvy's mass marketing now meets the science of Wunderman's direct marketing on the Web to create more effective marketing.

MASS MARKETING: NOT JUST AN END,
BUT A MEANS TO AN END

Maybe our expectations for mass marketing are just too high today. There was a day when ads could accomplish more—build brand awareness, generate leads or trial, motivate people to buy. But expecting mass marketing to build relationships with individual customers may be asking too much today. Besides, unless a marketer commits to a strategy that identifies each individual customer by name, address, and purchase history, it can never really know the health of its customer relationships.

Today's marketing environment is simply too noisy and not at all conducive to building relationships one at a time—especially when the orbit of mass-marketing messages doesn't always match up with the recipients' schedule and habits.

The job of mass marketing today is to continue to do battle with the noise and to identify and recruit prospects for a brand—not just to generate sales, but also to *feed the funnel.* Building customer relationships requires one-to-one conversations. Addressable, one-to-one media enables a way to have a conversation with a prospect that is *requested, relevant,* and *respectful.* The combination is bound to produce more effective overall advertising—and isn't that what Unilever wants?

THE CENTURY OF CUSTOMER SHARE

Human nature usually drives us to do what is easiest, both as individuals and as part of a corporate body. The wholesale acquisition of customers in the 20th century was a one-time event in history because of the relatively unadulterated universe of virgin consumers. A steady stream of new customers made their way into the funnel from 1950 to 1975. Marketers today need to recognize that such a march into the land of milk and honey will never happen again. Competition for customers is increasingly difficult for advertisers and their agencies, and realistically, it will continue to be waged on the market share battlefield.

But advertisers and agencies need to fight the human-nature urge to pursue these elusive customers exclusively through mass-marketing means and begin to look at the acquisition of customers—and, just as importantly, at the retention of customers—as fully integrated marketing events.

The time has come for advertisers and agencies to embrace the concept of growth through customer share marketing efforts as an important and productive partner to all market share marketing efforts. Acquiring a higher percentage of each customer's business will gain momentum as a principle marketing focus for all companies in the 21st century.

4

THE CENTURY
OF CUSTOMER
SHARE

Farmer Jones grew corn for a big produce corporation, and each year the corporation demanded more and more from Farmer Jones. Year after year, the corporation expected him to out-produce the prior year's yield. So he planted more and more corn, and for a while was able to produce more and meet the goals set for him by the corporation. Ultimately, though, he reached a point where he was simply unable to produce any more corn for the corporation. So, he went into the city to talk to management.

"Over the last quarter century, I've worked these fields hard and have always been able to give you more from one year to the next," said Farmer Jones. "But I've reached my limit. I can't possibly even water the land that I've planted. So, my harvest will be flat this year compared to last."

Pausing for a minute, one executive offered what he thought was a solution to the shortfall. "How about if you watered the field with two syringes?"

Sometimes, mass marketing can feel as if you are watering a field of corn with a syringe: No matter how fast or hard you work, it's awfully difficult to reach every stalk and generate a yield. Farmer Jones' approach to farming had its limits, and the solution was not necessarily more syringes.

BATTLING FOR MARKET SHARE: EARNING CUSTOMER SHARE

The 20th century will go down in the marketing history books as the 100-year war for market share, when the brand preferences of millions of Americans was up for grabs. Like the Oklahoma boomers who rushed across the plains to lay claim to a piece of America, marketers battled each other for a piece of every American's pocketbook—one product at a time.

For an entire century, companies battled each other for three types of customers:

1. *Brand loyalists:* Customers who are not lured away at all, but instead remain loyal to their existing brand. Their loyalty might not even be based in logic, but more on an emotional, psychological attachment to the products that their parents used. Like being born into a family of Republicans or Democrats, it may take years, if ever, for an individual to make the decision to switch parties (or brands).
2. *Brand switchers:* Customers who are convinced by the promise of a product's advertising and retained by the product's fulfillment of that promise.
3. *Brand neutralists:* Customers who have no specific brand loyalty and, more often than not, buy products based on price.

Some companies can tell you exactly who their customers are by name. Others can also tell you what they bought each year. But most companies know only if sales are up or if sales are down—that after spending millions of advertising and marketing dollars, their market share went up or down.

Like respect, though, customer share is earned over time, not over a weekend. Acquisition initiatives—acquiring sales—play an important role. But most companies can point to no specific initiatives that are dedicated to retaining customers or growing the amount of business from existing loyal customers. Table 4.1 highlights the two major growth strategies—*market share growth* and *customer share growth*. Growth by growing market share was overwhelmingly preferred as the primary means of growth during the second half of the 20th century.

TABLE 4.1   Acquiring or Retaining or Growing Share?

Strategy	Sales Focus	Marketing Focus
Market Share	Acquisition	Mass
Customer Share	Retention/ Growth	Direct

© 2001 Customer Share Group LLC

When the business strategy is to grow market share, the means to accomplish that strategy is to employ mass-marketing tactics to drive acquisition. Mass marketing can help build brand loyalty and effectively help deliver a level of customer share, but that is very difficult to measure and much depends on the product fulfilling the promise that its advertising makes.

A dedicated customer share focus requires direct communication between company and customer. The sales focus, then, is on *retaining customers* and *growing customer share*—getting more from the customers a company already has.

There are many companies that have a 1 percent share of an enormous market and have spent millions trying to get to 2 percent. It's perfectly acceptable if you're not the market share leader. Not every company can be. But businesses of all sizes—from the corner store to a global conglomerate—can and should look at sales from a customer share perspective. The investment required to find, convince, and ultimately acquire customers can be significant. Adopting a customer share strategy requires that you look at your prospects and customers along a continuum, where the marketer methodically develops an ever-increasing level of loyalty.

In Table 4.2, the objective is to move as many individuals from unidentified prospects status on one end of the continuum all the way to lifetime customers on the other end.

TABLE 4.2 Customer Value Continuum

	Unidentified Customers	Identified Customers	One-Time Customers	Repeat Customers	Lifetime Customers
Value	$0	$0	$40	$120	$10,000

© 2001 Customer Share Group LLC

It can be helpful for businesses to look at their prospects and customers categorically—from *unidentified prospect*, to *identified prospect*, to *customer*, to *repeat customer*, to *lifetime customer*. Is she a one-time customer or a repeat customer? What does she contribute annually? What's the value of a lifetime customer? This is the way the airlines have viewed frequent flyers for years. In such a model, customers can be viewed by level of contribution and treated on a quid pro quo basis—the more you give, the more you get.

In the airline scenario, customers who log 250,000 miles are treated differently than customers who fly 1,500 miles a year. The concept of creating a quid pro quo relationship with customers is a good one. The more a customer buys, the more they get. Sprite has essentially replicated this model with its *Rocket Cash* promotions.

For decades, the wholesale acquisition of customers was enough to sustain a business—but no longer. Acquisition is only one half of the equation necessary to sustain a business. Many businesses that haven't yet embraced customer share marketing see themselves as acquirers of millions of customers all at once. If you're selling over a billion drinks a day, one-to-one marketing might be a difficult concept to accept. But think of the impact on that business if its customer share marketing initiatives can help sell just one more drink a year to its existing customer base. The economic impact could be in the billions of dollars.

Getting more from your loyal customers is not difficult. Your customer share marketing initiatives have to be clever, but more importantly, they have to be *requested, relevant,* and *respectful* in order to successfully move prospects and customers along the customer value continuum. The bigger the company, the more loyal customers you have. The more loyal customers you have, the more you can sell to customers you already have by converting one-time customers to repeat customers and repeat customers to customers for life.

Smaller companies can be very successful and very profitable owning 1 or 2 percent of a large market. But their sales focus *must* be on retention, their marketing focus *direct,* and their business strategy on *growing customer share*—getting more from the loyal customers they have already acquired.

CUSTOMER SHARE VERSUS MARKET SHARE

A company that is market share-focused is constantly beating the bushes for new customers. All resources are spent trying to find more sources of revenue. In a company that is customer share-focused, all energy and resources are dedicated to getting 100 percent of the business from each of the customers served.

Table 4.3 shows that both Company A and Company B have captured a 50 percent share of a particular market, with each company generating $2,500 in sales. However, the respective paths to generating that $2,500 were quite different. While Company A had four times as many customers as Company B, Company B captured four times as much from each customer, or 100 percent of each of its customers' business.

TABLE 4.3 Customer Share Versus Market Share

Company	Number of Customers	Revenue Per Customer	Total Revenue	Market Share	Customer Share	Number of Tramsactions
A	100	$25	$2,500	50%	25%	100
B	25	$100	$2,500	50%	100%	25

© 2001 Customer Share Group LLC

Company B's customer share strategy helped to convince less to give more, while Company A's market share strategy resulted in more customers giving less. When you consider both the marketing and transactional costs associated with Company A's 100 customers, versus only 25 for Company B, it becomes clear which company is more profitable.

CUSTOMER SHARE: BEYOND RETENTION

We've heard the word *retention* used quite a bit since the Web was birthed, but what does it really mean? How does it translate into action? Acquisition actions can be identified, described, and quantified: advertising, promotions, sweepstakes, public relations, direct mail, affiliate marketing programs, search engine optimization. But this is generally not so with retention programs. What are your retention programs, specifically? Can you articulate or list them? More importantly, what are your customer share programs that are not designed just to keep customers, but to grow the amount of business you receive from each customer? The time has come for all companies to adopt alternative ways to water the field— ways that complement and support mass-marketing efforts.

WHY CUSTOMER SHARE?

Halloween was a very big night in my house when I was growing up. We lived in one of those neighborhoods with dozens of homes that you could easily cover in no time. We knew some of the neighbors really well, and others we didn't know very well at all. But my favorite stop on Halloween was always at Mrs. Grogan's because she always gave me the most candy. Handfuls of big candy bars, not the little ones—the full-size Snickers, Milky Ways, and Three Musketeers.

Wasn't there a kind old lady on your street who gave you two handfuls of candy? Why did she do it? Because over time a relationship had been built. She brought soup over to you when you were sick. You shoveled her walk during that blizzard. She knew you, liked you, and she was more than pleased to give you more. This is the same type of loyalty that customers feel for companies that pay attention to them and are respectful of them.

SIX REASONS WHY COMPANIES NEED A CUSTOMER SHARE FOCUS

The thousands of dotcom businesses that crashed and burned were not around long enough to be concerned about developing retention strategies. But companies like Coca-Cola and Pepsi have been around for a long time and have very loyal customer bases. They both have customers worth retaining—every company does. But not every company has retention or customer share initiatives that are designed to keep and grow a customer's business.

Here are six reasons why companies need to bolster their customer retention and customer share efforts, and why the Web should be at the center of those efforts:

1. *Cost of acquisition is high.* Increasingly, customers have become distrustful, especially when burned by new companies. It is very expensive to (a) find customers, (b) convince them to trust you, and (c) convince them to give you their money by placing an order. This is a process that takes time and investment. One of the most expensive investments a company can make is acquiring new customers. Doesn't it make sense to protect that enormous investment with specific, direct, effective, and affordable retention efforts?

2. *Cost of retention is low.* This process, ironically, takes far less time and far less money. For 20 percent of the cost to acquire a new customer, you can retain an old one. You do the math. Doesn't it make sense to be focusing more on making your customers feel good about you so that you can ultimately sell more to them? What are you doing to help insure that the customers you already have will be your customers for life? Do you know the lifetime value of one of your customers? Wouldn't it be worth it for you to capture all of it?

3. *Cost of churn is exorbitant.* With so much focus on acquisition, retention of customers gets far less focus today. But even less attention is paid to the cost of churn; that is, what it costs to replace a lost customer. Even if you replace each customer you lose with a new customer, you are still falling behind because of what it costs to acquire that customer. In such a scenario, your top line would be flat, but your bottom line would suffer because of the increased cost of acquisition.

4. *Cut through all the noise.* Whether you are the market share leader or are one of a dozen companies chasing after the leader, you are all fighting the noise of the market. Getting noticed is expensive. Can you outspend the market leader? Or does it make more sense to spend more on retaining the loyal customers that you already have? Which communications scenario would be easier for you: standing in Times Square at midnight on New Year's Eve and trying to get the attention of the entire crowd, or taking one person into a quiet restaurant for a one-to-one dinner? Competing with a noisy crowd is a job for mass marketing. But direct, one-to-one marketing is focused, and when it is *requested, relevant,* and *respectful,* it can be enormously effective. Think of it this way: A child who is tutored one-to-one can learn at a rate more than five times faster than 25 children who are taught by one teacher.

5. *Customer share marketing is direct, measurable, and inexpensive.* The Web makes it possible to develop inexpensive and direct initiatives that are designed to retain customers. Inexpensive and direct is a powerful combination that really only existed at retail prior to the Web. It's your grocery store butcher who knows that you like to have a prime rib cut every Thursday night or the dry cleaner that knows that you like extra starch in your shirts. The Web must be at the center of your retention efforts because you can create effective permission-granted customer touches that are *requested, relevant, respectful,* and measurable for pennies.

6. *Customer share marketing complements market share marketing.* Market share marketing on the front end: communicating to the masses, building brand, and driving prospects and customers to brick-and-mortar stores, to call centers, and to the Web. Customer share marketing on the backend, communicating one-to-one with qualified prospects and customers who have granted permission for you to send them messages on an ongoing basis.

MARKET SATURATION

Overconsumption, consolidation of businesses, and technological improvements to products have all contributed to pushing consumers to saturation levels. TVs are so well made that you might buy only two in your lifetime. That's why Sony Electronics markets and sells dozens of consumer electronic products worldwide. Is Sony selling more products to more people, or is it selling more Sony products to a loyal Sony customer base?

Does Sony know that I am loyal to Sony products? Does it know that I own a Sony TV, a Sony stereo, a Sony Walkman, a Sony answering machine? It doesn't, but it should. If Sony began a permission-granted conversation with me, wouldn't it have a good shot at selling me a new Sony PC, Sony floppy discs, a Sony camcorder, a Sony mini-disc recorder, or any of the dozens of other products that it markets?

The financial objective for all companies is the same: Deliver increased sales and profits. There are a number of ways to accomplish that objective. Acquiring new customers was the major focus of the first 80 years of the 20th century. Cutting costs associated with acquiring those new customers was one of the major focuses of the last 20 years of the 20th century.

If every man, woman, and child on the planet is consuming your products, there's only one place to go in order to increase sales and profits: to your existing customers.

RANDOMLY BUILDING P & G HOUSEHOLDS?

Brands are built one at time in this country. Enormous budgets are allocated to individual brands to fight the market share battle in an effort to win brand loyalty, one product at a time. It's category against category. That's the way the war has always been fought. Year in, year out, the battles continue, but is anyone looking at who might be winning or losing the war? Who is taking the longer view, realizing that ultimately there are a limited number of customers to acquire, a limited number of competitors to acquire, and a limited number of line extensions to launch?

To illustrate the point, let's take a field trip to my house. If you go through the cabinets in our home, you would find the household products listed in Table 4.4.

TABLE 4.4 Share of Household Products

Category	Osenton Household	Company	Competitive Brand	Company
Dishwashing Detergent	Sunlight	Unilever	Cascade	P & G

TABLE 4.4 Share of Household Products (*continued*)

Category	Osenton Household	Company	Competitive Brand	Company
Window Cleaner	Windex	S. C. Johnson	Formula 409	Clorox
Hard-surface Cleaner	Comet	P & G	Soft scrub	Clorox
Laundry Detergent	Wisk	Unilever	Tide	P & G
Fabric Conditioner	Downy	P & G	Snuggle	Unilever
Paper Towels	Bounty	P & G	Scott	Kimberly Clark
Bathroom Tissue	Charmin	P & G	Scott	Kimberly Clark
Facial Tissues	Kleenex	Kimberly Clark	Puffs	P & G
Bar Soap	Dial	Dial Corp.	Ivory	P & G
Tooth Paste	Crest	P & G	Mentadent	Unilever

© 2001 Customer Share Group LLC

Would Procter & Gamble be interested in knowing that 50 percent of the products in our household are Procter & Gamble products? Wouldn't it be worth it to the company to leverage the considerable share of customer that it has in our household to capture some or all of the other 50 percent of household products that we use? Conversely, would Unilever or Kimberly-Clark—two companies with brands already in the home—have an interest in leveraging their respective 20 percent and 10 percent customer share positions to muscle categories away from Procter & Gamble?

GENERATING INCREMENTAL SALES FROM CUSTOMERS YOU ALREADY HAVE

The Web also provides some marketers with the opportunity to begin to improve the quality of their sales in another way—by becoming retailers themselves. The Web offers manufacturers such as Timberland a way to add a direct sales channel to their sales mix, in many cases for the first time. More and more manufacturers are beginning to add their own e-commerce initiatives, eliminating, at least in part, the middleman and delivering higher margin, direct-to-manufacturer sales.

In the 20th century, a market share orientation fed the top line. In the 21st century, a customer share orientation will feed both the top and bottom lines. Market share is an open battle for customers played out on the local and national airwaves, pages, and banners. Customer share is a private email conversation between you and your customers who have essentially said directly to you, "I like what you're doing." There are thousands of companies out there who are spending too much time waging market share battle when all along they are fighting in a customer share war.

Big or small, all companies are in a position to use the Web as an offensive weapon to grow customer share. For a fraction of what it takes to wage a nuclear market share war, you can use the Web to mine more profitable dollars from your existing customer base.

GROWING CUSTOMER SHARE: UNLOCKING CUSTOMER LOYALTY

Now that the dotcom fog has lifted, it's time for companies of all sizes, with established customer bases, to begin to take advantage of the Web's unique characteristics, not only to acquire new customers, but also to retain and sell more to the customers they already have.

As the first two-way communication channel since the invention of the telephone, the Web offers boundless opportunities to increase sales and profits for most companies. However, in order to fully maximize the Web, mass marketers must now acquire or develop the skill set of direct marketers such as cataloger L.L. Bean. Advertisers that have for decades become adept at acquiring customers through mass-marketing initiatives can now use the Web in an affordable and practical way to retain customers and grow customer share, essentially using direct marketing tactics through the combined use of the Web and permission-granted email marketing.

Prior to the Web, one-to-one marketing, though targeted, was expensive and usually required significant investments in designing a physical piece that could be printed and mailed to a customer. For companies like Campbell Soup, whose products can be found in up to 90 percent of all U.S. homes, the cost of postage alone would preclude them from any realistic use of direct mail.

For many established companies, direct contact with customers is a brand new concept. The Web provides an opportunity for these companies to meet customers face-to-face, many for the first time. It also gives them the chance to begin to build one-to-one relationships with loyal customers for the purpose of capturing customers' lifetime value—earning every relevant sale in their company's category for the rest of the customers' lives.

2

UNLOCKING THE POWER OF CUSTOMER LOYALTY

For decades, the world's leading marketers have invested millions of dollars acquiring customers, building brands, and growing customer loyalty. Stored customer loyalty has never been actively mined to unearth profits from customers that have long been faithful to a brand or company.

Now the Web is enabling companies to develop a practical and affordable means of complementing market share initiatives with one-to-one customer share initiatives that are designed to sell more to a company's most loyal customers.

CHAPTER 5

MARKETING ONE-TO-ONE COMES OF AGE

Have you ever had a "good talking to"? Maybe you stayed out past your curfew and you ran into your father when you were tiptoeing across the kitchen floor. A good talking to is a one-way conversation. You are spoken *to,* or *at.* You are expected to listen, not talk. We don't like to be talked *to.* It makes us feel small and insignificant. We avoid getting a good talking to at all costs.

The nature of mass marketing is largely to talk *to* as many people as possible, an effective way to get the attention of your unidentified prospects. The nature of direct marketing is largely to talk *with* prospects and customers on a one-to-one basis—a conversation *with* identifiable prospects and customers.

THE WEB PLUS EMAIL: A "WITH" COMMUNICATION CHANNEL

The Web, all by itself, is another one-way, mass communication tool, just like television, radio, and print. It's definitely a *to* medium. In fact, one could argue that as a mass-marketing vehicle, the Web is even less effective than television because the user largely comes to the Web not to be entertained, but to search and find. People don't go to the Web to have something done to them—to be informed and entertained. They go to the Web to inform and entertain themselves. This is an important distinction, and a rather challenging one psychologically and logistically for marketers that are not used to the consumer driving the utility of a medium.

Now add the ability to communicate one-to-one with individuals by email, and the Web becomes the most powerful direct marketing weapon the world has ever seen. The combination of the Web with email makes for a very dynamic *with* medium, educating consumers and communicating with them in two directions.

BACK TO THE FUTURE

The practice of promoting the sale of goods one-to-one is certainly not a new one. Direct marketing actually predates Gutenberg's invention of the printing press in 1453, when seed and nursery fliers were distributed across Europe. The nursery and gardening "catalogs" made the trip across the "Pond" to the colonies before the country was a country, and in 1771 the first colony-based catalog was published by William Prince of Flushing, New York, promoting the sale of fruit trees.

Benjamin Franklin, the first significant printer in the colonies, published a catalog of nearly 600 books in 1744 in what was essentially the forerunner to the modern-day book club. Companies like Tiffany & Company (1845), Orvis (1856), Montgomery Ward (1872), and Sears, Roebuck (1886) all have a long-standing tradition as direct marketers, promoting their wares through catalogs or fliers over a century ago.

Ironically, both Ward's and Sears started as direct marketers before they ventured into retail—and with good reason. It was a relatively inexpensive way to get started in business, avoiding the enormous capital outlay that a self-directed retail model required. For Richard Sears, it was a way to find out if he could sell a box of watches by mail.

Within 6 months, he had made more than $5,000 and he gave up his job as a railroad station agent to start what would later become an American marketing phenomenon. Ward's wasn't as lucky as Sears at the retail game, however, and sadly closed its doors in 2000.

THE WEB AS AN OFFENSIVE MARKETING WEAPON

Figure 5.1 represents the universe of marketers that are using the Web to promote their products and services. As you move from right to left on this chart, the level of Web marketing sophistication increases. The laggards, on the extreme right, represent companies that ultimately made the move to the Web defensively, reacting to what everybody else was doing because they felt they had to.

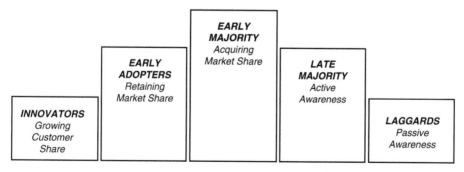

©2001 Customer Share Group LLC

FIGURE 5.1
Marketing adoption continuum.

On the other hand, the innovators such as Frito-Lay, on the extreme left, represent companies that are using the Web as a strategic offensive marketing weapon. These innovators are complementing their market share marketing initiatives with customer share marketing initiatives, working their own permission-granted email lists to help drive incremental sales.

Over time, marketers will move from right to left on the continuum as they become more comfortable with and more proficient at one-to-one customer retention initiatives. Companies progressively move through the continuum, graduating from one level to the next:

- *Laggards:* Engaged in passive awareness, doing little more than building a Web site.
- *Late majority:* Engaged in active awareness, minimally promoting their sites with URL tagging on packaging and existing advertising.
- *Early majority:* Engaged in proactively acquiring market share. It is at this stage that marketers begin to view the Web as a marketing weapon, actively advertising online and perhaps using third-party opt-in email to reach new prospects in an effort to increase market share.
- *Early adopters:* Engaged in all of the above, but have also added specific customer retention initiatives to the mix and have aggressively built a permission-granted email database for the purpose of retaining the customers they already have.
- *Innovators:* Engaged in all of the above, but are strategically using their permission-granted email marketing initiatives that are specifically designed to increase business from loyal customers—actively growing customer share.

Any company that has a Web site falls into one of these categories on the Web marketing continuum A small investment in retention goes a long way toward creating a deeper relationship with customers and a willingness to spend more with you. Where is your company?

ETHICAL ONE-TO-ONE MARKETING

Ethical marketers were forced to deal with the fallout from unethical marketers that blatantly sent unsolicited commercial email, or spam, to unsuspecting consumers and businesses alike in the 1990s. Though businesses soon learned how to build firewalls in the servers to prevent most spam from making it to employees' desktops, consumers haven't been so lucky. By 1999, the heightened focus on spammers caused the formation of numerous special interest groups as well as legislation designed to protect consumers from email that was not *requested, relevant, or respectful.*

Fortunately, the advent of permission-granted email marketing has helped to bring a new level of respect to the use of commercial email for ethical marketers. Permission is helping to improve the use of commercial email, not just because it is the right thing to do, but also because it's simply more effective.

ONE-TO-ONE MARKETING:

TARGETED AND MEASURABLE

Unlike mass marketing, where it is difficult to target and nearly impossible to measure its effectiveness, one-to-one marketing allows for both. In their pre-Web best-selling book *The One-to-One Future: Building Relationships One Customer at a Time,* Don Peppers and Martha Rogers gave us a glimpse of the future of marketing, where share of customer— not share of market—becomes an increasingly important means of growing a business profitably. This book does a great job of articulating the benefits of marketing conversations that are directed to a single, identified individual who oftentimes is already loyal to a product or brand. It's a must-read for any marketer.

The early pioneers of one-to-one marketing utilized the United States Postal Service as their means of both marketing to prospects and customers and delivering the goods. Direct mail, then, was their primary means of marketing and distribution. Though the cost of printing and mailing catalogs and fliers has grown consistently over the last 100 years, direct mail has always had two major benefits:

1. *Targeted.* Messages are addressed to individuals. Most often, the list contains both customers and prospects, and the targeted nature of direct mail helps to cut through the clutter of the thousands of commercial messages that consumers receive each day.
2. *Measurable.* A given number of pieces are mailed and a given number of customers respond—usually within the first 10 days. The outcome of most direct mail campaigns is fairly predictable, and depending on the mix of house names to rented/leased names, response generally falls in the 1 to 3 percent range. "House list" names generally respond at a much higher rate.

But as effective as direct mail is, it can't deliver all of the unique and powerful marketing benefits that the Web and email can deliver.

LEVERAGING LOYALTY

The marketing combination of having a tell-all Web site with the immediate and interactive nature of email is not only targeted and measurable, but also faster and cheaper than any other means of direct marketing. It is the combination of these four characteristics that now make it possible and practical for marketers of all sizes to create ongoing conversations with their customers one at a time:

1. Targeted
2. Measurable
3. Faster
4. Cheaper

These characteristics now make it possible for long-time mass marketers like Johnson & Johnson, Procter & Gamble, and Coca-Cola to link an effective one-to-one marketing back-end to their more traditional mass-marketing one-to-many marketing front end to complete a marketing strategy that seeks to grow market share through mass-marketing tactics, and at the same time, seeks to grow customer share through one-to-one direct marketing tactics.

Prior to the Web and email, customer share marketing was cumbersome, impractical, and expensive for most companies. Now companies of any size, from the Fortune 100 to the local wine shop, can communicate directly with the people who have been their loyal customers for years.

If your universe of customers is relatively finite, then customer share marketing is an important growth strategy for your business. If you are a B2B company with only 50 prospective customers in your universe, then customer share marketing can help you mine more business from those 50.

On the other end of the spectrum, if you are a B2C company that literally targets everyone in the world—6 billion prospective customers—and your global penetration and distribution is significant, then a customer share marketing strategy that is designed to sell more to your existing loyal customers can yield a significant and highly profitable increase in sales. The powerful benefits of targeted, measurable, faster, and cheaper, one-to-one marketing campaigns, finally gives marketers of all sizes, a practical and affordable means of fulfilling the promise of marketing segmentation.

Now overlay a fifth element—permission—and you add to your marketing arsenal a new means of communicating with prospects and customers who have requested that you send them future email messages.

THE POWER OF PERMISSION

Table 5.1, from Jupiter Media Metrix, compares retention initiatives that are direct in nature and are sent to inhouse, permission-granted lists with acquisition initiatives that are indirect in nature and can be either mass-marketing efforts, such as banner advertising, or direct marketing efforts, such as sending direct mail to a "cold" list of rented names.

TABLE 5.1 Retention: Faster, Cheaper

	Retention		Acquisition			
Metrics	E-mail	Direct Mail	E-mail	Direct Mail	Sponsorships	Banner
Variable Prod.	$0	$50	$0	$50	$0	$0
Media CPM	$0	$0	$200	$110	$25	$15
Delivery CPM	$30	$500	$0	$500	$0	$1
CTR	10%	N/A	7%	N/A	1.5%	0.5%
Conversion	5%	3%	2.5%	1%	2.5%	2.5%
Cost/Conversion	$6	$18	$114	$66	$67	$128
Execution Time	3 Weeks	3 Months	3 Weeks	3 Months	3 Weeks	3 Weeks
Response Time	48 Hours	3 Weeks	48 Hours	3 Weeks	48 Hours	48 Hours
Up-Front Creative Costs	$1K	$20K	$1K	$20K	$1K	$3K

© 2000 Jupiter Media Metrix

Retention, or permission-granted, email is defined as messages that are sent to customers who have given permission directly to you—not to a third party—to send them information on your products or services. By definition, these messages are *requested, relevant, and respectful* to the recipient.

The benefits of retention email are obvious. Not only is it targeted and measurable, but it also carries with it some other attractive additional benefits:

1. *Lower cost to create and produce:* Variable production costs, delivery costs, and up-front creative costs are all significantly lower than any of the alternatives.
2. *Faster execution time:* On average, it takes only 3 weeks to prepare and execute a retention-based email campaign, as opposed to 3 months for a direct mail campaign.
3. *Faster response time:* On average, it takes only 48 hours to receive a response from customers, while it

takes up to 3 weeks to receive the same level of response from a direct mail campaign.

4. *Lower cost per conversion:* By far the lowest cost to convert into a sale. The quality of the list in direct marketing has always been a major factor in generating outstanding response rates. This statistic underscores the effectiveness of working a permission-granted, or retention, email list.

The incredibly targeted and focused nature of a customer share marketing strategy allows marketers to pinpoint their prospects and customers, not by age, gender, and Household Income (HHI), but by name, address, email address, birth date, product usage, special interests, and more. The benefit to this type of invited and personal means of commercial communication is obvious: It is designed to have a quiet, focused, relevant, one-to-one conversation with prospects and customers about information that interests them.

Creating these one-to-one, permission-granted messages helps marketers cut through the noise and clutter, allowing them to engage in a form of personal marketing that actually is a throwback to the simpler days when the proprietor of the general store knew who you were, when you shopped, and what you liked.

A SYMPHONY OF NOISE

Mass marketers work hard to get the attention of their prospects and customers. The unfortunate thing is that a single ad—like a single note from an oboe in an orchestra—has to fight all the other ads that are all playing at the same time.

Think of all the world's greatest orchestras crammed into Carnegie Hall. The London Symphony next to the New York Philharmonic next to the Berlin Philharmonic next to the Philadelphia Orchestra next to the Chicago Symphony, and so on. And each orchestra is playing a different classical piece. . .

all at the same time. London plays Mozart, Philadelphia plays Beethoven, Berlin plays Wagner, Chicago plays Brahms, and so on—thousands upon thousands of individual notes trying desperately to reach your ear. The output is so overwhelming that you cover your ears. It is far from harmonic and produces a cacophony that is deafening. No one is served in this scenario—not the *sender* or the *receiver.*

CUTTING THROUGH 300,000 YEARS OF ORIGINAL DATA

According to a recent study from the School of Information Management (SIMS) at the University of California, Berkeley, humankind will generate more original information in the next 3 years than was created in the last 300,000 years.

So, marketers have a choice: Fight the "Content Big Bang," as the study suggests, or begin an entirely new type of communication with prospects and customers that attracts a center-of-the-target audience to a Web site and seeks their permission to communicate directly with them.

Messages that are not requested are most often irrelevant and disrespectful to the recipient and are being tuned out, especially in an email format. Email that is *requested* by the recipient, *relevant* to the recipient, and *respectful* to the recipient will cut through the clutter of commercial messages that bombard consumers on a daily basis.

ACQUIRING AND RETAINING CUSTOMERS ONE AT A TIME

The idea of acquiring customers one at a time is not generally how marketers and their agencies think. The terms *acquisition* and *retention* have been around for a very long time and have been the primary focus of magazine circulation directors for many decades. *Town & Country* magazine has been acquiring and retaining subscribers or selling and renewing subscriptions for over 150 years.

But acquisition and retention only recently became part of the general business parlance with the birth of thousands of new businesses on the Web. Unfortunately for most of them, the retention of customers never became a real issue.

But as more and more established businesses begin to use the Web to strategically market to their best prospects and customers, the Web will increasingly be used as a retention and customer share marketing device. According to Jupiter Media Metrix, retention email is poised to explode over the next 4 years from a measly $164 million industry in 1999 to a projected $7.3 billion in 2005—a whopping 44-fold increase in annual spending in using email to retain customers.

Acquisition has historically been defined as acquiring a sale, but it can also describe the acquisition of permission from prospects and customers in order to send them future messages by email. Certainly, the objective of most marketing initiatives is to acquire as many sales as possible. But if you can't acquire a sale, acquire permission. Acquiring the privilege of communicating with a prospect or customer in the future creates a second chance at influencing him or her. It creates a second level of sell.

Think of your acquisition marketing initiatives as efforts that *feed the funnel* with prospects and customers that will help you build your own permission-granted list. Think of your retention marketing initiatives as efforts that *work the list* of prospects and customers that have granted you permission to send them messages and are resident in your permission-granted database.

Since online transactions are not practical for most companies in the service industries, acquiring permission—using their sites as qualified-lead generators—should be a primary goal for such companies. Capturing the names, email addresses, and permission from interested prospects and customers allows service industry businesses, such as real estate companies and car dealers, to create relevant, outbound, permission-granted email marketing programs that fill very specific consumer preferences.

BUILDING LONG-TERM LOYALTY

A customer share marketing focus is not necessarily about online sales. It's about maximizing your relationship with every customer who you can identify and with whom you can begin to have a conversation. It's about using all of your sales channels to help capture permission-granted email identities: sign-ups at your retail locations; WWW taglines on all packaging, delivery trucks, and advertising. Ultimately, it's about creating customized permission-granted email initiatives—the most efficient relationship-building marketing tool that is designed to build loyalty one customer at a time.

A customer share marketing focus takes a long-term view of generating sales from customers. The ultimate objective: capturing the lifetime value of each customer. Increasing the share of business from each customer also helps to fight churn—replacing lost customers with new customers. All businesses experience some level of churn. Building customer relationships one at a time is the best strategy to replace lost customers with growth from the loyal customers that reside in the company's permission-granted email database.

NOW EVERY COMPANY IS A DIRECT MARKETER

If your company has a Web site, you have entered the world of direct marketing. Your customers have an easy and direct way to communicate with you. Now you have to decide what to do as a direct marketer. Will you be reactive and develop your Web marketing initiatives as a defensive measure? Or will you go on the offensive and use the Web and email to enhance your relationship with your best prospects and customers? If you decide not to take a proactive approach to customer acquisition and retention, you can be fairly certain that your competition will. The Web is a great equalizer and can rapidly level the playing field for competitive businesses. Who would have guessed that the world's largest bookstore in 2000 did not even exist in 1994?

More and more of the world's leading marketers are beginning to wage the war for share on two fronts: the battle for market share and the battle for customer share. The battle for customer share is a quiet one. You won't be reading too much about it in *Ad Age* or *Adweek* or *iMarketing News* because customer share marketing is about private conversations, not public ones.

A customer share marketing focus will become an increasingly important part of your marketing strategy, if it isn't already,

- even if you haven't started collecting your own list of permission-granted email addresses,
- even if you haven't started to convert your mailing list to an emailing list,
- even if you haven't sent out one permission-granted email.

Many companies are in a position now to embrace the opportunity to communicate one-to-one with their prospects and customers, beginning a process that will result in a measurable increase in the amount of business they earn from each customer.

SELLING AND DISTRIBUTING DIRECTLY TO CUSTOMERS

The unique energy that can be created by the Web and email is causing manufacturers of all kinds to rethink how they sell and distribute their goods. Many companies are beginning to take responsibility for both selling and distributing their products directly to customers.

This new responsibility creates new opportunities and challenges for both manufacturers and their reseller partners. A higher premium is being placed on owning and developing the customer relationship. As more manufacturers move into retail, managing customer relationships becomes a high priority for the first time ever.

6

SELLING DIRECT COMES OF AGE

The overwhelming majority of consumer products sold in the United States have been purchased through the wholesale or reseller channel. We typically don't buy our string beans from Green Giant, our lawnmowers from Lawnboy, or our televisions from Sony. Historically, we've purchased our string beans from Safeway, our lawnmowers from Sears, and our televisions from Circuit City.

Even though only a small fraction of the more than $6 trillion sold at retail in 2000 went directly to manufacturers, the lure of increasing margins by selling direct is definitely gaining momentum. The interactive nature of the Web has been the catalyst helping to feed the trend. We now can buy PCs directly from IBM and Dell, shoes directly from Bally and Timberland, and CDs directly from Universal Music and BMG

Entertainment. Selling directly to end-users, keeping $1 out of every $1 instead of sharing up to half of it with a wholesale or reseller partner, has manufacturers rethinking their sales channels and in many cases becoming retailers themselves.

THE GENERAL STORE

In the years immediately following the Civil War, catalog mail order grew into a significant industry. The hub of catalog mail order was the Midwest, where farmers were discontent with the low prices they would receive for goods that they sold to the local general store. It was this discontent that led to the formation of the National Grange of the Patrons of Husbandry, which served as the primary organization that represented the voice of the farmer. Their singular battle cry during the early years: *Eliminate the middlemen.*

But the general store model—a one-stop location where people could buy the products of hundreds of manufacturers—had become an institution in this country well before 1800. The model was borrowed from rural England as a way to efficiently transport and sell supplies to remote areas without constructing costly manufacturing all over the country. In the 17th and 18th centuries, most of the manufacturing was based in the eastern part of the United States, making it necessary to establish general stores as the primary means of distributing and selling a variety of products from a variety of different manufacturers as the country was settled from East to West.

This reseller model made good sense as an efficient way for manufacturers to grow without unnecessarily tying up huge amounts of capital in constructing manufacturing facilities across the country. So the general store, or reseller, model was embraced early on and became the primary means of distributing and selling products in this country.

Even though chain department stores helped push out the general store in the early part of the 20th century, the model for companies such as Montgomery Ward was still the same— sell and distribute someone else's products.

RESELLER AS MIDDLEMAN

In the traditional general store model, the reseller is placed between the manufacturer and the customer. In essence, the manufacturer has outsourced its relationship with customers to the reseller, as illustrated in Figure 6.1.

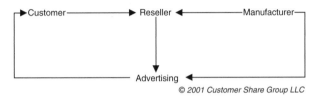

© 2001 Customer Share Group LLC

FIGURE 6.1
Reseller as retailer.

The reseller, not the manufacturer, manages the relationship with the customer. For example, Macy's services the customers when they show up at a physical location. Macy's takes an order at its call center from a customer ordering out of a Macy's catalog or from a customer ordering online at Macys.com. Macy's fulfills that order and Macy's handles customer service on that order, including returns. That's a lot of customer touches that a manufacturer has essentially "outsourced" to a reseller partner.

In the end, Macy's largely builds and owns the customer relationship. Since it controls the customer touch, there's nothing to stop Macy's from cross-selling or upselling a customer into another manufacturer's line. When the manufacturer abdicates control over the customer touch, it gives up control over the ability to build trust and a relationship directly with a customer.

THE EROSION OF THE GENERAL STORE MODEL

Toward the end of the 20th century, the general store, or reseller, model was in trouble. The days when resellers charged high prices to farmers were long gone, with most surviving department stores battling it out based largely on discounted prices. Department stores such as Montgomery Ward, Lechmere, Caldor, HQ, just to name a few had all closed their doors. Wards, one of the oldest direct marketers in the country, filed for bankruptcy at the end of 2000, unable to differentiate itself in a world of specialty stores such as Best Buy and Circuit City and mega-discount chains such as Wal-Mart and Target.

One of Ward's chief competitors for much of its 128-year life, Sears, Roebuck & Co. similarly battles for its life, trying to determine what kind of company it will be in the 21st century. The days of selling everybody everything are over at Sears. It's more likely that Sears will play to its strength and focus its efforts in the major appliance area—especially since Sears, under the Kenmore brand name, sells its own private label appliances that are exclusively manufactured for Sears by Whirlpool.

The health of the reseller model on the Web may even be worse than that of offline resellers, if that's possible. Scores of startup e-commerce resellers formed and folded over the first 6 years of the Web's life. Amazon.com, the undisputed heavyweight champ of B2C Web resellers, leads the pack in burning through cash—losing an astonishing $1.4 billion in 2000 alone, nearly twice the loss from the prior year. Though their losses appear to be shrinking as a percent of sales and promises of near-term profitability abound, there's one undeniable fact: The business of selling someone else's products on the Web is a very difficult one.

One has to wonder: Are we seeing the beginning of the end of the reseller model?

THE MANUFACTURERS' PERSPECTIVE

Manufacturers, such as Timberland, are carefully looking at their channels and realizing that in the channels they control, their margins far exceed those that they generate through the reseller channel. Certainly, the lion's share of the more than $6 trillion generated annually through retail will continue to flow from that channel. For companies such as Timberland, distributing and selling through resellers represents an inexpensive, if not greatly profitable, means of getting the boots and gear out there.

If you are running the show at a major shoe company, adding e-commerce over the Web as an additional sales channel is probably a no-brainer. You will be adding a more profitable channel to your mix as well as a sales environment that you control. You will still sell in thousands of reseller shops around the country, because it represents the largest portion of your top line. But as more and more consumers turn to the Web out of convenience, you will be there displaying what you want, the way you want to display it—and probably selling against the reseller Web sites that carry your products.

SELLING SHOES

There are basically six ways for shoe manufacturers to sell their goods:

1. Through a manufacturer's own brick-and-mortar location, such as Kenneth Cole,
2. Through a reseller's brick-and-mortar location, such as Bloomingdale's,
3. Through a manufacturer's own catalog by calling a toll-free number or through mail order, such as Cole Haan,
4. Through a reseller's catalog by calling a toll-free number or through mail order, such as Macy's By Mail,
5. Through a manufacturer's own e-commerce site, such as Bally.com,
6. Through a reseller's e-commerce site, such as Nordstrom.com.

Table 6.1 details the variety of different sales channels that some of the leading shoe manufacturers use to sell their shoes.

TABLE 6.1 How They Sell Their Shoes

Manufacturer	Own Retail Store(s)	Reseller Retail Store(s)	Own Catalog Mail/Call Center	Reseller Catalog Mail/Call Center	Own E-Commerce	Reseller E-Commerce
Avia	No	Yes	No	Yes	Yes	Yes
Bally	Yes	Yes	No*	Yes	Yes	No
Cole Haan	Yes	Yes	Yes	Yes	Yes	Yes
Dexter	Yes	Yes	No	Yes	Yes	Yes
J & M	Yes	Yes	Yes	Yes	Yes	Yes
Keds	Yes	Yes	No	Yes	Yes	Yes
K. Cole	Yes	Yes	Yes	Yes	Yes	Yes
Nike	Yes	Yes	No	Yes	Yes	Yes
Nine West	Yes	Yes	No	Yes	Yes	Yes
Rockport	Yes	Yes	Yes	Yes	Yes	Yes
Sebago	No	Yes	No	Yes	Yes	Yes
Timberland	Yes	Yes	No	Yes	Yes	Yes

Eliminated print catalog in Fall 2000
© 2001 Customer Share Group LLC

Only 4 of these 12 major shoe manufacturers use every sales channel on the chart to move their products. The majority of these shoe manufacturers—10 out of 12—have invested in their own brick-and-mortar retail locations, while *all* of them sell through their reseller partners' brick-and-mortar retail stores. Interestingly, though, these manufacturers let their reseller partners fund the lion's share of shoe marketing when it comes to producing and mailing printed catalogs, with only 4 of 12 funding their own catalog marketing efforts. There definitely seems to be a trend away from manufacturer-produced catalogs in favor of manufacturer's own e-commerce sites on the Web. Timberland is a good example—the company has never produced and mailed its own catalogs, but instead invested in Timberland.com as its principle direct marketing initiative.

When it comes to e-commerce, all support their own direct-to-manufacturer efforts on the Web. Interestingly, only one—Bally—seems to have made the conscious decision not to sell online through e-commerce resellers and instead has essentially created an online exclusive for Bally products at Bally.com.

MANUFACTURER AS RETAILER ON THE WEB

The Web debuted and made it easier for the manufacturer to become retailer. It also allowed manufacturers to circumvent the reseller and communicate and sell directly to their customers, many for the first time. See Figure 6.2.

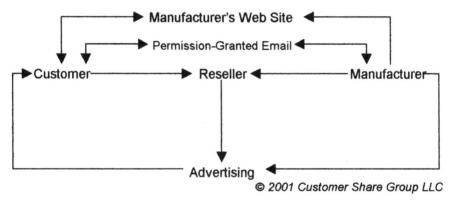

© 2001 Customer Share Group LLC

FIGURE 6.2
Manufacturer as retailer.

By obtaining permission to begin an email conversation with customers, the Web marketing model allowed manufacturers to connect directly with their customers and get to know them better. This strategic move was a significant one and has caused many companies to seek help in the management of what could be millions of customer relationships after essentially abdicating this role to resellers for decades.

Though this has already provided a relative boon to the customer relationship management (CRM) community, marketers of all kinds that are using the Web to grow sales are also realizing that the capture, storage, and analysis of customer intelligence is just one piece of an overall communications program with a company's best prospects and customers. The careful and productive use of the intelligence represents uncharted waters for most parties involved and requires marketers to proceed with caution.

THE DECISION TO SELL DIRECT

L.L.Bean, the Freeport, Maine, institution and manufacturer and marketer of clothing and supplies for outdoor types, decided to sell direct right from the outset in 1912. Bean sent out a four-page mailer promoting his *Bean Boots* to out-of-state sportsmen, and the rest is history. Its famous 24/7 Freeport retail store was added in 1917, and in 1925 a full line of apparel and sporting gear was added when Bean sent out its first full-sized catalog.

By the time the Web appeared in 1994, Bean already had over 80 years of direct marketing experience and was exceptionally proficient at all the skills required of a manufacturer that sells and distributes directly to its customers: managing a database of names; mailing catalogs; managing a call center; managing inventory; picking, packing, and shipping; handling returns; and customer service. Bean did it all. So Bean's move to the Web in 1995 was a fairly seamless event. The Web simply represented another source of orders for the company—a new channel through which it communicated, sold, and fulfilled.

DELLVISION

Michael Dell's vision to build a personal computer empire based on selling his products directly to consumers has certainly paid off. Dell was the top performing stock of the 1990s, averaging nearly a 100 percent annual improvement in the stock price. When Dell was launched in 1984, there was no Web, so direct meant pushing customers to a call center, where a Dell customer care representative handled the touch and closed the sale.

Later, the move to the Web was a natural one for Dell, as it was for L.L. Bean, since it was already experienced with selling and distributing directly to customers one at a time. Today more than 50 percent of Dell's $32 billion in annual sales are captured on the Web—representing more than $50 million a day.

Dell's vision of the Internet, according to its 2000 Annual Report: The Internet, the purest and most efficient form of the direct model, provides greater convenience and efficiency to customers and, in turn, to Dell.

Though PC sales have stalled in recent years, and Dell has been criticized for some its marketing tactics in order to keep sales flowing, the leading direct marketer of PCs still finds a way to keep more of the margin with which it has to play, and consistently ranks as the profit leader in its industry.

NAVIGATING THE ADDITION OF THE DIRECT CHANNEL

Timberland is another company that launched by selling boots, but not directly to the public. Timberland first sold its waterproof leather boots as part of the Abington Shoe Company before changing the name of the company to Timberland in 1978. A decade later, it opened its first retail store in Newport, Rhode Island.

At the turn of the new millennium, Timberland products were largely sold through resellers around the world and through about 60 of Timberland's own specialty retail stores and outlets. As a company, it had never ventured into direct marketing, never investing in a catalog. Unlike L.L. Bean, Timberland had virtually no experience selling and distributing its gear directly through consumer catalogs and call centers through which consumers could place orders. So, its move to add the direct e-commerce channel in the summer of 2001 required some soul-searching and some sensitivity regarding their wholesale partners.

Sensitive about the possibility of creating channel conflict by adding a direct sales channel, Timberland managed the process of entering the e-commerce arena very carefully. Timberland communicated its e-commerce plans to wholesale partners both by letter and in person in late Fall 2000— 9 months prior to the expected launch of Timberland.com.

From a pricing standpoint, Timberland also took the high road and determined that it would sell products on its Web site at the manufacturer's suggested retail price (MSRP) to avoid price competing with its existing channels. Additionally, the Web site included a store locator that directs customers to the nearest brick-and-mortar retail store.

A LARGER SHARE OF CUSTOMER

Even though the company is most well known for its footwear products, Timberland has evolved into a head-to-toe lifestyle brand in recent years by adding apparel and gear lines to its offering. But because its products are often sold at footwear-only stores, the opportunity to capture an increased customer share has been limited.

The Web also gave Timberland the opportunity to more broadly position the brand and to sell across all product lines, something that is not always possible in the wholesale channel.

The addition of its own complete-line e-commerce Web site has created greater cross-selling and upselling opportunities that have helped Timberland significantly outperform its average offline retail sale of $75, more than tripling that average in its first 2 months of e-commerce sales.

FIVE BENEFITS OF SELLING DIRECT

For manufacturers, the lure of selling direct to customers is a powerful one, especially for those companies that have been underperforming. Direct communication with customers allows for an increased opportunity to:

1. *Control the touch.* It's *your people* answering the telephone. It's *your people* answering customer service email or chatting live. You hire them and you train them. When you outsource your customer touches, you give up the hands-on opportunity to insure that your customers are being handled exactly the way you want them to be handled. It's your reputation and your brand equity that's on the line. The last thing your customers need is a surly contact that has an eye on the clock because the third shift is about to end.

2. *Control the message.* It's your vision. It's your message. You want customer care contacts that fully understand your vision, your message, and your products. When you control the message, you know what's being said or written. Companies would be horrified if they spent a morning listening to outsourced call center conversations or reading chat messages or outbound emails. You think they know your message and represent you the way you want them to represent you? Think again.

3. *Gather customer intelligence.* Firsthand, one-to-one contact provides the best opportunity to keep your finger on the pulse of your customers. Whether it's by telephone, through email, or in person, your conversations can be two-way, and if your people are curious or are trained to listen, you will learn a lot about your customers' habits, attitudes, and preferences.

4. *Grow customer share.* If your people are trained to help resolve customer problems, you have a natural way to sell more products. For the long term, building loyalty and trust with your people should be your primary goal. For the short term, cross-selling and up-selling, when done appropriately, can help greatly improve average order sizes. But be very careful. Trying to sell products to people who don't need them can result in alienating customers and putting their trust at risk.

5. *Improve the margin.* Becoming proficient at all of the above can help improve a manufacturer's margin. The

fact is that a move to a direct sales model alone can greatly improve the margin by eliminating a reseller's percentage of each sale. Some marketers feel that a significant increase in marketing spending is necessary to successfully sell its own products online. But as a marketer's permission-granted email database grows, marketing costs can actually drop as one-to-one marketing initiatives become more and more productive.

A NEW CHALLENGE FOR RESELLERS

The Web has created both new opportunities and new challenges for resellers. The migration of manufacturers to the Web to sell directly to their prospects and customers creates a leak in the reseller dam. If you're a reseller, you have to feel the nibble on your business that the Web has enabled: the slow drip of sales leaking off of your shelves and onto the shelves of the manufacturers you represent.

Brick-and-mortar resellers must focus on the most important marketing element that they control: managing the customer relationship. Nordstrom made that decision a long time ago, well before there even was a Web, delivering an in-person customer experience like no other brick-and-mortar reseller. The company has also successfully replicated that customer-centric sensibility in all of its e-commerce applications.

The Web has created a breakpoint opportunity for manufacturers, and some are taking advantage of it. In 1994, none of the 12 shoe manufacturers listed in Table 6.1 sold their products over the Web. Now they all do.

What does this mean for the reseller? Like the manufacturers, they need to create and mine the customer touches as they always have, giving customers a reason—beyond price—to link with them either online or offline. Nordstrom works hard at this, and it shows.

MAXIMIZING CUSTOMER TOUCHES

Every day of the year, customers create an overwhelming number of touch points with companies by visiting them at retail, calling their call centers, logging onto their Web sites, or sending them mail or returns. Each time a customer comes in contact with a company, a customer touch is created—an opportunity for the company to either *enhance* or *erode* its relationship with the customer.

Many of these touches go unnoticed by the company. These are lifeblood interactions between your company and the people that buy your products or services. Do you feel 100 percent confident that your customer touches are world class? Are your customer touches hurting you, or helping you?

7

MAXIMIZING YOUR CUSTOMER TOUCHES

The Golden Rule

Sell good merchandise at a reasonable profit,
treat your customers like human beings,
and they will always come back for more.

—Leon Leonwood Bean, 1912

Leon Leonwood Bean sold 100 pairs of his boots in the spring of 1912 and attached a tag to each pair guaranteeing 100 percent satisfaction. Within weeks, 90 of the 100 boots were returned because the rubber soles were separating from the leather uppers. Bean quickly refined the boots and replaced all 90. He not only made good on his promise, but also won the loyalty of his fledgling customer base.

Bean lived by his own golden rule and treated his customers as human beings, resulting in an ever-growing community of Bean boot owners. So in 1925, when he introduced a line of outdoor apparel and sporting gear to his loyal customers through his first-ever full-sized catalog, his customer share exploded, and he sold more than he ever imagined he would to his most loyal customers.

As an outdoorsman himself, Bean intuitively knew that by thinking like an outdoorsman, he was able to serve his customers in a way that he would want to be served. He knew that he had a particularly high degree of customer knowledge, since he was one, and he used that knowledge to sell more and more items to his growing list of satisfied customers.

CUSTOMER SHARE GIVES WAY TO MARKET SHARE

Ironically, at about the same time Bean was pioneering the concept of customer share, Henry Ford was putting the finishing touches on his assembly line that paved the way for mass production and the ability to rapidly create and sell cars to as many people as possible. The mass marketing roar of market share drowned out the quiet finesse of building customer share one customer at a time.

To a great degree, mass marketers abandoned the concept of full service in favor of moving quickly to generate more sales to more people. In the process, the concept of selling and serving one customer at a time was replaced by the easy pickings of a people that had sacrificed much during a depression and a world war and were now anxious to acquire the things that they had previously only dreamed about. Marketers and their agencies, poised to drive hungry consumers into the stores of retailers, managed the tidal wave of interactions between customers and companies like never before during the 1950s and 1960s.

CUSTOMER TOUCHES DEFINED

The success of luring more than a generation of Americans to indulge themselves created an ever-increasing number of one-to-one contacts—or customer touches—between companies and individual customers, or as L.L. Bean put it, human beings. These customer touches occur in the following ways: in person, over the telephone, through the mail or other physical delivery services, through email, or through live customer care chat on your Web site, as listed in Table 7.1.

TABLE 7.1   Know Your Customer Touches

Type of Touch	Where	What	With Whom
In-Person*	Retail	Product Info	Salesperson
		Check-out	Cashier
Outbound Telephone*	Call Center	Telemarketing Issue	Telemarketing Rep
		Resolution	Customer Service Rep
Inbound Telephone*	Call Center	Orders/Info Issue	Telesales Rep Customer Service Rep Resolution
Outbound Mail/Delivery	Marketing Dept. Customer Service Fulfillment Center	Direct Mail Letters Packages	Marketing Rep Customer Service Rep Fulfillment Rep
Inbound Mail/Delivery	Marketing Dept. Customer Service Fulfillment Center	Orders Letters Returns	Marketing Rep Customer Service Rep Fulfillment Rep
Outbound Email	Marketing Dept Customer	Retention Email Issue Service	Marketing Rep Customer Service Rep Resolution
Inbound Email	Marketing Dept. Customer Service	Action/Orders Issue Identified	Marketing Rep Customer Service Rep
Live Online Chat*	Web Site	Product Info Questions	Web Salesperson Customer Service Rep

Live Customer Touches
© *2001 Customer Share Group LLC*

Every time a customer comes in direct contact with a company, a customer touch is created—an opportunity for a company to *enhance* or *erode* its relationship with that customer. From the company's perspective, it is:

■ A salesperson responding to a customer's question about a washing machine, or a cashier collecting money from a customer at check-out.

■ A telemarketing rep calling a customer about credit card debt consolidation, or a customer service rep calling back a customer about the status of an order.

■ A telesales rep taking an order, or a customer service rep providing clarification of return policies.

■ A marketing department rep sending out a direct mail piece, a customer service rep sending a resolution letter, or a fulfillment rep sending out a package that fulfills an order.

■ A marketing department rep receiving an order from a customer through the mail, a customer service rep receiving a complaint letter, or a fulfillment rep receiving a returned product.

■ A marketing department rep sending out permission-granted email, or a customer service rep sending out an email that resolves an issue.

■ A marketing department rep receiving an order from a retention email campaign, or a customer service rep receiving a complaint from a customer via email.

■ A Web salesperson chatting live with a customer on the Web site, answering questions about a product or resolving an issue.

Every time a customer touch occurs, you are either *enhancing* or *eroding* the relationship between you and your customer. Outsourcing these important opportunities at customer interaction can be risky. By outsourcing your customer touches, you lose control of those touches. When you lose control of customer touches, you run a much higher risk that your customer touches will be *erosion touches* instead of *enhancement touches*.

The customer touches that are followed by an asterisk (*) in Table 7.1—in-person, outbound and inbound telephone, and online chat—represent *live* customer touches—in which one human being is communicating in real time with another human being—over the telephone or over the Web through live chat. These touches are particularly critical, since there is a heightened expectation on the part of the customer for immediate and successful resolution. Your representative is, in a sense, on the spot to perform. After all, he or she is making an impression, good, bad, or indifferent.

A customer touch is an opportunity to make a good impression and to build upon the relationship. Take the opportunity, but remember that a computer's keyboard is often the tool for communicating in the information economy, and sometimes speaking a simple word like received, for some people, is easier than spelling it.

EMAIL, CHAT LITERACY

Communicating through email and live online chat with customers shifts the communication playing field from spoken word to written word and can expose otherwise hidden inadequacies. When speaking the word *received,* as an example, your customer care representatives don't have to remember "i before e except after c." But when communicating through a keyboard, they do.

Some customer service emails are embarrassingly sprinkled with poor grammar and even worse spelling. This may seem like a trivial point, but every time a customer touch occurs, some type of impression is made with a customer. The last thing that you want is to unnecessarily create *erosion touches* because of someone's sloppiness, laziness, or legitimate inability to communicate effectively through the written word. Pay attention to how your employees communicate with your customers, and don't assume that just because people have great communication skills over the telephone, it necessarily translates to the keyboard.

Though all customer touches are critical in building customer loyalty, trust, and ultimately a lifetime relationship, *live* customer touches are an opportunity for your best people to shine. Sadly, though, we have historically compensated many of the employees that control our customer touches on the lower range of the pay scale, relative to the balance of the workforce. Think about your own business, and the people in your organization who come in contact with customers, day in and day out. To a great degree, it's their ability to appropriately manage those customer touches that ultimately determines your success or failure.

OUTSOURCE CRAZY

When I first became CEO of *The Sporting News* in 1989, I was very surprised to find that the company had outsourced its call center operation to some enormous industrial outpost in the middle of nowhere. Think about it: All of those sports fans that were calling to subscribe, renew, or even cancel were being handled by people six states away from the heart and soul of the operation in St. Louis. Those lifeblood customer touches—those invaluable opportunities to enhance the brand, gather customer intelligence, cross-sell and upsell—were offloaded in the late 1980s to save a little money.

When I visited the subscription fulfillment center for the first time, I was amazed at the size of the place: acres of cubicles inhabited with telephone operators ready to answer the next call. This place handled all subscription-related inbound calls for many of the major magazine publishers in the United States.

I wanted to spend the day speaking to—and especially listening to—the shifts of people that were representing our product over the telephone. We set up training sessions for each of the three shifts of operators and presented the nuts and bolts of our story, our mission, our heritage, details on each of our core products, and our vision for the future.

I was greeted by the telemarketing shift manager, who told me that no publisher had ever visited them. At the time, I didn't think much about that statement, but later on began to realize that if CEOs experienced what I was about to experience, they would be on the next plane to this complex. Since we had about a million customers at the time, I thought it might be a good idea to listen to what some of them had to say.

So I pulled up a chair right beside an operator who had just started his shift so that I could observe some inbound calls on our 800 number. The first call came in. The computer screen in front of him identified that the caller had dialed an 800 number for *Redbook*.

The next call came in for a needlework & crafts magazine, then a woodworking magazine, then an art magazine, then a car magazine, and then finally a call for *The Sporting News*. The caller wanted to know where to buy a *Sporting News Baseball Register,* an annual book of stats on all the players in major league baseball.

"I'm not sure. Maybe you could check your local bookstore or library. Or you could call the company in St. Louis."

The operator was flying by the seat of his pants. Making things up just to get the caller off the telephone. Not only was this probably a sales opportunity lost, but the operator also dispelled any notion that the customer was in fact calling *The Sporting News* directly by saying that they could call "the company in St. Louis." This outsource example demonstrates that when the questions or conversation get specific, the outsourced customer touch is not so seamless, and it becomes obvious to the customers that they are not talking to someone at the company's headquarters.

This experience helped me to learn that outsourcing customer touches is a dangerous practice. I also learned that one outsourced call center is basically the same as all the rest. Therefore, changing from one outsourced call center to another is most often an exercise in futility like firing your ad agency and hiring another. For a limited number of products and for special promotions that basically drive order-givers to order-takers, outsourcing can work. But for ongoing sales operations that require customer care representatives to engage customers and build relationships, no source will be able to compete with your own staff.

THE DOWNSIDE OF OUTSOURCING CUSTOMER TOUCHES

You may think that a customer care rep is a customer care rep. But that is not the case. Even though technology can help make touch points appear seamless, it becomes abundantly clear to customers when they are not communicating with a savvy inhouse rep. After you get past the novelty of having the ability to chat live with a rep online, if the person is not someone who intimately knows your story or your products, then you create potential *erosion touches.*

There is cool technology on the Web right now that allows you to chat live with e-reps. But in some cases, customers talk to an offloaded touch, to someone in a call/Web center somewhere, completely disconnected from the mother ship. It becomes obvious fairly early in the conversation when you engage rental reps in detailed conversations about the products they represent. Their product knowledge is thin and becomes exposed. Not a good thing for the manufacturer. The sad and damaging thing is that many of these types of erosion touches occur without the manufacturer ever knowing—and you can almost hear the drip, drip, drip of customer relationship erosion of your offloaded customer touches.

In many ways, the concept of Henry Ford's assembly line that was designed to automate work perpetuated a mindset that technology can manage most of the tasks humans perform. Even today, we see customer relationship management (CRM) software making qualitative claims that it cannot possibly deliver, such as service companies that claim they have permission-based or permission-granted services. By definition, that's impossible.

Customer intelligence is extremely important, and there are scores of companies and software products that can help you capture and analyze the online habits and behaviors of

your customers. But the strategic use of personal information—especially in this medium—can be tricky.

USING TECHNOLOGY
AND GOOD JUDGMENT

Always remember that your customers are human beings.
That's not to say that you won't use intelligence to properly
court their business, but you don't do it out of desperation,
because your mission is to land not just the next sale, but a
lifetime full of sales. Also, think of the 3Rs when considering
the use of captured personal data—or at least two-thirds of the
equation. While it's impossible for you to have every strategic
marketing nuance requested by the customer, will your intended use of intelligence be *relevant* and *respectful?* If you
answer this question honestly, you'll know what to do.

The bottom line is this: Customers are human beings.
Managing customers requires other human beings who say
hello, who thank people, who check on availability, who suggest a better color for fall, who research a problem and email
you back, who email you or call you back promptly with a resolution to a problem—the type of work that a computer will
probably never be able to do. Is anyone really impressed anymore when they receive an autoresponder? That might have
worked once, or in certain limited applications, but an auto-
matically generated form email usually doesn't do much anymore to enhance a customer relationship. The customer
simply wants resolution, not a promise that someone is working on the resolution.

When you have technology or human beings outside of
your company handle your customer touches, you give up a
great deal:

■ The probability of having a representative that knows
everything there is to know about your products.

■ The probability of gaining a high level of new intelligence about your customers.

- The probability of attaining a high level of customer issue resolution.
- The probability of attaining relevant and successful up-selling and cross-selling opportunities.
- The probability of creating high customer satisfaction.
- The probability of minimizing customer frustration.

TABLE 7.2 Customer Touches: Inhouse or Outsource?

	Outsourced	Inhouse
Product Knowledge	Low	High
Customer Intelligence Gathering Capability	Low	High
Expeditious Resolution Capability	Low	High
Cross-Sell/UpSell Capability	Low	High
Customer Satisfaction	Low	High
© 2001 Customer Share Group LLC		

Companies need to look at the impact of outsourcing customer touches from two perspectives:

- What does it *save* in terms of lower costs? (20th century perspective)
- What does it *cost* in terms of lost revenue? (21st century perspective)

The abdication of customer touches has been practiced for centuries. After all, that's what the general store was all about: the outsourcing of the distribution and sale of products to a reseller somewhere far, far away from the factory.

COORDINATING CHANNELS, CUSTOMER TOUCHES

A number of brick-and-mortar and catalog retailers originally viewed their Web site operations as distinct and separate from other channels within the same business. But it didn't take long to realize that a catalog channel and a Web channel are simply sources of orders placed directly with the company—some by telephone, some by mail, and some over the Web.

Two of the world's leading retailers realized enormous efficiencies when they integrated their own catalog and Web fulfillment operations. Bloomingdale's, a division of Federated Department Stores, formed a separate division—Federated Direct—to manage the integrated back end of *www .bloomingdales.com* and Bloomingdale's By Mail, and *www .macys.com,* and Macy's By Mail did likewise. The integration helped to insure a more consistent customer experience across all customer touches.

CAPTURING AND MANAGING CUSTOMER DATA

In looking at the location of the various customer touches in Table 7.1, it becomes clear that customer data exists at every touch point: at retail, in the call center, on the Web site, in the marketing department, customer service department, and fulfillment center.

The purpose of this book is to focus specifically on marketing—on the myriad of issues directly related to using the Web to acquire and especially retain customers. Technology is obviously critically important to enabling this type of direct interaction with customers. But because technology continuously changes—as will your technology needs—we make no specific recommendations for technical systems here. Instead, it is vitally important for you to work closely with your IT department to articulate your processes and initiatives so that they can help develop the systems that work best for your overall marketing strategy. This way, you should be able to manage your customer data in a secure yet flexible environment that makes accessing data and reports easy for analysis and use.

You will want to be able to access data so that you can use it for outbound customer share marketing initiatives. Make sure that you are able to access and use the stored data as often as you need it and in the formats you need it. For example, you may create a weekly e-newsletter that is delivered by email every Sunday night. Each week, you will need to be able to create a clean file of your email list or lists that:

1. Suppresses the opt-outs
2. Adds the new permission-granted registrations from all sources: retail, call center, mail, and Web
3. Isolates third-party opt-in email addresses if using acquisition email concurrently with your own permission-granted email database

This process can be coordinated inhouse or by using an application service provider (ASP) and is just a small example of the coordination necessary to drive effective, requested, relevant, and respectful customer marketing campaigns.

BRAND RESPONSIBILITY

If you are putting a single pair of boots in a box and shipping it to an individual for the first time, then you are taking on new responsibilities that will either enhance your brand's strength or erode it. Pick, pack, and ship the wrong boots: erosion. Pick, pack, and ship the wrong size boots: erosion. Send a notice saying that the boots are on back order: erosion. Send the boots in 3 weeks when you promise them in 7 to 10 days: erosion. When you play in the direct game, there are additional responsibilities that many companies have essentially outsourced to the wholesale or reseller channel since the advent of the general store.

Every time you "touch" a customer, you have the opportunity to either build on the trust that you've developed with that customer or erode it. Moving to a direct sales model is very exciting and most likely will help you greatly improve the margin of every sale. But it comes with its share of new responsibilities. The game has exponentially changed for companies that decide to add the direct sales channel to their mix. If you are up for the challenge, it offers an opportunity for you to grab market share, and more importantly, begin to grow your customer share.

MOVING CUSTOMER TOUCHES INHOUSE

Abercrombie & Fitch realized in fairly short order that it needed to control and manage the customer touches for its children's apparel Web site *www.abercrombiekids.com* in order to provide a more consistent customer experience end to end. So, the New Albany, Ohio-based apparel retailer made the move to bring order management, fulfillment management, and customer service inhouse in mid-2001 to help improve its ability to manage inventory, modify orders, meet delivery expectations, and centralize their call center, to name a few benefits. Any of these customer touches can either enhance or erode a company's relationships with its customers, and A & F has decided to bet on its own staff instead of someone else's as more likely to deliver enhancement touches.

With this important move, Abercrombie & Fitch is making the statement that the ability to provide world class customer touches is not only a priority for them, but also is viewed as part of A & F's core competencies.

CUSTOMER TOUCHES:
A CORE COMPETENCY

John Nordstrom struck gold twice in his life. First, as a teenager, he made his way to the Klondike in Alaska near the turn of the 20th century, and 2 years later returned to Seattle with over $13,000 that he had earned from a goldmine stake. In 1901, he and a partner opened a shoe store in downtown Seattle with a business philosophy that was based on exceptional service. It was that exceptional service that led to a second goldmine stake—the overwhelming success of customer-centric Nordstrom stores nationwide.

Some of the greatest companies in the world were started by people who sold one product at a time to one customer at a time. Companies like Nordstrom, L.L. Bean, Orvis, Tiffany & Co. all have heritages of great customer service. There was a time when customer touches were considered a core competency for businesses. But especially over the last 20 years of the 20th century, many people handling customer touches inside the company were reengineered out of the company. Management consultants and outsourcing and "rightsizing" experts convinced many companies to outsource operational functions that—according to the experts—were not part of a company's core competency.

I recently ordered four shirts from Nordstrom. The shirts arrived promptly, were in good condition, were the right size, matched the description in the catalog, and fit perfectly. I was a satisfied customer.

Shortly thereafter, I received the following handwritten note from the operator who had taken my order over the telephone:

> Mr. Osenton,
> It was a pleasure serving you recently and I hope your four
> shirts arrived safely. My husband bought the very same
> shirts last summer and loves them. Hope you do too.

This represents one of the great Hall of Fame customer touches. Do you think for a second that Nordstrom's doesn't consider customer touches a core competency? John Nordstrom made that decision over 100 years ago, and it is a major factor in creating a meaningful point of difference between Nordstrom and other department stores that essentially carry the same products.

CUSTOMER EXPECTATION: RESOLUTION BY EMAIL WITHIN 6 HOURS

Rightly or wrongly, there's an expectation in the minds of consumers that issues related to their purchases online will be resolved by companies quickly. A survey by Jupiter Media

Metrix suggests that up to half of all consumers expect problems that they have communicated by email to be resolved within 6 hours of alerting the marketer.

Further, the study showed that 25 percent of all customer email is not answered at all. Consider what would happen to a brick-and-mortar business if one in every four customers that walked up to an in-store rep asked a question and was completely ignored.

Such mishandling of basic customer service issues not only creates erosion touches, but also drives the cost of customer service through the roof as unsatisfied customers end up calling the call center on the company's dime.

PERMISSION, PRIVACY, AND PROTECTION

Taking care to treat both customers and their information with the utmost respect will go a long way toward convincing customers that you have their best interests at heart. The company that goes the extra mile and initiates actions that are in the best interest of customers will likely have customers who return to buy again. The careful handling of customers is really an art form whose foundation is *respect.* Treat customers with respect and you will earn their trust. Earn their trust and they will reward you with their loyalty.

Because the unique characteristics of the Web allow marketers an inside view of customers' personal and private information, it is critically important for marketers to raise the ethics bar relative to their interactions with customers or give up any hope of building long-term relationships and customer share strategies.

Issues of permission, privacy, and protection of customers' personal information are not only important legal issues, but important marketing issues as well. Actions that compromise the trust between customer and company are simply counterproductive to the concept of capturing the lifetime value of a customer.

CHAPTER

8

PERMISSION, PRIVACY, AND PROTECTION

I was astonished recently to open up my sixth grader's Friday Folder to find a solicitation for a manners course being offered to all students in the local grade school. For a mere $150, you could send your child to a week of manners training presented by a local *manners expert*. It was like a soccer camp for pleases and thank yous.

At first I was outraged that someone might think that I wasn't doing my job as a parent and that my kid was clueless when it came to manners. But then I realized that regardless of how this boot camp for behavior originated, it happened for a reason. It made me reflect on how truly devoid our culture has become of the simple courtesies and manners that most of us prefer.

From our classrooms to our boardrooms, we want what we want when we want it. In the business world, we want sales over the short-term, and we want them at almost any cost, including the long-term alienation of the customers who ultimately pay our salaries.

ASKING PERMISSION

It makes so much sense to respect your customers enough to ask for permission to send them email. For most of the 20th century, marketing to customers required nobody's permission. It just required money, and lots of it. Remember the master-slave paradigm? Master speaks, slave listens. Master sells, slave buys. Not any more. The rules have changed, and the Web has been a catalyst at the center of that change.

By asking for permission from your prospects and customers, you send them an important message about the way you treat your customers. Your adherence to the rules of permission is an indication as to how you do business and underscores your respect for customers' privacy. Prospects and customers have a right not to receive unwanted email, even if they are repeat buyers.

Permission is a critical component for marketers wishing to grow sales by growing their share of business with the customers they already have. Email without permission is simply less effective, not to mention annoying to the people you should care about most.

PERMISSION ISN'T ASSUMED—
IT'S GRANTED

The folks at a popular online music store recently sent me a flurry of very commercial, very desperate-sounding emails that, purely and simply, were designed to move product. In the past, I had purchased CDs from this online store, but had never granted them permission to send me email on any subject. They assumed that because I bought something, I would be interested in hearing about other things that they had to sell. They assumed that I gave them permission to send me email, but never asked me the question: Would you like to receive information from us about future specials and new product offerings?

This may sound a bit like splitting hairs, but there will be people who buy from you who prefer not to receive any commercial email from you. Assuming that they do is simply disrespectful of your customer and could easily lead to an erosion of trust and a breakdown in your relationship or, worse, losing a customer altogether.

In the early days of the Web, it was—and to some extent still is—like the Wild, Wild West. There were no rules. You could send anything you wanted to anyone you wanted as many times as you wanted just because you could. But the cries of outraged consumers quickly followed, rightfully condemning the invasion. Permission isn't something that is taken or assumed. Permission is granted. It's a privilege—the privilege of being able to communicate one-to-one with a prospect or customer about something that he or she finds interesting.

SHADES OF PERMISSION

Permission comes in three different shades, like a traffic light: red, yellow, and green (see Table 8.1). Red represents spam: those emails that are not requested, most often irrelevant, and always disrespectful that—despite all the legislation and consumer protection efforts—still find their way into our inboxes. *Red means stop immediately.* Spam is worse than junk mail. It's like breaking into someone's house. You're inside someone's computer trying to sell something that has not been requested and is probably not relevant. You are disrespecting the recipients with unsolicited commercial email. Get out of their computer, get out of their house, and get out of the business of marketing this way.

From a marketing standpoint, uninvited contacts by email are not nearly as effective as email that is sent with the recipient's permission.

TABLE 8.1 Shades of Permission

Form of Marketing	Permission Acquired From	Permission Acquired How
Spam (red)	No One	Not At All
Opt-In (yellow)	Third Party	Indirectly
Permission (green)	Customer	Directly

© 2001 Customer Share Group LLC

Yellow represents opt-in email marketing. *Yellow means proceed with caution.* There is still much confusion around the definition of opt-in. For our purposes, an opt-in list is a list of email addresses that is secured from a third-party list broker. Opt-in email can be a great way to target prospects for acquiring sales and permission. However, just because prospects have given permission to someone else, doesn't mean that they've given it to you. Make sure you secure permission directly from your prospects and customers.

Look at it this way. Opt-in email marketing is like proxy dating. One person asks another out on a date, but instead sends someone else in his place: "Good evening. I'm Bill. Fred sent me. I know you agreed to go out with Fred, but since I kind of look like Fred, he thought you might want to date me instead."

Opt-in email marketing can often be viewed by the recipient as spam, because consumers can't always remember where they registered, when they registered, with whom they registered, or what they expected to receive in return. For this reason, opt-in email is not nearly as effective as permission-granted email. Opt-in usually performs about as well as direct mail sent to a rented list. Permission-granted lists can often outperform opt-in lists by as much as a 10 to 1 ratio.

It's difficult to build a relationship with prospects if they remain in the opt-in state. Until you are able to convince a prospect to say yes to you and he or she becomes part of your own permission-granted database, conversations with this person will be random, fleeting (if at all), and expensive, since you'll probably have to rent this name from a third party every time you use it.

Work with third-party list brokers to develop your acquisition email efforts, but know exactly what you are getting. In most cases, opt-in aggregators have taken steps in the registration process to qualify the prospects as interested in learning more about the type of product or service that you sell. If the list is a good one for your industry, it should yield a fair number of prospects—and even customers—who grant permission directly to you.

Green represents permission-granted email marketing. *Green means it's okay to go.* The prospects and customers that you place on this list are *your* people. They've said yes to you. Take special care of these people. This is the list that you will have conversations with over time, transforming prospects to customers and customers to customers for life. These are the people that you will begin to look at from a customer share perspective. They're the people who surf through your Web site, browse through your brick-and-mortar retail store, and thumb through your catalog on a regular basis. They're also the people who could potentially buy from you again and again, over the course of a year or a lifetime. They can be part of your revenue picture 10 years from now. Like loyal magazine subscribers, they keep coming back without a lot of prompting or investment on your part. They renew because you have spent the time and effort to retain them and in the process have built a level of trust that is often rewarded with repeat business.

EMAIL TRIAGE

If you send and receive email, then you know all about email triage. The typical consumer goes to his or her email inbox and opens it up to see what messages have been delivered since the last visit. As the eye scans down the list, email triage begins: DELETE NOW, DELETE NOW, READ LATER, DELETE NOW, DELETE NOW, READ NOW, DELETE NOW, READ LATER, DELETE NOW, READ LATER. Depending on how much email a consumer receives, this process can take a matter of seconds.

Unless email can be easily identified as invited in by the recipient, it will achieve an extraordinarily low open rate.

Unfortunately, spammers can generate enough response from the millions of emails they gather and send, to generate enough of a return to make it worth it. Even a small fraction of a percent response rate can generate enough cash to support a spammer for another day.

If a spammer sent out 10 million unsolicited emails selling a $50 product, and the response rate to that email was only one-tenth of one percent, that campaign would generate 10,000 orders, or $500,000 in revenue. This is one of the reasons that spam has not become extinct. Fortunately, though, to operate this way is very expensive—especially when you consider that 9,990,000 people of the 10 million they emailed said no.

On any given day, a consumer might check their email inbox to find an offering of messages that looks something like the list in Figure 8.1.

SUBJECT	SENDER	DATE
1. Now Save 70% on Life. . .	Hfuutrysj23@hejit.com	3/25/04
2. Better Than Viagra! And. . .	Ciiii99@veluuts23.com	3/25/04
3. Matt's Birthday	jmilford@ansuen774d.org	3/25/04
4. Interest Rates Have. . .	G3gg2g4@da2o84hfy.net	3/25/04
5. Want To Eliminate Bad Debt?	C9dhry@uue7rbf.com	3/25/04
6. Rice-A-Roni Newsletter	roni@ricearoni.com	3/25/04
7. New! 75 million Email. . .	Ndwyt35@ao2sith75b.com	3/25/04
8. Bonjour from Paris	jenny123@viva27fg748s.net	3/25/04
9. Lower Your Cholesterol	ns88ehrfs@aauetd6n.net	3/25/04
10. Gardening Tips	newsletter@burpee.com	3/25/01

© 2001 Customer Share Group LLC

FIGURE 8.1
Triaging email: Read or delete?

The 10 emails that this consumer has received are probably not all relevant to her. Some of them might be opt-in email. Some of the emails are just blatant spam efforts. But emails 3, 6, 8, and 10 are special to this consumer and were triaged as READ during the email triage process. These emails will be opened and read because they are requested, relevant, or respectful to the recipient. Emails 1, 2, 4, 5, 7, and 9 don't even get opened because they are recognized as hostile, company-centric attempts to generate sales.

Email 3 is an email from the recipient's sister concerning her son's birthday. Email 6 is an e-newsletter from Rice-A-Roni that was requested by the recipient. Email 8 is from the recipient's daughter, who is living in France. Email 10 is a monthly e-newsletter on gardening from the Burpee Seed Company.

The consumer treats all of the READ emails the same and groups invited commercial email from companies to whom she has granted permission with emails from her sister and daughter. That is where smart, ethical marketers want to be—as if they were part of the recipient's family and welcomed into the home.

RETURN ON INVESTMENT

For many decades, many billions of dollars have been spent in the United States, marketing every product and service under the sun, and much of it without being able to measure its effectiveness. Then along comes the Web and return on investment becomes the mantra of many marketers in the information economy. It's very appropriate to measure the impact of your acquisition efforts. It's especially important to measure the return you get from investing in email marketing to third-party opt-in lists.

But once you have converted a prospect or customer to a name on your permission-granted list, measuring ROI against retention efforts becomes much less relevant since you own the names, and sending email to them—at least from a cost per thousand (CPM) standpoint—is $0. ROI is an acquisition metric, not a retention metric. By all means, measure the effectiveness of your acquisition efforts, but don't obsess over measuring the effectiveness of your retention efforts.

The purpose of retention email is to build a relationship over time, not to sell a product every time you touch a customer. By building a relationship over time, you will condition your prospects and customers to be much more willing to consider commercial offers when you determine that the time is right. Retention marketing requires finesse and sensitivity—not a sledgehammer over the head.

OPT-IN LIST FOR ACQUISITION, PERMISSION LIST FOR RETENTION

You should have short-term and long-term objectives for your email marketing initiatives (see Table 8.2). Acquisition email is short-term in nature and is often tied to a specific event, campaign, or promotion. The recipients of acquisition email are opt-in names that are rented from a third-party email list broker. The objective of acquisition email is to acquire sales and/or permission in order to communicate in the future by email. In Chapter 10, "Feeding The Funnel," we will explore the fundamental elements of identifying and driving prospects to your Web site for the purpose of acquiring short-term sales and long-term permission.

TABLE 8.2 Opt-in for Acquisition, Permission for Retention

Type of Email	Recipients of Email	Objectives of Email
Acquisition	Opt-In List	Short-Term Sales
	List	Acquire Permission
Retention	Permission-	Long-Term Sales
	Granted List	Build Loyalty/Trust

© 2001 Customer Share Group LLC

Retention email is longer term in nature and can be viewed as a throwback to the art of letter writing. It generally reads like a letter from a friend and usually involves a much softer sell. The recipients of retention email are people who have granted permission directly to you for the right to send them information. The objective of retention email is to retain your customers' business and grow the amount of business from each customer by building on a foundation of trust and reliability. In Chapter 12, "Working the List," we will cover the basics of permission-granted email marketing campaigns that are designed to build long-term customer relationships and a greater share of your customers' business.

WHO'S ON FIRST? YES, WHO IS ON FIRST?

Don't try to trick or confuse your prospects and customers into granting you permission. Negative option practices that ask you to check the box if you *do not* want to receive email can be confusing. Such practices can even be perceived as deceptive when, for example, an uninvited e-newsletter shows up in a consumer's email inbox.

Use the positive option approach by asking your prospects and customers to check a box if they want to receive information by email. Though this may be a more conservative approach to acquiring permission, you can help prevent potential future problems and confusion by including only those prospects and customers who request to be a part of your permission-granted list.

Another positive option is to have the Yes box checked for the customer, requiring them to uncheck it if they prefer not to grant permission. This is a very popular technique and usually results in generating the highest permission-granted rate.

In keeping with the respect theme, you should also make it easy for prospects and customers to opt out of receiving your emails. There is nothing more annoying to prospects and customers than being ignored or, worse, tricked by a company. As David Ogilvy said half a century ago, consumers are not morons, so don't treat them that way. Make opting out easy and uncomplicated. After all, your retention efforts should be focused on people who want your information. There's no upside to promoting to people who have decided that they are not interested. Increase your chances of turning prospects into customers and customers into customers for life by limiting your list to those people who have expressed—and continue to express—interest in what you sell.

CUSTOMERS AND PROSPECTS GRANT PERMISSION

There will be customers who buy from you who *will not* grant you permission, and there will be prospects who don't immediately buy from you who *will* grant you permission. It's important to track the variety of categories in your database. Work closely with your IT professionals to design the appropriate database capability that allows you to capture data in specific "buckets" that can easily be used later in outbound marketing efforts.

Over time, you will develop a host of buckets based on the many different ways that you define as important characteristics and habits of your prospects and customers. If you are involved in e-commerce, you will be able to create dozens of buckets that define your individual customers in many different ways. But as it relates to permission, there are probably three primary buckets that describe your prospects and customers:

- Customers who have granted you permission
- Customers who have not granted you permission
- Prospects who have granted you permission

Prospects who have not granted you permission are probably names that you don't own and that probably shouldn't reside in your database.

THE FIVE DON'TS
OF COURTING CUSTOMERS

In many ways, the increasing use of permission has reintroduced good manners to the art of courting a customer. Its practices are firmly grounded in common sense and old-fashioned common courtesy. But as in any type of courtship, there are some definite do's and don'ts when navigating the waters of relationship building. The following is a list of the pitfalls to avoid when courting your prospects and customers:

1. *Don't confuse opt-in with permission.* When a prospect or customer responds directly to you and agrees to receive future emailings from you, you have been granted permission. With a list of opt-in names, permission has probably been granted to someone, just not directly to you. Use opt-in names in your acquisition efforts as a way to create a sales event and to acquire permission. Remember, the two acquisition objectives in using opt-in names are to capture one-time sales and permission. The two objectives in using permission-granted lists are to build loyalty and to generate long-term sales.

2. *Don't scare people.* As a general rule of thumb, people do not like to be scared, especially by companies who might capture their credit card information, home address and telephone number, social security number, and mother's maiden name. Think through the use of cookie technology and weigh the upside versus the downside of having the ability to welcome customers back. Remember the brick-and-mortar general storekeeper: Eventually, he says, "Hello Mrs. Smith" when she comes in to the store. Mrs. Smith doesn't freak out when the storekeeper addresses her because a relationship has been established over time. But Mrs.

Smith might feel a little uneasy if the second time she entered the store, she was called out by name.

3. *Don't hide behind legalities.* It's always important to be in compliance with the law. I received a piece of spam recently that, at the end, stated that it was in compliance with Senate Bill 1618, Section 301. It didn't make me feel any better about receiving a piece of spam. Certainly be aware of the changing laws governing electronic communication. Laws usually are created because people are abusing a right. Legislation occurs because of abuse by spam artists. If your own email marketing efforts follow the simple and sensible guidelines of the 3 Rs, then it's highly likely that you will be in compliance with the law. It's unfortunate that we need such laws to protect the privacy of consumers. But most often, the laws are not nearly conservative enough, especially as it relates to spam. There are two simple rules to live by relating to your email marketing efforts:

A. Don't send email to people who have not requested it.

B. If they ask to be removed from your list, take them off immediately, or at least before the next emailing.

Unfortunately, if you aggressively use opt-in lists in your acquisition efforts, it's very likely that you will rent the same name over and over again because consumers often register for numerous promotions or e-newsletters, sometimes using a variation on their name or different email addresses. It's important to practice diligent email list hygiene, such as deduping, to avoid the continuous delivery of unwanted emails. But sometimes, this can be difficult, especially with registration-happy consumers.

4. *Don't disrespect your permission-granted customers.* These are your frequent flyers. Always treat them

with the utmost respect, and they will happily continue to do business with you. Think through how often you want to communicate with them. Think through how you want to serve up commercial messages to them. Be helpful to them by providing advice. Ask for their feedback.

5. *Don't ever rent your permission-granted list.* Other companies will pay good money for all of the hard work that you've done to build a relationship with a customer. The work you do now will pay off for you in a decade if you are true to your customers and protect their privacy and their relationship with you. Look at your ever-growing permission-granted email list as an important link to your future sales. Increasingly, this list will gain value and soon will be viewed as much more than just an emailing list. The permission-granted email database will gain in importance as a meaningful revenue stream for companies, no different than the subscriber list for a magazine. Your permission-granted database is an ever-increasing company asset that can, over time, increase the value of your company. Protect it.

To illustrate the point, major corporations are now debating the issue of ownership and use of permission-granted email lists when companies merge or are acquired. If Bank of America acquires Fleet Bank, does it also acquire permission along with the actual ownership of the list of names and email addresses? The answer is a qualified yes. Respecting the acquired customers, email communication explaining the change, first from the incumbent bank and then from the acquirer, is the appropriate way to alert those on a permission-granted email database that they will soon be receiving messages from a new entity. After that, the acquirer can outbound to the acquired permission-granted list with its normal email and e-newsletter offerings, always giving the prospect or customer the ability to easily opt out at anytime.

ACQUIRE PERMISSION TO AVOID MOST PRIVACY ISSUES

Any activity that threatens our ability to grow the level of trust with our prospects and customers is counterproductive to our objectives of capturing the lifetime value of a customer and is a real marketing issue. Every time they come in contact with prospects and customers, marketers have an opportunity to either enhance or erode the level of trust that exists between them and their customers. By practicing the 3 Rs, marketers can avoid most of the issues related to a customer's privacy.

PRIVACY AND SECURITY OPERATIONALLY

The purpose of this book is to focus on the marketing activities that help you generate more sales and more profitable sales. Breaches in privacy and security can dramatically erode the trust that you have built with a customer. These issues require in-depth discussion and understanding on the part of those handling the marketing as well as of those on the operational side of a site.

Though it's not possible to fully do justice to the subjects here, it's important to touch upon some of the key security and privacy issues that can create marketing problems because the erosion risk is so high.

Here are some red flag areas that can be particularly sensitive and require your close attention:

1. *Credit card information.* This information must be treated as sacrosanct and must be managed in the most secure environment possible. Mishandle a customer's credit card information and you'll probably lose that customer—or multiple customers—for good.
2. *Personal information.* Similarly, customers trust that you will protect their personal information, such as

names, addresses, telephone numbers, social security numbers, birth dates, PIN numbers, passwords, mother's maiden name, and email addresses.

3. *Purchasing information.* There's plenty of good data that can be very helpful in generating incremental sales down the road, but using this information is tricky. Be very careful how you use this intelligence, especially after the transaction takes place.

4. *Click trail information.* You certainly should mine and study the habits of the customers that interact with your Web site to gain a deeper understanding of patterns and trends that could help you improve your ability to close online sales. Just be very careful how you use this information. If your prospects or customers feel as though you're spying on them, their trust may be irreparably damaged.

5. *Cookie technology.* The Web scares a lot of people with its nifty technology. Make sure you clearly display your cookie policy on your site, but even more importantly, weigh the downside erosion potential against the upside enhancement potential when using cookie technology. Is it worth it? If it makes navigating your site easier for consumers without scaring them, then it's probably a good thing. But be careful. Practicing the science without the art can sometimes damage customer relationships—when the intent is to enhance them.

6. *Fraud.* Using another person's credit card to purchase goods over the Web can be a real issue for e-commerce. But systems, software, and processes designed to prevent fraud are improving every day. The most widely used preventative action is the use of address verification systems that match a customer's credit card billing address with the ship-to address. This can even be done in real time, especially if online fraud is a pervasive problem for you.

7. *Global marketing.* This may seem like an odd place for this entry, but not all countries approach marketing the same way that the United States does. Because

you are essentially a global marketer when you hang out a shingle on the Web, it's important to be aware of local laws that may impact your ability to grow your customer base. For example, it is illegal to offer discounts or other types of promotional claims, such as lifetime guarantees, in Germany, while those types of practices are common in the United States. On another issue, the First Amendment of the Constitution ironically protects companies and individuals who wish to sell Nazi memorabilia, while that practice is forbidden in Germany. Simply put, it's important to know your market and the laws and customs governing that market, wherever it may be. Standards and practices relating to email marketing greatly vary from jurisdiction to jurisdiction around the world and, more often than not, are far more restrictive than current policies in the United States. Be aware of the specific laws in all the countries where you do business.

Though many of the preceding issues are not directly the responsibility of the people who design your acquisition and retention marketing programs, missteps involving these operational responsibilities can become real marketing issues and can create erosion touches. This also underscores the importance of creating a close working relationship between the marketing and operational sides of your business, especially with your IT department, in teaming up to help prevent issues.

CUSTOMER SHARE MARKETING

Ever walk into a Ritz-Carlton hotel and approach any member of the staff? I'm always amazed at how I'm treated. Staff members are completely attentive and always at the ready to serve you. They have no other agenda. They're never on their way to someplace else. What a pleasure it is to be treated like that. That type of treatment makes an indelible impression and lays the groundwork for the next time a customer is in town and needs a room.

The folks at Ritz-Carlton determined a long time ago that theirs would be a customer share strategy in filling rooms and in selling pricey ancillary services to a relatively finite universe of loyal guests who prefer and can afford high-end living and demand the attention. Their target audience is certainly not the masses, and for the most part, they use very targeted, upscale media to lure guests when using media at all. They practice a very focused form of customer marketing that is beginning to gain traction as a one-to-one marketing complement to a marketer's one-to-many mass marketing efforts.

Customer share marketing focuses on mining more from the customers you already have. It takes advantage of the unique benefits of the Web and email to deliver permission-granted messages that are designed to communicate one-to-one with your best prospects and customers. Customer share marketing is integrated with market share marketing to deliver end-to-end marketing coverage that results in capturing a larger share of each of your customers' business.

Getting more from your best customers starts with identifying them by name and email address, and by acquiring permission to communicate with them through email. The unique characteristics of the Web and email now make this process easy and affordable for companies of all sizes that have something to say—and sell—to what previously have been anonymous consumers for most companies.

9

CUSTOMER SHARE MARKETING

I spent a number of years on the other side of a one-way mirror watching sports fans talk about the products that they used to educate themselves about their favorite sports, teams, and individual stars. I was always amazed at the number of serious sports fans who renewed or even extended their subscriptions well before they expired, and some without any prompting at all on the part of the company.

These were the customers in the very center of the target—the most profitable customers in the database—because they kept coming back, year after year, without any arm-twisting, convincing, or expense on the part of the company.

I once received a telephone call from a subscriber who wanted to take advantage of a special promotion by extending his subscription for 14 years! Think about that. He wanted to take advantage of an offer that would save him money on his favorite magazine by essentially prepaying for more than 750 issues—or well into the new millennium!

Though this is an extraordinarily rare case, it dramatizes the bond that can be built between a customer and a brand over time. Because the editor of the publication had once taken this subscriber's call and followed up with a personal letter, he was a customer for life. Maybe even beyond life!

CUSTOMER SHARE MARKETING: TAPPING CUSTOMER LOYALTY

Historically, the acquisition of customers has been an offensive marketing initiative that requires a thoughtful strategy, a step-by-step plan, and a lot of money. The retention of customers, on the other hand, has rarely been afforded such a deliberate, organized, and well-funded process. More often, retention has been the by-product of a string of acquisition or branding campaigns, or has been gained through the satisfactory fulfillment of the promise that a product's advertising makes. If the advertising claims that the product takes out the toughest stains and succeeds in doing so, there's no better means of retention than the successful delivery of a promise that provides a solution to a customer's problem.

The development of an orderly, outbound, offensive strategy specifically designed to retain customers is rare indeed. Many of today's marketers would be hard pressed to even articulate what their specific retention or customer share initiatives are, or even if they had any.

Customer share marketing is the development of an orderly, outbound, offensive marketing plan that is designed not only to retain customers, but also to grow customer share—increasing the amount of business each customer does with your company. Customer share marketing goes beyond the retention of customers to build trust with each customer on a one-to-one basis. Customer share marketing is the art and science of:

- Driving your best prospects and customers to your Web site by using all relevant online and offline marketing initiatives.

- Capturing permission from both prospects and customers who have expressed an interest in learning more about what you have to sell.

- Using that permission to initiate thoughtful conversations by email with prospects and customers for the purpose of enhancing customer relationships and building trust between buyer and seller.

- Creating appropriate commercial opportunities through permission-granted email efforts for the purpose of increasing the amount of business with each customer.

These four major actions define the practice of customer share marketing. It starts by using all forms of online and offline marketing to drive prospects and customers to your site: running ads and promotions, sending direct mail, renting email lists, sending opt-in email, and partnering with other sites to drive their traffic to your site via an affiliate marketing program.

In Table 9.1, you can see that some of these initiatives are dedicated and budgeted Web marketing initiatives, such as the development of online advertising or opt-in email campaigns. Other mass-marketing initiatives, such as URL tagging in national advertising or on product packaging and retail shopping bags, simply take advantage of the substantive and widespread marketing energy that only mass-marketing efforts can generate.

TABLE 9.1 The Elements of Customer Share Marketing

Four New Ps	Purpose
1. People	Identify Your Customers
2. Preferences	Identify Their Product Usage
3. Permission	Obtain Their Permission
4. Precision	Communicate One-to-One

© 2001 Customer Share Group LLC

Once prospects arrive at your site, it's about engaging them with relevant content and encouraging them to sign up for one of several permission-granted programs, such as e-newsletters, email updates on specials and new product announcements, contests, sweepstakes, and polls.

Ultimately, it's about creating outbound, permission-granted communications with your prospects and customers, sending them messages that are engaging and entertaining, while motivating from a sales perspective. Though many companies still view email—even permission-granted email—as a nice, customer service-oriented outreach program to prospects and customers, you will learn later in the book that some major marketers are effectively using email to move the needle on incremental sales, both online through e-commerce for companies such as Nordstrom and offline through increased brick-and-mortar retail sales for companies such as Pepsico's Frito-Lay brand.

Customer share marketing in no way replaces market share marketing, but instead works in tandem with market share marketing efforts to create a second opportunity to sell to interested prospects and customers. Customer share marketing moves the marketing conversation to a quiet, one-to-one place, delivering messages that are more relevant to recipients.

THE 3 RS OF CUSTOMER SHARE MARKETING

Customer share marketing is an effective way to begin focused and dedicated retention programs—for some companies for the first time ever. Customer share marketing allows companies to build retention efforts that fully respect recipients by limiting their messages to those that are requested, relevant, and respectful:

1. *Requested.* Think of all the direct mail that you get every day in your mailbox. Most of it is not requested and probably none of it would qualify as permission-

granted. This is also true of many of the emails we receive. The way for marketers to avoid any confusion is simply to ask for permission *directly from the prospect.*

2. *Relevant.* The more relevant your messages are to the recipient, the more likely they will continue to welcome messages from you into their inbox. Random solicitations are most often irrelevant to the recipient. If a gardener receives information on gardening, that's relevant. But if a person living in a penthouse in New York City randomly receives information on gardening, then the message is probably neither relevant nor effective.

3. *Respectful.* Gone are the days when marketers can just muscle their way into people's lives because they have something to sell. Customers have been treated like slaves for a very long time. The time has come for marketers to treat customers the way they would treat their own mothers on Mother's Day. They want to be treated with respect. That's what customers want. They want information on the products that *they* want when *they* want it. If they want to be taken off the list, take them off. This dynamic represents an enormous paradigm shift for traditional advertisers and their agencies, but is a natural next step in the evolution of marketing.

The 3 Rs are designed to help marketers adopt communication practices based on respect and common sense that will lead to capturing a larger share of a customer's business.

MORE FROM THE CUSTOMERS YOU HAVE ALREADY ACQUIRED

Once you've decided that at least some of your marketing efforts need to focus on attracting more business from customers you already have, then you've basically decided that customer share marketing makes sense for your business. Customer share marketing complements market share marketing in that it can leverage the energy and attention that market share marketing creates in building brand, driving short-term sales, and driving interested consumers to a company's Web site. Once there, it's up to marketers to develop clever ways of capturing the identity, email address, and permission from prospects who have prequalified themselves.

While market share marketing utilizes mass-marketing vehicles such as television and print to reach as many prospects as possible, customer share marketing accomplishes just the opposite—using direct marketing vehicles to reach only those prospects and customers that have identified themselves as interested in what you have to sell. Market share marketing seeks no permission, while customer share marketing exclusively involves permission-granted messages.

Market share marketing is most often about generating the next sale, while customer share marketing is more about generating future sales, perhaps across the entire lifetime of the prospect or customer. If one of your products sells for $40, the quantitative perspective of market share marketing is focused on a $40 sale, and success is largely viewed on the basis of generating as many $40 sales as quickly as possible.

The quantitative perspective in customer share marketing is quite different and focuses on capturing all sales that this customer will generate for this category for the rest of her or his life. So instead of looking at a prospect or customer as a $40 opportunity, customer share marketing views a prospect or customer as a $10,000 opportunity (see Table 9.2).

If you can successfully blend your market share efforts with customer share efforts, you can create two levels of selling: one for today and for tomorrow. Consider the expense associated with convincing a customer to give you $40 approximately 250 times over the course of her or his lifetime.

TABLE 9.2 Pay Me Now or Pay Me Later

Marketing Focus	Sales Objective	Sales Objective Quantified
Market Share Marketing	Next Sale	$40
Customer Share Marketing	Lifetime Sales	$10,000
© 2001 Customer Share Group LLC		

Remember the guy who prepaid for 750 issues of a magazine? For 14 years, there was virtually no marketing expense associated with that customer—just revenue. Your customer share initiatives should work to eliminate some of the convincing you must do over a customer's lifetime so that a higher percentage of those $40 sales occur out of loyalty—loyalty that you've built with a customer on a one-to-one level over the course of time.

THE ZEN OF CUSTOMER SHARE

Western culture tends to look at life as if it were a 100-meter dash, while Eastern culture tends to look at life as a 26.2-mile marathon. In the West, we are driven to deliver results *today*. In Eastern Culture, goals and results are often viewed over generations and decades. (See Table 9.3.)

A market share orientation typically takes the view that business is conducted as a series of millions of little battles to be won or lost, while value is gained from outside the core—by acquiring new customers. A customer share orientation, on

TABLE 9.3 Acquisition More—Retention Better

	Cultural Orientation	Marketing Orientation	Revenue Goals	When Hungry	When Tired
Market Share	West	Mass	More	Sell	Sell
Customer Share	East	One-to-One	Better	Eat	Sleep
© 2001 Customer Share Group LLC					

the other hand, takes the view that business is conducted as a war that is fought over a lifetime and takes advantage of energy that has already been created, perhaps even by a prior generation. Customer share marketing redirects that energy, leveraging years of brand loyalty and goodwill to create more value from inside the core—by retaining and growing business from loyal customers.

In Western culture, the system of financial support overwhelmingly supports attacking the enemy (competition) to win sales today rather than methodically enlisting the help of thousands of individuals, who are loyal to your brand, to defeat the enemy over time.

Historically, for every $100 we spend on advertising products and services, less than $20 is dedicated to retaining the customers we already have. That's $80 out of every $100 dedicated to acquiring new customers—convincing prospects to try our products and services for the first time or to switch back from a competitor's product. An inordinate amount of time and money is spent trying to find and convince new customers, while the customers that we have already acquired are greatly ignored.

To a large degree, this thinking is backwards. More often than not, marketers reward the hardest to find, hardest to acquire, hardest to keep customers with discounts and premiums, while the most loyal customers, who for years have paid full freight for products and services, are not rewarded for their loyalty. Doesn't it make sense to reward the most loyal of all customers?

The airline industry figured that out decades ago. The time is now for other industries to begin to look at their customers by level of contribution, rewarding the most loyal based on their level of annual contribution to the company. Doesn't it make sense for Unilever to view their revenue sources this way—from most valuable to least valuable?

What would happen if we turned the marketing tables and spent $80 out of every $100 spent on marketing on the retention of customers instead of on the acquisition of customers? What would happen if we invested heavily in the customers and repeat customers in the two inner circles in Figure 9.1?

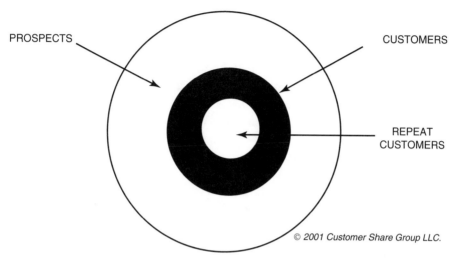

FIGURE 9.1
Waging war outside and inside.

What would happen if the majority of marketing spending was designed to grow the business from existing customers by providing relevant incentives for them to buy all relevant product categories from the same marketer?

LIFETIME VALUE

What's the lifetime value of an average consumer for all household care products? $10,000? $20,000? What about family care? Pet care? Lawn care? This radical notion helps to dramatize that much more can be done to care for the people we've already acquired by creating one-to-one conversations with them. An increase in retention spending—even a minimal increase—serves as an insurance policy against all the customers you've spent years and invested millions to acquire.

A lifetime value focus requires a customer share orientation that looks at individual customers and households differently. It requires companies like Procter & Gamble to use their significant marketing might to build rich customer databases for the purpose of executing customer share marketing strategies. The objective of these strategies would be for P & G to dominate household share, essentially creating the concept of P & G families—households where the overwhelming number of products are from Procter & Gamble.

It requires engaging in customer share marketing strategies that look at the household territorially, not one brand at a time, but across as many categories as possible. It also requires a more corporate view by coordinating synergistic marketing strategies, above the brand level, that result in selling more of what a marketer has to sell. Ultimately, the goal would be to horizontally expand P & G's household share with campaigns designed to insure that at least some of the individuals in a household:

- Brush their teeth with Crest.
- Wipe their counters with Bounty.
- Wash their clothes with Tide.
- Treat their fabrics with Downy.
- Wash their dishes with Cascade.
- Wash their bathrooms with Comet.
- Wash their floors with Mr. Clean.
- Wash their hair with Head & Shoulders.
- Wash their bodies with Ivory Soap.
- Snack on Pringles.
- Protect their babies with Pampers.
- Treat colds with Nyquil.
- Settle their stomachs with Pepto-Bismol.

Presently, the products that inhabit a household are there because loyalty has been won—or passed down from generation to generation—on the brand level, not the corporate level. If a company currently holds customer share dominance in a household, that corporate dominance has, to a great degree, been achieved randomly through the strength of the individual brands. Customer share marketing allows companies to shape a strategy that helps them leverage the inherent strength of their individual brands to increase their penetration across all relevant brands: leveraging a customer's brand loyalty to a laundry detergent to sell them fabric softener; leveraging a customer's brand loyalty to toilet paper to sell them napkins and paper towels.

Customer share marketing provides another weapon in the war to increase sales and profits, but in no way replaces market share marketing. Instead, it offers a relatively inexpensive complement that helps consistently deliver more from loyal customers, helping to fight the revenue churn of uncommitted brand loyalty.

THE YIN AND YANG OF MARKETING

Market share marketing and customer share marketing are complementary actions with the same overall objective: to generate more sales and profits. While market share marketing creates unprecedented reach in helping to identify and drive prospects, customer share marketing creates targeted, one-to-one conversations with those prospects. While market share marketing works to drive sales this year, customer share marketing helps to deepen customer relationships, laying the groundwork for sales a decade from now.

Customer share marketing fulfills the promise of segmentation—building a one-to-one relationship with each customer based on relevance to each customer. Customer share marketing can truly accomplish what 20th century marketers intuitively knew was the next logical step in the evolution of marketing. They were simply unable to deliver on the promise of segmentation using the available 20th century mass marketing tools. All of that changed with the advent of the Web and email.

Table 9.4 demonstrates the extreme yet complementary differences between market share marketing and customer share marketing. Though market share marketing still plays a critical role in reaching the masses most efficiently, its effectiveness has come and gone. On the other hand, customer share marketing's time is just beginning. Market share marketing's primary mission was to build and sell one brand at a time to as many people as possible, most of them unknown and unidentified. Customer share marketing's mission is just the opposite—sell as many relevant brands to each customer, all of them known and identified.

TABLE 9.4   The Yin and Yang of Marketing

Marketing Type	Marketing Perspective	Marketing Style	Marketing Scope	Sales Perspective
Market Share	Mass	Without Permission	One Brand	Next Sale
Customer Share	Direct	With Permission	Many Brands	Lifetime Sales

© 2001 Customer Share Group LLC

The objective of customer share marketing is to isolate your prospects and customers and to begin a conversation with them about what interests them, relative to your product or service. You will have prospects on your list who will grant you permission, but have yet to purchase anything from you. These are great leads, since they have prequalified themselves as interested in what you do or sell. From this point forward, your objective relative to these prospects would be to turn them into customers, and then repeat customers, and then customers for life.

Customer share marketing is about being smarter with your advertising efforts. It's not necessarily about greater creativity, better writing, bigger ads, louder ads, or even more ads. It's about using both mass marketing and direct marketing to draw on the brand equity and customer loyalty that you have built over the course of many years and many budgets. Customer share marketing is about selling more to the customers you already have by creating an action-oriented bridge out to the future with one-to-one messages that are requested, relevant, and respectful.

BUILDING A MARKETING PLAN FROM THE INSIDE OUT

In many ways, some of the most effective means of communicating or marketing are still the simplest. In Figure 9.2, one-to-one communication in level one represents the most targeted means of influencing a sale. All of the efforts in level one are direct, one-to-one marketing initiatives that can pinpoint individuals who have expressed an interest in what you sell.

In level two, though these are not direct marketing tactics, marketing through niche media represents a way to communicate with groups of enthusiasts who are brought together based on a common interest. For example, gardeners are drawn to Gardening Magazine, HGTV and *gardenweb.com*, making these perfect environments for marketers such as Miracle-Gro to get the attention of relatively large groups at the center of the target prospects.

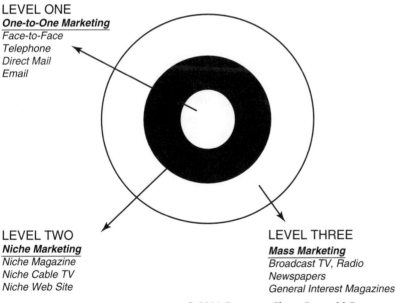

LEVEL ONE
One-to-One Marketing
Face-to-Face
Telephone
Direct Mail
Email

LEVEL TWO
Niche Marketing
Niche Magazine
Niche Cable TV
Niche Web Site

LEVEL THREE
Mass Marketing
Broadcast TV, Radio
Newspapers
General Interest Magazines

© 2001 Customer Share Group LLC

FIGURE 9.2
Three Levels of Marketing Penetration

In level three, we see the mass-marketing channels that deliver reach. If you have a product that many different kinds of people consume, such as cars, food, real estate, movies, music, and insurance, mass media can reach and drive new prospects to your Web site as well as touch and influence existing loyal customers.

Major advertisers are demanding better results from the campaigns that their agencies create and place. During the 20th century, most advertisers used the tactics in levels two and three to influence and sell to customers. But increasingly, companies are moving toward the center of the circle in Figure 9.2 by creating one-to-one campaigns with their own customers.

Historically, advertisers and their agencies built their marketing plans from the outside in—starting in the outer ring in level three with mass marketing and moving in toward one-to-one marketing. This was largely because advertising agencies viewed themselves as creators of great advertising as opposed to developers of integrated marketing strategies, plans, and campaigns. But that's changing. Slowly, the many disparate pieces of marketing are at last beginning to come out of the same company as traditional ad agencies broaden their skill sets in the direction of one-to-one and customer share marketing.

Building marketing plans from the inside out is not only a helpful exercise for large companies and brands, but also a practical one for small to mid-size companies that don't necessarily have the marketing budgets to even consider mass-marketing vehicles. The civil engineering firm that calls on the entire universe of only 50 prospective customers will start—in Figure 9.2—with level one in the center of the circle by calling, visiting, direct mailing, and emailing their way toward sales. Ultimately, they may run an ad or two in trade magazines or on trade Web sites in level two, but it's probably not practical for them to even consider level three.

A major national brand, on the other hand, is more likely be active across all three levels, but still should think through marketing to prospects and customers from the inside out—from one-to-one marketing *out* to one-to-many marketing.

CUSTOMER SHARE MARKETING:
GETTING STARTED

The sooner marketers begin to practice customer share marketing, the sooner they will be able to engage in a cost-effective program that draws on the equity that their brands have built over time. It's simple for any marketer—big or small, B2B or B2C—to get started by answering these simple questions:

- What are we specifically doing to build market share? Make an inventory of the current marketing initiatives that are designed to help you build market share.
- What are we specifically doing to build customer share? Make an inventory of the current marketing initiatives that are designed to help you build customer share.

Take advantage of the significant energy that your market share marketing efforts create by designing a mass marketing/direct marketing plan that communicates with your prospect and customer base on multiple levels. Think of your combined market share and customer share efforts as part of a four-step communication process:

1. *Drive prospects and customers to your Web site.* Leverage your mass marketing efforts, either directly or indirectly, to drive prospects and customers to your Web site.
2. *Capture identity and permission.* Create a number of clever, relevant, and helpful reasons on your site, such as e-newsletters, email updates, sweepstakes, or contests, to convince prospects to identify themselves by providing their email address as well as granting permission to receive future communications by email.
3. *Build your permission-granted list.* Continually feed your permission-granted database with new prospects and customers every day. This list will become increasingly valuable as each day passes. Protect it, and share it with no one.

4. *Work the list.* This is your opportunity to build customer relationships as well as a second level of sell by sending helpful and relevant messages to your prospects and customers. Think of what you would say to just one prospect or customer if you met face-to-face. What would you say? Would you sound like an impersonal annual report, or like a friend from next door who provides good advice? How can you be helpful to prospects and customers and not totally self-serving to your sales objectives? How can you speak with them from the right side of your brain?

This important customer share orientation starts with the belief that traditional means of mass marketing can only do so much in its role as a workhorse in battling the noise of thousands of daily commercial messages that bombard our senses. By definition, mass marketing is designed to speak to the masses, not to individuals one at a time. That is the province of direct marketing—the world that Orvis and Tiffany's are practicing in their third centuries.

Growth by customer share is not a *random act of marketing,* but a calculated, controlled use of the science of direct marketing using the Web and email to communicate with people who have identified themselves as interested in what you have to say or sell.

DRIVING PROSPECTS AND CUSTOMERS: FEEDING THE FUNNEL

Before your company can fully engage in customer share marketing, you need to develop your own permission-granted email list. The first step in building that list is to take an inventory of all of your mass-marketing initiatives and determine which ones can directly or indirectly help you acquire permission from the thousands of prospects and customers that move in and out of your marketplace each and every day.

Next, make sure that your Web site is the beneficiary of the enormous marketing power that you generate each year through the sum of all of your mass-marketing efforts. Picture a huge funnel feeding prospects and customers that have seen your online advertising and acquisition email efforts, but also continually see your URL on television commercials, in magazines and newspapers, on buses, shopping bags, boxes, billboards, in press releases—in short, anywhere and everywhere, especially wherever your mass-marketing efforts appear.

Feeding your funnel helps to rapidly build your list. Once you have built your own list, then you'll be ready to work the list by serving up requested, relevant, and respectful messages to people who have identified themselves as potential customers for life.

For decades, companies have spent billions of dollars to convince consumers to buy what they have to sell. Now, the Web makes it possible for companies to grow short-term sales—online or offline—as well as to develop permission-granted email databases to help deepen customer relationships on the way to growing long-term sales.

Learn how the world's leading companies and brands are using the Web to acquire sales and permission as part of the first step in creating one-to-one conversations that result in growing customer share.

10

FEEDING THE FUNNEL: HOW TO ACQUIRE CUSTOMERS AND PERMISSION

I grew up in New England, the maple syrup capital of the United States. Every February, when temperatures started to rise, my father would pull out the rusting cans and taps, and we'd head out to our backyard to tap the big maples.

Each day when I got home from school, I'd run out to check the buckets, hoping to find a bucket full of sap so we could start the boiling process. Finally, as temperatures rose, the sap began to run, quickly filling each bucket with the clear, watery stuff. I was so excited the first time I saw an overflowing bucket of sap that I couldn't wait for my father to come home to start boiling the first sap of the season. So, I took things into my own hands.

I poured four buckets of sap into our largest pot, turned on the burner, and started to stir the mixture with a big wooden spoon. The thought of thick maple syrup just made my mouth water. After about two hours of stirring, the pot full of sap was nearly gone. I was able to scrape a small sample off the bottom of the pot. It was sweet, but considering all the work that went in to producing a teaspoonful of syrup, not all that satisfying, and certainly not enough for even one serving of pancakes.

When my father came home and saw the pot on the stove, he just shook his head. He later told me that it takes about 40 gallons of sap to make one gallon of maple syrup—about one quart of syrup for every tree. That was just way too much work for an impatient adolescent. After that, I left the boiling to him.

ACQUIRING SALES: LEFT SIDE OF THE BRAIN

The process of generating sales is much like making maple syrup—it takes a lot of prospects to convert just one into a customer. And the cost of acquiring customers—the people who actually buy your products or services—continues to escalate. That's why companies like Unilever are questioning the return on their marketing investments. How can mass-marketing initiatives become more cost-effective? How can Unilever's $3.5 billion short-term annual investment generate more?

For years, researchers have studied the wonders of the human brain. Some have even speculated that we have two brains because of the very specific functions controlled by the left and right hemispheres of the brain.

It is believed that the left side of the brain is more dominant for abilities such as logic, conformity, rules, calculations, and math: many of the characteristics that are expected of participants in the world of business. The right side of the brain, on the other hand, is considered to be more dominant for creativity, emotion, and nonconformity.

Most of us live our lives on the left side of the brain, where logic dictates an orderly movement forward, largely delivering what is expected of us, day in and day out. What is expected of us in business, day in and day out, is more sales. Sometimes we deliver on that, and we are rewarded. Sometimes we don't deliver on that, and we are fired. Sometimes market conditions deliver it for us, and we are rewarded—and sometimes market conditions prevent us from delivering it, and we are fired.

We are most often so focused on the need to generate new sales *now* that we forget about the work that we can concurrently do now to help pave the way for future sales. Western culture predominantly dictates that we must achieve more and more each year, especially when it comes to top-line revenue. But we are so focused on generating sales for next quarter's results that we rarely have the time to think of the future. Too little time and effort is focused on retaining and expanding business with customers that we have spent years and millions to acquire.

Because of the significant and ever-increasing cost of acquiring customers, it's especially important now for marketers to begin to think—and act—on both sides of the brain, taking care of today's sales (left side) while laying the groundwork for tomorrow's sales (right side).

Acquisition initiatives are usually short-term, mass-marketing efforts with the overall objective of improving market share. Retention initiatives are usually long-term, one-to-one efforts designed to grow customer share (see Table 10.1). The left side of the business brain has most often dictated that the road to increased sales and profits is through the increase in market share. Rarely have increased sales and profits been the result of any sustained or focused effort to grow customer share.

Prior to the Web and email, there really was no practical way to market one-to-one with customers. Direct mail and outbound telemarketing were too costly and too slow to communicate with a universe of customers on an ongoing, consistent basis. Add to this that many companies don't even know who their customers are beyond a demographic description, and the historic track record of companies to consistently generate retention or customer share marketing efforts has been lacking.

TABLE 10.1 Acquisition and Retention

Marketing Initiatives	Sales Perspective	Marketing Perspective	Growth Perspective
Acquisition	Short-Term	Feed the Funnel	Market Share
Retention	Long-Term	Work the List	Customer Share

© 2001 Customer Share Group LLC

If you are successful at growing your customer share, and in doing so your sales increase at a rate faster than your competition, then your market share will also increase. When this happens, both sides of the brain are happy. The only difference is that the incremental sales generated from existing customers through customer share initiatives will be more profitable. This is because your long-time investment spending to build loyalty has preconditioned customers to know you, to trust you, and to consider offers from you as part of a relatively inexpensive permission-granted marketing program.

It is important now for marketers of all sizes to create dedicated and measurable customer share initiatives that complement their market share initiatives. The reason is simple: to create a competitive advantage. A specific customer share marketing strategy that works in tandem with your market share marketing strategies can help insure that you leverage your past, present, and future marketing investments to more directly leverage the loyalty that you have built to generate incremental sales.

Though the fight for market share on a category-by-category basis has been waged for decades, the fight for customer share has just begun.

ACQUIRING SALES AND PERMISSION: RIGHT SIDE OF THE BRAIN

Not every prospect that you touch with your marketing efforts will result in a sale today or this week. But if your marketing efforts offer an easy way for prospects to identify themselves and grant you permission, then you have an opportunity to generate another valuable yield short of a sale—permission. Permission gives marketers a second shot at conversion through ongoing, one-to-one messages that are requested, relevant, and respectful.

Cincinnati-based Procter & Gamble markets over 300 products to more than 5 billion consumers in 140 countries and spends nearly $4 billion a year to acquire its sales. For nearly two centuries, P & G has successfully driven sales by developing more products and selling them in more countries to more people since the company's humble beginnings as candle makers in 1837.

Now, more than 175 years since the company was started, P & G products are purchased by more than 85 percent of all people on earth. Is it possible that the manufacturer of Tide, Cascade, and Pampers has reached a market share saturation point? With unit growth flat in 1999 and up only 4 percent in 2000, would P & G benefit from a dedicated customer share focus? After all, $4 billion can buy a lot of permission.

The building of trust and share of mind has historically been the job of brand advertising: waves and waves of Coke ads followed by Pepsi ads in an effort to muscle mind share one point at a time. But brand advertising is also at risk of being swallowed by a raging sea of commercial messages, requiring advertisers to spend more, enabling frequency levels that help break the noise barrier.

Taking the time to build a bridge to future sales by creating one-to-one conversations is not something that most companies have ever done. It takes time and hard work. Mass marketers think in terms of marketing to millions of people all at once. After all, wouldn't it be easier to reach 20,000,000 people in 30 seconds on Monday Night Football? It certainly can be an easier way to reach millions of people, but is it the most effective way to build customer relationships today? When you consider the challenge of getting the attention of the average American adult today and the sizable out-of-pocket cost of mass media, the idea of marketing one-to-one with a CPM of $0 has a great deal of appeal.

A circulation director at any paid circulation magazine knows the value of working a list as well as anyone. For some popular magazines, as much as 60 to 70 percent of readers renew their subscriptions, some without any prompting or expense on the part of the publication. One of the reasons that this works so well for magazines is that the customer receives a customer touch each week or each month by receiving the publication itself. These frequent requested, relevant, and respectful customer touches help to truly build a relationship with a customer over the customer's life. The objective of customer share marketing is exactly the same—to deepen the relationship with the customer, something that is just too difficult for mass marketing alone to accomplish today.

FEEDING THE FUNNEL

Think of your Web site as an enormous funnel (see Figure 10.1) into which you drive as many prospects as possible through your acquisition efforts. Some of your mass-marketing efforts will directly drive prospects to your site through the promotion of your Web site, using both offline efforts, such as print and broadcast advertising, promotions and sweepstakes, as well as online efforts, like banner advertising, sponsorships, portal partnerships, and affiliate programs. As a customer share marketer, your first objective is to drive as many unique visitors into that funnel and onto your Web site as possible for two important reasons:

1. *To acquire sales.* Short-term transactions, either online or offline, are the direct result of mass-marketing efforts.
2. *To acquire permission.* Not everyone who shows up at your site will (or even can, in the case of many service sites) buy something at that moment. If you can't acquire a sale, at least acquire the permission to begin a conversation with prospects. By visiting your site, prospects have essentially prequalified themselves as interested in what you do. Don't let the opportunity to efficiently talk one-to-one with prospects escape.

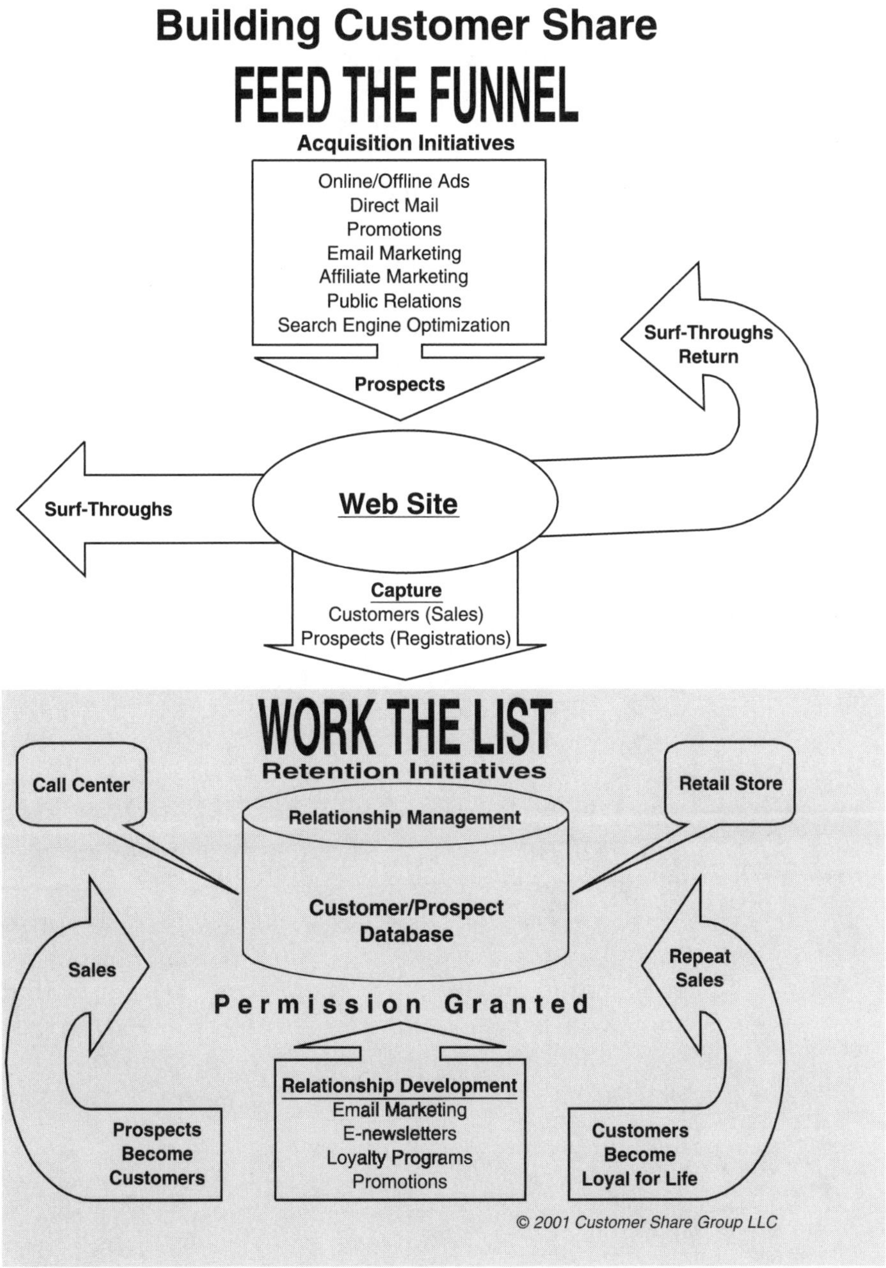

Building Customer Share
FEED THE FUNNEL
Acquisition Initiatives

Online/Offline Ads
Direct Mail
Promotions
Email Marketing
Affiliate Marketing
Public Relations
Search Engine Optimization

Prospects

Surf-Throughs Return

Surf-Throughs

Web Site

Capture
Customers (Sales)
Prospects (Registrations)

WORK THE LIST
Retention Initiatives

Call Center

Retail Store

Relationship Management

Customer/Prospect Database

Sales

Repeat Sales

Permission Granted

Prospects Become Customers

Relationship Development
Email Marketing
E-newsletters
Loyalty Programs
Promotions

Customers Become Loyal for Life

© 2001 Customer Share Group LLC

FIGURE 10.1
Feed the funnel, work the list.

Once you drive them into the funnel, unique visitors will fall into one of four progressive categories based on their actions:

1. *Surf-throughs (unidentified).* Some of your unique visitors will simply enter your site, look around, and surf through. These visitors are like the people who walk into a Macy's brick-and-mortar retail store, browse for a while, purchase nothing, and walk out. These surfers do not identify themselves by buying products or signing up for a sweepstakes or other promotion. They simply surf through and may or may not come back. Tracking software can give you clues as to the patterns and trends of these prospects, which may help you identify a problem and correct it—such as abandoned shopping carts at the point where shipping costs are calculated. But as for specifically identifying this prospect by name and email address, your ongoing feed-the-funnel activities will have to do the work to draw them back into the funnel in the future.

2. *Prospect registrations (identified).* Some prospects are not ready to buy but demonstrate a level of interest by signing up for a promotion or e-newsletter and provide their email address as well as permission to send information by future email. Though short of acquiring a sale, if you acquire permission, you acquire an opportunity for future sales.

3. *Prospects become customers (identified).* When prospects buy for the first time, they become customers and identify themselves in the process. Make sure that you, acquire permission along with the sale. Don't assume that just because they have purchased something from you, they want to receive email from you in the future.

4. *Customers become repeat customers (identified).* These are your frequent flyers—the people who come back again and again. They are your most profitable customers because your customer share marketing initiatives have been informative, helpful, and most of all requested, relevant, and respectful.

Each category represents a progressive deepening in your relationship with a prospect or customer and a heightened level of commitment to you on behalf of the customer—a direct correlation to your respectful treatment of them.

CAPTURING NAMES
AND PERMISSION ONLINE

Once your mass-marketing efforts do the job of driving prospects and customers into the funnel, your objective is to capture their identities and permission, and you can do that in two ways: (1) Sales transactions, and (2) Sign-ups and registrations.

Here are some of the most popular ways of capturing identities and permission:

1. *E-newsletters.* Scheduled outbound messages that provide helpful information, hints, and suggestions are very popular. These don't have to be long, wordy newsletters. One page of interesting and helpful information is enough. Their frequency depends entirely on how unique and timely the information is. If you are distributing information like stock quotes, then daily makes sense. If you are delivering information related to a single event, once a year might be sufficient. But for most businesses, monthly is a good frequency.

2. *Updates and specials.* Email notification of specials, clearances, new product availability, or other information that would be of interest to the customer is popular and can be effective for moving product.

3. *Contests and Sweepstakes.* Capturing permission through sweepstakes and contest sign-ups is a great way to rapidly build your own list, especially if the promotion is supported by offline and online advertising initiatives.

Remember not to assume that customers are providing permission simply because they make a purchase. Make sure that you ask for permission as part of the checkout process. You should also prominently display a link to your privacy policy so consumers can quickly review how you handle outbound email communications as well as their confidential information.

CAPTURING NAMES AND PERMISSION OFFLINE

Not all email addresses and permission need to be captured online. There are a number of ways for you to capture both email addresses and permission in an offline environment. Consistent with the customer touches chart in Chapter 7, "Maximizing Your Customer Touches," you will have opportunities to capture email addresses and permission at all touch points, including your brick-and-mortar retail stores and your call center. Providing inexpensive incentives can be a good way to convince people to sign up. Just make sure, before you initiate a plan, that you are committed to the effort and that someone has responsibility for it.

I recently had my car serviced at the local Volkswagen dealership, and while I was sitting in the customer lounge waiting for my car, I noticed a sign-up sheet taped to the counter. *Sign up for Free Information by Email.* The dealership was collecting email addresses and permission from walk-in customers in its service department. But judging by the very worn and yellowed condition of the sign-up sheet that was completely filled out with names and email addresses, this initiative had completely run out of steam.

Too often, executives of an organization attend seminars and conferences and come back to the business with great ideas to help improve marketing, but fail to communicate the importance of the initiative to the rank and file. So, Joe the Service Manager simply gets a directive without an explanation. These initiatives often die a slow death after someone spills coffee on the sign-up sheet that's been taped to the counter for four months. Make sure you communicate the importance of capturing email and permission to everyone in your company, not only as a way to save money, but also as a way to boost sales. Make sure all of your employees understand and make the commitment to help the effort.

It is also imperative to follow up on your permission capturing initiatives, not just to input the data, but also to fulfill the expectation that you have now created in the minds of your customers. It is unlikely that I will be receiving anything from my Volkswagen dealership anytime soon, based on the lack of follow-up to the sign-up process initiated at its retail location. One of the biggest mistakes companies make in utilizing the Web is to first raise a customer's expectations and then fail to deliver.

Whatever your method of sign-up, remember that you have created an expectation in the mind of the consumer that he or she will receive something from you, like an e-newsletter or emails that announce special offers. Follow up quickly and consistently. Too many companies trumpet the introduction of a new e-newsletter only to realize that they have to create a second, a third, and a fourth e-newsletter after the first one has been produced and sent. Don't commit to an outbound program until or unless you are ready or staffed to consistently generate unique and helpful information that will be relevant to your prospects and customers.

CONVERTING YOUR MAILING LIST TO AN EMAILING LIST

If you haven't started the process of collecting email addresses and permission from your existing customers, you need to start today. There is little debate that permission-granted electronic messages will be as common for communicating commercial messages to consumers as first and second class mail was in the 20th century, as long as the messages are requested, relevant, and respectful. The sooner you can build your own list, the sooner you can begin to inexpensively communicate—both ways—with your prospects and customers. If you have retail locations, create clever ways to naturally weave the process into typical customer touches.

Another way to get started quickly is to begin a conversion process around the names and street addresses of your current customer base. Many companies have a significant mailing list of names and street addresses and a relatively small list of email addresses. Certainly, a dedicated direct mail effort to your mailing list for the purpose of conversion to email addresses makes sense, but can be very costly. Even sending a postcard to 100,000 addresses can cost more than $30,000.

There are a number of ways to convert mailing lists to emailing lists without incurring unnecessary costs. For example, you can piggyback other initiatives, such as billing statements and product shipments, and offer an incentive to provide email addresses and permission. If many of your customers are local and you have their telephone numbers, outbound telephone calls by your staff during slow periods can help you convert your mailing list to an emailing list over time. Programs like this may be slow in building, but are extremely cost-effective. Your goals in the feed-the-funnel phase of customer share marketing should be to

1. *Drive* as many prospects and customers to your Web site as possible, and
2. *Capture* the identity and permission from as many prospects and customers as possible to aggressively build your permission-granted database.

Make sure that you look at outbound efforts as another opportunity to create a customer touch as opposed to just getting something that you want from the customer. Think through what your staff members might say if contacting customers by telephone. Remember, this is a call out of the blue. Disarm the customer by letting them know that you are updating your files so that they know that the call is a customer service call and not a sales solicitation. Review the information in Table 10.2 to insure that you have created an appropriate means of capturing identities and permission across all of your touch points. You could be capturing information at all of these points. Are you?

TABLE 10.2 *Maximize All of Your Customer Touches*

Type of Touch	Where	What	With Whom
In-Person*	Retail	Product Info	Salesperson
		Checkout	Cashier
Outbound	Call Center	Telemarketing	Telemarketing Rep
Telephone*		Issue	Customer Service
		Resolution	Rep
Inbound	Call Center	Orders/info	Telesales Rep
Telephone*		Issue	Customer Service
		Resolution	Rep
Outbound	Marketing Dept.	Direct Mail	Marketing Rep
Mail/	Customer	Letters	Customer Service
Delivery	Service Fulfill-	Packages	Rep
	ment Center		Fulfillment Rep
Inbound	Marketing Dept.	Orders	Marketing Rep
Mail/	Customer	Letters	Customer Service
Delivery	Service Fulfill-	Returns	Rep
	ment Center		Fulfillment Rep
Outbound	Marketing Dept.	Retention	Marketing Rep
Email	Customer	Email	Customer Service
	Service	Issue	Rep
		Resolution	
Inbound	Marketing dept.	Action/Orders	Marketing Rep
Email	Customer	Issue	Customer Service
	Service	Identified	Rep
Live Chat*	Web site	Product Info	Web Salesperson
		Questions	Customer
			Service Rep

Live, one-to-one customer touches
© 2001 Customer Share Group LLC

Avoid problems down the road by communicating your customer share marketing strategies to all of your employees. Make sure they understand the importance of these initiatives for the health of the company. Whenever possible and practical, the CEO should communicate these types of strategic initiatives to underscore their importance.

FEEDING THE FUNNEL:
BEST PRACTICES

The Web is making it easy for companies to develop their own permission-granted email databases that they are using to deepen relationships with their customers. Some of the world's leading companies and brands, such as Johnson & Johnson, American Express, and Minute Maid, are using the Web to acquire sales and permission as part of the first step in creating one-to-one conversations that result in growing customer share.

Learn specific customer share marketing tactics through a collection of more than 30 mini case studies that describe how nationally branded marketers are successfully feeding their own funnels.

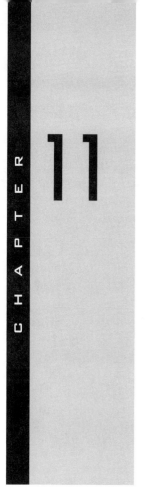

11

ACQUIRING CUSTOMERS AND PERMISSION: BEST PRACTICES

Advertisers spent more than $134 billion to promote their products and services in the United States in 2000, according to *Advertising Age*. That's nearly $500 for every man, woman, and child in the United States. To put that investment into perspective, with $134 billion in promotional investment each year, you could theoretically reach everyone in the United States:

- 500 times by telephone
- 2,000 times by postcard
- 50,000 times by email

Though sending an email to every person in the United States every 10 minutes for an entire year is neither practical nor advised, it does underscore both the efficiency of email as well as the enormous investment that advertisers are making each year to convince people to feel good about a brand, take action on that brand, or both. Like it or not, direct marketing, in the form of the Web and email, has raised the specter of return on investment. Unilever wants to know how its $3.5 billion of annual advertising spending can produce more—and it's a perfectly good question to ask.

A $134 billion investment obviously helps to sell a lot of products and services for America's companies. But how much permission is it buying at the same time? Capturing permission from the people who are moved by your advertising to take action—visit the retail store, go to the Web site, call your toll-free line—is a marketing imperative today. Even if you have no plans to use the names, you must aggressively capture information and permission from the people you drive into your funnel.

The reason: Most companies will engage in one-to-one, permission-granted communications in the future. It's no longer a matter of *if*—it's now simply a matter of *when*.

How the World's Leading Marketers Feed the Funnel

Feeding the funnel and then capturing identity and permission are the first steps in acquiring customers. Using predominantly—but not exclusively—mass-marketing techniques, marketers purchase time and space in front of the eyeballs that the media attracts. Increasingly, nationally branded advertisers are seeing the value in creating a second level of sell by leveraging their advertising investments to help create future direct, targeted, measurable, inexpensive, and fast communication with their best prospects and customers.

The following examples demonstrate how the world's leading marketers are feeding the funnel, identifying their best prospects and customers, and capturing permission with the help of online and offline advertising.

ADVERTISING

From a 30-second spot on the Super Bowl to targeted banner ads on a network of e-newsletters, paying for access to your target audience through media that attracts lots of eyeballs is still one of the most efficient means of driving the masses into your funnel.

Advertising initiatives both offline and online, such as sponsorships, portal partnerships, integrated marketing programs, direct mail, promotions, acquisition email marketing, affiliate marketing, search engine optimization, and banner and tile advertising, are all effective drivers of prospects and customers. Learn here how leading marketers are creating campaigns that generate an "afterlife" in the form of permission-granted email campaigns that are primarily designed to build a relationship.

OFFLINE ADVERTISING

No matter how you look at it, the lion's share of advertising by far is done offline in an effort to build brand and to motivate consumers to take action. Even though the noise levels are reaching a powerful crescendo, advertising on television, radio, and in print is still the most efficient means of reaching the masses with a singular message.

Some marketers, such as automakers, use mass-marketing vehicles such as network television to reach the largest possible number of prospective buyers. Other advertisers, such as Miracle-Gro, are able to use niche media, such as Home & Garden Television (HGTV), to reach the most likely prospects to buy and use their products. In either case, the specific identities of the viewers, readers, or surfers are unknown until they identify themselves as interested in the product or service that you provide by asking for more information by email. The pre-Web parallel to this action was probably when consumers requested a catalog either through the mail or over the telephone. Not surprisingly, prospects requesting catalogs convert to customers at a much higher rate, but not as high as you might think. Less than one-third of all catalog requests result in an actual order, which further underscores the need to create a relevant connection with the prospect on an ongoing basis.

Following are examples of how leading marketers are using offline advertising to direct prospects and customers to their Web sites in order to capture sales and permission.

BAND-AID® Brand Adhesive Bandages Targets Gardeners. BAND-AID® Brand Adhesive Bandages used offline advertising that targeted gardeners as a group who commonly cut and scrape themselves as part of their passion for the activity they love most. This is a clever way to target individuals who have a high probability of using the company's products. The company teamed with Walgreens drugstores by creating point-of-sale displays intended to motivate gardeners to register for a sweepstakes at *www.walgreens.com*.

- *Objectives:* To increase sales and to develop a permission-granted database for use in future emailings.
- *Strategy:* To target a large group of enthusiasts who often scrape and cut themselves as part of the activity—in this case gardeners. Create a sweepstakes promotion during the heavy gardening season that coincides with an overall increase in outside activity and a general need for BAND-AID® Brand products.
- *Tactics:* Promoted the sweepstakes by running advertising in programming that attracts gardeners, including television spots on HGTV and the Do-It-Yourself Network as well as at the corresponding Web sites for those networks, *www.hgtv.com* and *www.diynet.com*. Aisle displays were also utilized at participating Walgreens to specifically promote sign-up at the Web site. Additionally, Walgreens highlighted the sweepstakes as part of its ongoing circular marketing efforts. BAND-AID® Brand also supported the effort with free-standing inserts in newspapers across the nation.
- *Analysis:* A very good example of how a major, nationally branded advertiser can create a second level of sell

by driving prospects and customers to the Web to provide both personal information as well as permission to send future emailings. This campaign combines a number of complementary offline and online vehicles to drive traffic, including the power of program and content compatibility of cable television and Web sites, the targeting capabilities of direct mail, the reach of newspapers, and the immediacy of point-of-sale. The promotion was also coordinated with the launch of the new BAND-AID® Brand Web site at *www.bandaid.com*.

BMW Used Offline Ads to Drive Prospects to View Online Film Shorts. Automaker BMW took a very different approach to promote its line of cars by creating a series of five short rich-media films directed by some of Hollywood's most popular directors. The six-minute films were streamed over *www.bmwfilms.com* and were designed to appeal to BMW's target audience, the vast majority of which research their car purchases online before buying offline. Offline advertising campaigns in newspapers, magazines, and on television helped to dramatically boost unique visitors at the site. Visitors were asked to provide their name, email address, zip code, and country, as well as given the option to grant permission, as a prerequisite for viewing the shorts. The cost of the campaign came in under what the automaker has spent on developing a traditional all-offline campaign.

- *Objectives:* To entertain, generate interest, and capture permission from potential buyers of BMW's line of cars.
- *Strategy:* To use "out-of-the-box" thinking to create an integrated campaign that drives the target audience online for an entertaining online commercial experience.
- *Tactics:* Tapped some of Hollywood's hottest directors—and some stars as well—to produce five film shorts that could be viewed online at *www.bmwfilms.com*. Drove BMW prospects and customers to the site to view the films by running trailers for the movies on television and in theaters, as well as print ads in the entertain-

ment sections of a host of local newspapers. The films were also copied onto DVDs and distributed to BMW customers by mail.

■ *Analysis:* This campaign provides a great example of how traditional advertising is changing. BMW used offline advertising to drive prospects and customers online to see its product in action. By using some of Hollywood's top action-adventure directors, BMW was able to create six-minute ads that were not only entertaining, but also demonstrated all the performance capabilities of the driving machine in action, all within the cost of an average offline campaign.

Sports Authority Builds Email Database with Offline Advertising. Sporting goods retailer The Sports Authority has used the power and efficiency of reach to help feed its funnel and build its own database of permission-granted email addresses. By offering prospects and customers an opportunity to win a $1,000 shopping spree through its own freestanding insert in Sunday supplements leading up to Father's Day, the Fort Lauderdale-based retailer successfully drove traffic to its Web site for two purposes: (1) to generate short-term sales by suggesting appropriate gifts for dads, and (2) to aggressively capture names, email addresses, and permission from prospects and customers visiting the Web site. The Sports Authority cleverly uses its permission-granted database in conjunction with offline advertising as a way to work the list by adding very directed, one-to-one marketing energy to a campaign. A good example is its day after Thanksgiving event that highlights the 6 AM DOORBUSTERS promotion. Each email carries a link that enables recipients to locate the nearest Sports Authority brick-and-mortar location.

■ *Objectives:* To generate short-term sales at brick-and-mortar retail outlets or at *www.thesportsauthority.com*. To aggressively capture permission from prospects and customers in order to add to its emailing list of over 500,000 names.

- *Strategy:* To use mass-marketing tactics to reach as many prospects and customers as possible during the period leading into Father's Day—a key gift-giving holiday for sporting goods retailers.
- *Tactics:* Utilized the reach and efficiency of freestanding inserts through Sunday newspapers in key markets around the country to reach over 15 million consumers per insertion.
- *Analysis:* An outstanding example of how a company that is completely committed to the future of communication by email uses the benefits of mass marketing to feed its funnel for the purpose of building its own list and an opportunity at a second level of sell. This integrated use of the Web yields great results for the sporting goods retailer—from driving short-term sales both online and offline to actively building its database asset. This is also another example of a company that could greatly benefit from a robust CRM or eCRM strategy that matches customer buying habits with future outbound email messages.

ONLINE ADVERTISING

Though criticized for not living up to expectations, online advertising is still a great way to reach the people you want to reach when they are already online. Historically, we have based our expectations around online advertising on three false assumptions: (1) Early click-through rates could be sustained after the novelty of clicking through wore off, (2) Conversion rates—when applicable—could also be sustained, and (3) The tidal wave of dotcom ad spending would indefinitely feed the monster. Using banner, tile, and other space-related advertising to drive prospects and customers to your Web site to acquire sales, sales leads, and permission can be another effective way to drive target audiences to a site. We also became very conversion-oriented relative to online ads, largely because we could—asking the question, So, how many sales did it generate?

When click-through and conversion rates universally dropped, we heard from agencies and online media that advertising was an effective online branding tool. The fact is that online advertising is another means through which companies can communicate their marketing messages. Online ads are another tool through which advertisers can reach and influence target audiences. If your target audience is online, you should be there, especially when inventory is high and bargains can be negotiated.

Following are examples of how leading marketers are using online advertising to drive prospects into the funnel.

New York Life Insurance Company Used Web to Generate Leads. New York Life, headquartered in New York City, used the Web to generate leads for its insurance sales agents nationwide. As a service company that relies on a consultative process with clients through one-to-one offline discussion, New York Life viewed the Web and email as tools both to generate near-term leads and to build a permission-granted email list of prospects and customers. The company historically has used direct mail, DRTV (Direct Response Television), and referrals from existing policyholders to generate leads. In its first online effort, the company ran banner and tile advertising on sites targeted to women. Clicking through the ads brought prospects and customers to a landing page at *www.newyorklife.com* that was designed to educate women on the benefits of planning for their financial future around life's major events.

- *Objectives:* To use the Web to generate leads from women for New York Life insurance agents nationwide and to develop a permission-granted email list of prospects and customers for future email campaigns and e-newsletters.
- *Strategy:* To help educate women about the need to plan for the financial future, especially around life's major events. To demonstrate how a variety of New York Life insurance products may help them accomplish their financial goals.

- *Tactics:* Rotated a dozen banner and tile ads on sites that attract women, such as *www.discovery.com, www.women.com,* and *www.insure.com.* The ads focused on some of the major events in a woman's life, including marriage, childbirth, financing their child's college education, and retirement. The ads ran during the summer months.
- *Analysis:* A great example of how a service company can use the Web to generate leads for its sales agents for offline follow-up, and in this case, complement its existing mechanisms for lead generation. Many service-related businesses resisted using the Web to generate leads during the Web's early years because of the perception that the Web was primarily a place for online transactions. But this perception is rapidly changing. Big companies and small, B2C as well as B2B, are using the Web to (1) describe the service and its benefits, (2) provide a way for individuals to identify themselves and grant permission, and (3) generate a consistent and planned communication program out to prospects and customers, regardless of the size of the company, the type of industry, or the number of prospective customers.

Business Week Promoted Special Issue with Online Rich-Media Ads. *Business Week* promoted its *Business Week 50 Special Issue* by running online rich-media ads. The ads ran on the Finance section of the heavily populated portal site Yahoo! and allowed surfers to view streaming video, stock quotes, company profiles, and other information simply by mousing over elements of the ad. The technology essentially gave *Business Week* an opportunity to provide more relevant content on the surface of the banner ad by utilizing a rich-media technology that enabled the publisher to do much more within a standard 468 x 60 pixel banner ad.

- *Objectives:* To drive prospects to the *Business Week 50 Special Issue* section of the Web site. To capture subscriptions or permission, or both, from prospects who clicked through the ad to the Web site. Also, to drive newsstand sales of the special issue.

- *Strategy:* To reach the target audience in an online environment that was consistent, editorially, with the content delivered in *Business Week* and to use rich-media technology to increase the amount of information delivered in the banner ad without requiring the prospect to click through to the Web site.

- *Tactics:* Used rich-media technology in banner ads to expand the delivery of site content to a targeted audience of prospective readers. Educated prospects with mouse-over technology that allows the advertiser to create an ad that contains much more content than a traditional banner ad to help increase the likelihood of click-through to the Web site.

- *Analysis:* A good example of using the technology to say more to prospective customers—in this case subscribers—in an environment that was consistent with the demographics of the business publication. This is also a good example of using a high-profile special product to try to entice prospects into the fold on a regular basis. Also, this is a classic example of using a high-profile event or product to drive trial. Using the online ad environment and rich-media technology allowed *Business Week* to create more than just an interactive ad—an ad with dynamic elements that allowed the advertiser to include multiple content-related messages to broaden the appeal to prospective subscribers without first having to click through to the site.

Portal Partnerships

For advertisers with a healthy budget, perhaps one of the best means of advertising online is partnering with major portals like AOL and Yahoo!. If volume is what you're after, then few vehicles will deliver more traffic than the major portals. One in every three Americans—or 95 million people—visits a search engine or major portal every month, according to Nielsen/NetRatings.

Portal partnerships often integrate a number of advertising, promotional, email marketing, and merchandising elements that most other sites simply can't match in terms of reach. Marketers can take advantage of promotional tools, such as banner, tile and interstitial advertising, rotating merchandise teasers on the home page, and specific banner and tile placement on relevant areas of a portal, such as the music section.

Following are examples of how leading marketers are using portal partnerships to drive prospects into the funnel.

American Airlines Partnered with AOL for Million Mile Sweeps. American Airlines and America Online teamed up to create a promotion that included an online sweepstakes designed to drive memberships for the Fort Worth, Texas-based airline's frequent flyer program. The promotion, dubbed the Win A million Miles Sweepstakes, offered entrants a weekly opportunity to win one million AOL AAdvantage miles. Winners could redeem their miles for travel as well as for merchandise, such as consumer electronics products, books, and music. In order to sign up for the chance to win, consumers had to provide their AAdvantage when registering. Current AAdvantage members could simply enter their name, zip code, email address, and AAdvantage number to enter. Nonmembers could easily sign up for membership for free within the context of the promotion. The sweeps was part of a larger promotion entitled Your Summer Getaway that was designed to drive summer travel on American Airlines as well as to increase AAdvantage memberships.

- *Objectives:* To dramatically grow memberships in American Airlines' AAdvantage frequent flyer program. To grow the inhouse permission-granted email list.
- *Strategy:* To provide consumers with a compelling incentive to become members in American's AAdvantage program.
- *Tactics:* Created a partnership with one of the leading Web portals to take advantage of the enormous traffic generated there daily. Created a sweepstakes that gave

away one million miles each week for four weeks to AAdvantage members who registered for the sweeps. Promotion was prominently announced on AOL's home page on the day it kicked off. Campaign was also supported by banner advertising that rotated through the top of the Travel section of AOL.

■ *Analysis:* An example of how an advertiser with a healthy budget can channel traffic through its funnel, capturing permission, and in this case, driving member sign-up for its Customer Rewards frequent flyer program. This promotion also provided incentives and rewards not only for its new customer acquisitions, but for existing AAdvantage customers as well. This last point is sometimes lost in promotions where the new members get an incentive, while existing loyal members are often overlooked. That's an old economy way of thinking: rewarding the people who have marginal interest in what you do or sell for trying you out. Rewarding the people who reward you with their loyalty requires retention spending. But the investment is worth it, because it takes five times as much to acquire a customer as it does to retain one.

Six Flags Partners with AOL to Promote Theme Parks. Six Flags Theme Parks and America Online partnered to create an integrated marketing campaign designed to drive prospects and returning customers to its 31 locations across North America. One of the elements of the Thrill Seeker Summer promotion allowed Six Flags to reach 250,000 of AOL Moviefone's opt-in email subscribers with the opportunity to enter a sweepstakes based on a number of summer movie releases. The sweepstakes highlighted action-adventure movies such as Tomb Raider, starring Academy Award winner Angelina Jolie, to underscore the excitement and adventure themes at Six Flags Parks. The sweepstakes coincided with the release of six action-adventure movies, with the winners receiving four free passes to any of the Six Flags locations.

■ *Objectives:* To drive paid admissions and ancillary sales during the height of the theme park season.

- *Strategy:* To promote the addition of 11 new roller coasters that were hyped as the "hairiest" the world has ever seen. Align with a partner who can bring reach with the target audience in an atmosphere that coincides with the park's adventure and excitement themes.
- *Tactics:* Created a summer-long sweepstakes that coincide with the release of six action-adventure films: *Swordfish, Tomb Raider, Kiss of the Dragon, Original Sin, American Outlaws,* and *John Carpenter's Ghost of Mars.* The sweepstakes was promoted throughout the summer through emails to Moviefone's opt-in list of over 250,000 e-newsletter subscribers. Banner ads ran on AOL Moviefone as well as on other AOL/Time Warner sites, such as Netscape, CompuServe, and AOL Entertainment. Banner ads for the AOL service ran on the Six Flags home page at *www.sixflags.com.* Also, AOL collateral material promoting sign-up for the service was distributed at the parks.
- *Analysis:* This is an example of a well-planned marketing initiative that involves both online and offline advertising, acquisition email marketing, and retention email marketing all integrated into one program. It is also a good example of an advertiser aligning with a site that has very similar target audience demographics and using a sweepstakes theme that borrows equity from the energy that major motion picture releases generate over the summer. This promotion not only yielded the short-term benefit of driving prospects and customers to Six Flags' parks, but also created a second level of sell by capturing permission from participants that can be used for future promotions.

INTEGRATED MARKETING

Some of the most effective feed-the-funnel campaigns integrate a number of complementary marketing elements, usually weaving a common theme through multiple vehicles, both offline and online. Increasingly, advertisers are using cross-media strategies to reach their target audiences wherever they gather both offline and online. Following are examples of how leading marketers are using integrated marketing strategies to drive prospects into the funnel.

American Express and NBA Go Online and Offline to Promote Trivia Contest. Financial Services giant American Express teamed up with the National Basketball Association in developing an on-line trivia contest designed to promote American Express to the core fan base as part of its ongoing sponsorship of the NBA and its status as the official card of the NBA. The contest was promoted both online and offline and was designed to drive memberships for American Express cards and, short of that, capture permission from prospects interested in hearing more about American Express products and services.

- *Objectives:* To demonstrate the value of membership with American Express by providing special access and programs for card members. To acquire new American Express card members and to capture permission from both new and existing card members for the purpose of sending future emailings.
- *Strategy:* To promote the advantages of American Express membership to the core NBA fan base. To take advantage of the most exciting part of the NBA season by sponsoring a contest leading up to and through the playoffs.
- *Tactics:* Promoted the online trivia contest through a variety of online and offline marketing vehicles, including ads on *www.nba.com*, *www.yahoo.com* as well as on NBA.com TV and in print ads appearing in *NBA Stuff* magazine and *Hoop* magazine. The NBA Ultimate Player Video was used to reward existing card members and as an incentive for fans to sign up and compete in this 12-week contest. This helped identify interested card members and prospects, and enabled the company to obtain permission from both existing American Express customers as well as prospective customers through the contest registration process for future contact.

■ *Analysis:* One of the many examples of how American Express leveraged its longstanding relationship with the NBA as the league's official card. The sign-up process was respectful of consumers and utilized a positive option to indicate an interest in receiving future information via email from the NBA and American Express. Another example of NBA commissioner David Stern's golden touch in involving major, nationally branded advertisers to promote their products and services through the NBA. For American Express, this promotion represents another thoughtful execution from one of the world's great direct marketing and database marketing companies.

Murphy Oil Soap and Merry Maids Cleaning Service in Partnership. Murphy Oil Soap, a Colgate-Palmolive brand out of New York, and Merry Maids of Memphis, Tennessee, teamed up in a co-promotional effort aimed at their similar target audiences of 25- to 49-year-old women. The integrated marketing program involved both offline vehicles (newspapers, product packaging, collateral, and product samples) and online vehicles (Web sites, acquisition email, retention email, and e-newsletters). In addition, the companies developed an online sweepstakes that ran for five weeks, with an ongoing, cobranded e-newsletter developed as a result of the campaign, giving life to the promotion well beyond the initial push.

■ *Objectives:* To drive near-term trial and sales of Murphy Oil Soap. To drive near-term trial of Merry Maids home cleaning service. To drive collective prospects to either or both Web sites in order to capture mailing and emailing addresses, telephone numbers, and permission to send future messages by email.
■ *Strategy:* Create an online sweepstakes with the winner receiving a year of Merry Maids cleaning service. Create a cobranded, content-based monthly e-newsletter to be sent to the permission-granted list and to third-party opt-in lists, rented after the sweeps in an effort to continue to grow the permission-granted list.

- *Tactics:* Integrated the sweepstakes theme into freestanding inserts in over 30 million Sunday newspapers, which also carried coupons for Murphy Oil Soap. Sweeps also promoted at both *www.murphyoilsoap.com* and *www.merrymaids.com*. Additionally, Murphy's bottles displayed coupons offering discounts on Merry Maids services, while Merry Maids provided leave-behind samples and coupons for Murphy's in homes where they provide their services. Monthly e-newsletters were designed to provide legs for the cobranded promotion well into the future.

- *Analysis:* A terrific example of how two marketers, who appeal to the same target audience, put their heads together to create new energy for both brands. This win-win promotion allows Merry Maids to tie with one of its packaged goods suppliers to create exposure that borrows the enormous brand equity and loyalty that has been built over many years with Murphy Oil Soap. Murphy's, on the other hand, gets the opportunity for exposure as a product used by the Merry Maids service, but also enjoys the unique opportunity for in-home product samples as complimentary leave-behinds.

Land Rover Tapped Web to Drive Traffic for the New Freelander. Land Rover of North America used an integrated marketing approach to drive prospects to its Web site and generate pre-orders for its new sports utility vehicle (SUV), the Freelander. The promotion also highlighted a trend in automobile sales in which the Web is not only used to educate prospective customers, but also allows them to actually build and order a car to their own specifications prior to the car's availability. The Lanham, Maryland-based Land Rover of North America is a division of the Ford Motor Company.

- *Objectives:* To generate pre-orders and capture sales leads for retailers for the new Freelander SUV and to capture prospects' email addresses as well as permission to send future electronic messages.

- *Strategy:* Develop a standalone Web site, *www.free-lander.com* designed to inform and capture prospective buyers of the new vehicle. The site had customizable features allowing visitors to select options based on their own specifications and to pre-order the car online.
- *Tactics:* Integrated a variety of online and offline vehicles to promote the new site, including acquisition marketing initiatives such as banner advertising on sites that attract a 25- to 34-year-old demographic as well as third-party opt-in email marketing that targeted the same group. Retention marketing initiatives took the form of retention email to an inhouse permission-granted list, many members of which were already satisfied Land Rover customers. Consumers were also able to track the progress of their orders, similar to the process that Federal Express uses to track the progress of the delivery of a package.
- *Analysis:* An outstanding example of how a company can use the Web not only to inform and educate prospects, but also to create an improved overall sales experience by integrating the online and offline elements. During the first two months of the campaign, Land Rover was successful at lighting up the site by driving more than 16 million unique visitors who surfed through the Freelander site each month. This campaign was also very focused in terms of its online promotional outreach by appearing only on auto-related sites. Once again, Land Rover works extra hard to make the customer experience a special one and consistent with its brick-and-mortar reputation as a provider of high-end customer service.

DIRECT MAIL

One of the most effective means of delivering one-to-one marketing messages is through the use of direct mail. Though it can be costly to produce and deliver, direct mail can also pinpoint prospects in your target audience, sell them products directly, and drive them into brick-and-mortar retail locations or to your Web site.

Often equated with catalogers such as Sharper Image, direct mail can arrive in a variety of different forms, including fliers, coupon packs, and postcards. Increasingly, advertisers have turned to direct mail as a way to physically get their messages into the hands of likely prospects. Some marketers are even using direct mail to help convert a mailing list of prospects and customers into an emailing list of prospects and customers. This, too, can be quite expensive, but there's little debate about the effectiveness of the direct mail science. It is a very reliable—if not inexpensive—producer of results and is governed by the same relative laws of response as email.

Sending to a rented list generally yields a conversion rate of between 1 percent and 3 percent. The same generally holds true for rented opt-in email lists. House lists are different. Conversion rates can widely vary based on the offer, season, and quality of the house list. House mailing lists and permission granted emailing lists could generate conversion levels as high as 20 to 30 percent.

Following are examples of how leading marketers are using direct mail to drive prospects into the Funnel.

Ben & Jerry's Opted for Direct Mail to Help Drive Customers. Ice cream maker Ben & Jerry's partnered with supermarkets in sending a direct mail piece to several million shoppers nationwide to help promote the company's summer contest, Citizen Cool, as well as its newest ice cream flavor, Concession Obsession. The Burlington, Vermont-based ice cream maker will include a $1.00-off coupon in the mailings and will also drive prospects and customers to the company's Web site, *www.benjerry.com,* where they can nominate people who make outstanding contributions to their communities as part of the Citizen Cool contest.

- *Objectives:* To generate trial of the company's newest flavor of ice cream, Concession Obsession. To generate involvement in the summer promotion, Citizen Cool, and add to Ben & Jerry's database by capturing the names, email addresses, and permission of those making nominations and those who are nominated.

■ *Strategy:* To target shoppers in key markets to publicize two important summertime promotions. To drive prospects and customers to the company's Web site, to Ben & Jerry's own brick-and-mortar retail locations, and to supermarkets that carry their products.

■ *Tactics:* Teamed with supermarkets and utilized direct mail lists of shoppers for the purpose of sending them a direct mail piece that promotes trial of the new ice cream as well as participation in the Citizen Cool contest. The direct mail campaign was also supported offline with freestanding inserts in selected major metropolitan newspapers as well as radio spots in those markets.

■ *Analysis:* Ben & Jerry's demonstrates its understanding of how to effectively integrate the Web into the peak season promotions that both raise awareness and build trial. This campaign also underscores its corporate sensibilities as citizens who give back to society and the communities in which they live. This has been an important element in the philosophy of running this business. A by-product of the promotion is capturing email addresses and identities of Ben & Jerry's core constituents that will provide the basis for a second level of sell through emailings down the road.

PROMOTIONS

Often used as a way to generate excitement around an event or key selling season, promotions can help you quickly grow your permission-granted lists. The upside: Promotions can drive huge numbers of prospects to your Web site. The downside: There is a community of people who enter contests or sweepstakes and are motivated only by the chance to win a prize. Over time, however, you will be able to weed out these illegitimate prospects by servicing them with your scheduled emailings.

Promotions are still an effective way to entice your target audience into identifying themselves as well as granting permission. The upside far outdistances the downside, especially if you have an effective ongoing means of list hygiene. Following are examples of how leading marketers are using promotions to drive prospects into the funnel.

Frito-Lay Delivered Record-Breaking Sales with Summer of Cash Promo. Frito-Lay and sister company Tropicana Twister brand, both divisions of Pepsico, combined to generate record-breaking results with their Summer of Cash promotion. The 16-week promotion helped Frito-Lay set a retail sales record for the Memorial Day holiday sales week. The Plano, Texas-based Frito-Lay also captured more than 2 million names and email addresses online—10 times the number generated by any previous promotion. Participating Frito-Lay brands included Tostitos, Doritos, Lays, and Ruffles as well as Tropicana's Twister juice beverage.

■ *Objectives:* To accelerate sales during the April to June peak snacking season. To capture permission from participants for the purpose of future email promotions.

■ *Strategy:* Create a promotion that allows for a high incidence of reward, delivering the prize that consumers want most: cash. Encourage transactions around larger product sizes with an incentive that helps generate repeat purchases.

■ *Tactics:* Prominent in-store displays featured billionaire Donald Trump to create greater awareness of the $1,000,000 in real cash in Frito-Lay snack bags that graphically hyped the promotion as part of the packaging. Also placed a card inside snack bags that contained an "Activation Code" (also under bottle caps of Twister) that consumers could enter online at *www .fritolaycash.com* for the chance to win "Online Cash." Consumers had a 50 percent chance of winning between the in-bag cash and online prize pool. Online cash could be used to purchase merchandise at online e-tailers Sunglass Hut, Rumpus, FTD.com, eBags, and

Critic's Choice Video, who partnered with Frito-Lay on the promotion.

- *Analysis:* Great example of a peak-season promotion that hit a home run. Not only did Frito-Lay break a retail sales record due to the promotion, but also generated 10 times the number of online registrations and captured more permission than any previous promotion. More than 2 million consumers registered at the fritolaycash.com site, which will give Frito-Lay an enormous head start when it primes the pump in advance of its next promotion by outbound emailing to its now sizable—and ever-increasing—permission-granted list.

Juicy Fruit Moved Product, Built List with Gotta Have Sweet Spot Promo. Juicy Fruit gum developed a very clever integrated marketing program that gave customers the chance to win a variety of prizes in a number of different ways, including winning instantly by checking the inside wrappers of the gum. The Chicago-based Juicy Fruit, a brand of the Wm. Wrigley Jr. Company, gave consumers a second chance at winning by registering at *www.juicyfruit.com* and entering a unique password that was found inside the gum's wrappers. Additionally, consumers could play an online scavenger hunt on the gum's Web site, where they were challenged to answer simple questions by an animated character for the chance to win simple downloadable games or puzzles. After a consumer correctly answered a question, he or she was sent to one of nine Web sites—all targeting kids, teens, and young adults—to look for the Spot somewhere on the site. Once the Spot was found, the consumer was able to download a prize.

- *Objectives:* To drive mid-summer sales of Juicy Fruit gum by providing a fun, entertaining, and rewarding experience for the target audience.
- *Strategy:* To create a promotion that allowed consumers several chances to win prizes of interest to them. Utilize the Web as a sales facilitator at the core of a promotion during the heavy summer sales season. Develop a theme

around the gum's most important and unique consumer benefit: sweetness.

- *Tactics:* Created packaging that allowed consumers to win instantly or offered a second opportunity by visiting the gum's Web site to register (email and permission collection) and load a unique password. Partnered with Web sites such as MTV.com, Warner Brothers Online TV, Alloy.com, TeenPeople.com, CartoonNetwork.com, Katrillion.com, Nick.com, and ign.com to create a third opportunity to win by locating the "sweet spot" somewhere on the partner site. Supported the entire promotion with selected media, such as television, radio, and print, all designed to drive consumers to the gum's Web site.

- *Analysis:* A very creative way to partner with other sites that attract the advertiser's target audience in order to drive traffic in both directions—from juicyfruit.com to partner sites and from partner sites to juicyfruit.com. This is a good example of a campaign that works extremely hard on a number of levels: (1) It gets consumers' attention at point-of-sale through specially designed packaging and gives consumers the chance to win prizes instantly, (2) if consumers don't win instantly, it gives them an opportunity to visit the Web site to load a special password found on the packaging for another opportunity to win prizes, (3) it gives consumers the chance to play an online game that rewards success with prizes, and (4) it drives consumers to nine other partner sites as part of a value-added extension to advertising programs in cooperation with those sites that are designed to promote the campaign to the target audience.

Minute Maid Used Online Sweeps to Launch Simply Orange. Juice giant Minute Maid used the Web to create awareness and excitement around the launch of its new product Simply Orange. The Houston, Texas-based division of the Coca-Cola Company created a sweepstakes that helped position the new juice product as closest to fresh-squeezed and "100% unfooled around with." Prospects were driven to the brand's dedicated Web site, *www.simplyorangejuice.com*, to sign up for the sweepstakes, with the winner receiving an all-expenses paid trip to an "unspoiled" destination: Montana, Hawaii, Utah, or Alaska.

- *Objectives:* To build awareness and trial for Simply Orange as well as lay the foundation for future loyalty programs with the development of a permission-granted marketing database for the product. The Web site supported other communication elements—advertising, promotion, and public relations—as part of this integrated communications campaign.
- *Strategy:* To establish the positioning of Simply Orange in the crowded juice sector as closest to fresh squeezed through an attention-grabbing sweepstakes that underscored the product's purity by providing the winner with a trip to an "unspoiled" destination. To build a permission-granted marketing database as part of the promotion for the purpose of creating an ongoing dialogue with Simply Orange prospects and customers.
- *Tactics:* The 5-month sweepstakes coincided with the introduction of the product in stores and was supported with point-of-sale couponing and display, regional television spot advertising, and public relations activities in the northeastern part of the United States—a major orange juice consumption region.
- *Analysis:* This is a great example of a major nationally branded advertiser using the Web to help build a brand and support a product launch. In addition, the strategic effort created a second level of sell by building a permission-granted marketing database. Consumers will receive requested, relevant, and respectful communications from a brand that is part of the single largest nonalcoholic drink producer in the world, the Coca-Cola Company. Coke and its family of brands are clearly laying the foundation for customer share marketing.

Disney and Kellogg Partnered to Promote the Release of *Atlantis: The Lost Empire.* Bringing family and fun from the movies to America's breakfast tables, Kellogg USA and Walt Disney Pictures captured the magic and mystery of *Atlantis: The Lost Empire* with the first ever Disney-licensed cereal. Kellogg's Atlantis: The Lost Empire toasted oat cereal featured chocolaty pieces that revealed the Atlantean alphabet when added to milk. The limited edition cereal hit store shelves just prior to the film's release promoting free mail-in offers, an Atlantis interactive Web site as well as free package inserts on several other Kellogg's cereals. The promotion cleverly integrated online games and electronic greeting cards where kids could decode the Atlantean alphabet.

- *Objectives:* For Disney: To create awareness and drive consumers into theaters to see Disney's animated movie *Atlantis: The Lost Empire.* For Kellogg: To use the movie's theme to extend its ongoing commitment of bringing fun to breakfast. For both companies: An added-value incentive program that creates mutual consumer awareness.
- *Strategy:* Create a new cobranded cereal based on the movie that mutually promotes ticket sales and the purchase of Kellogg's cereals to extend fun at breakfast time while encouraging consumers to visit the Atlantis interactive Web site and participate in special offers.
- *Tactics:* Promoted the Web site and the movie on packages of Kellogg's cereals and Kellogg's limited-edition *Atlantis: The Lost Empire* cereal through inclusion of free-in-box Atlantean diving water toys, free on-pack interactive CD-ROMS, on-pack games, and a free CD-ROM mail-in offer. Advertising support came in the form of banner ads that rotated through *www.disney .com,* a highly trafficked entertainment portal for families.
- *Analysis:* Another great example of using offline marketing tactics to drive consumers to retail to purchase product. This promotion is also a good example of how a company can use the Internet to create cross-selling

strategies that help sell more products to customers they already have. For Kellogg, this promotion demonstrates a classic customer share marketing tactic, helping them to use the Atlantis promotion to sell more cereal.

Valvoline Created Online Sweeps to Help Build Permission Database. Automotive oil manufacturer Valvoline created a fishing-related sweepstakes and photo contest for its SynPower brand of products in an effort to aggressively add to their own permission-granted database that will feed a host of planned email efforts in the future. Lexington, Kentucky-based Valvoline found, through research, that a high incidence of men who buy their own automotive oil treatments and cleaners are also likely to be interested in fishing. The fishing theme, then, was used to help generate sales as well as permission for SynPower products through the creation of the SynPower Great Canadian Fishing Sweepstakes and the SynPower Big Catch Photo Contest.

- *Objectives:* To drive short-term sales and trial of SynPower products and to collect permission-granted email addresses from prospects and customers at *www.valvoline.com* in order to support future emailings.
- *Strategy:* To use a fishing theme to attract men in the 25- to 49-year-old target audience to register for a sweepstakes by providing personal information and permission. To drive in-store awareness for the SynPower line of products and to drive trial of those products with prospects that are using competitive brands.
- *Tactics:* Used point-of-sale counter displays to promote awareness of the Great Canadian Fishing Sweepstakes. Additionally, the company partnered with Finnish fishing lure manufacturer Rapala to develop a limited-edition premium lure that was packaged in specially marked boxes of SynPower products. Valvoline also developed the Big Catch Photo Contest to run in tandem with the sweeps and to provide an online viral element to help draw even more participants to the sweeps.

- *Analysis:* This is a good example of gaining new intelligence about customers in order to be able to match the high incidence of a special interest to the demographic of the individuals that typically buy the product. Valvoline was able to generate nearly a 90 percent permission rate among unique registrations to sweeps—an extraordinarily high rate of granted permission. Customer share marketing through email or other electronic messages makes perfect sense for such an audience, especially if the theme of the common passion is integrated into communication efforts. It's not difficult to imagine the scope of the content of email messages or e-newsletters that Valvoline can begin to develop with the permission-granted audience that it has captured.

Wyndham Hotels Used Sweeps to Help Build User Database. Wyndham Hotels & Resorts used a very targeted means of driving membership to its Wyndham by Request loyalty rewards program through its Wyn the Ultimate Vacation online sweepstakes. The Dallas, Texas-based Wyndham was determined to build a quality list of prospects and customers, avoiding wholesale registrations from online surfers who often sign up for contests with little or no interest in the product or service. Entrants registered to win a trip for a family of four to a Wyndham destination, such as a four-day trip to Orlando that included four passes to the Disney theme parks.

- *Objectives:* To grow the Wyndham by Request loyalty rewards program membership. Also to capture permission from those who sign up for the sweeps but do not become members at sign-up.
- *Strategy:* To create a promotion that focuses on travelers, particularly on travelers who often visit cities where Wyndham has properties. Also to create a viral element that allows registrants to essentially pass the promotion along to a friend or colleague.
- *Tactics:* Outbound permission-granted email to inhouse list of members and prospective members. The effort was also supported with limited online banner advertising.

■ Analysis: Though open to anyone who wanted to enter, this promotion provides a good example of some of the steps that can be taken to limit sign-ups and registrations to the target audience. By not widely promoting the sweepstakes through mass-marketing channels, Wyndham Resorts was able to focus primarily on travelers who frequent their hotels—center of the target prospects—for continuing to do so. Wyndham has been successful at converting about one-third of the sweeps registrants to members of its Wyndham by Request program. This is a great way to start building a permission-granted list from the core out, especially if marketing funds are limited.

ACQUISITION EMAIL MARKETING

Renting third-party opt-in lists for the purpose of emailing your message to people who have indicated an interest in the type of product or service that you sell can be a very effective way to drive prequalified prospects into your funnel. If you are building an acquisition and retention plan for the first time and you need to prioritize your spending, renting opt-in lists from reputable brokers should be one of the first initiatives that you consider, especially if you have a limited budget.

Opt-in lists are made up of people who have agreed to receive information, often on broad topics such as health or do-it-yourself, through any number of registration processes. Even though these folks have granted permission to someone else, it doesn't mean that they've granted permission to you. Though opt-in is not pure permission, it represents an effective means of targeting key prospects on a one-to-one basis and increases your odds of converting prospects to customers. Emailings to opt-in lists can be a very fruitful acquisition initiative, especially if you are in the process of aggressively growing your own permission-granted list.

Following are examples of how leading marketers are using acquisition email to drive prospects into the funnel:

Sony Pictures Targeted African Americans to Promote Movie Release. Sony Pictures tapped into BlackPlanet.com's opt-in email list to send emails to over 1.3 million African Americans to promote the release of *Baby Boy*. The emails came from John Singleton, the Academy-Award nominated screenwriter who also wrote *Boyz 'N the Hood,* and told recipients why he wrote the screenplay about the struggles of a young African American man growing up in south-central Los Angeles. The combination of sending an email from an accomplished African American screenwriter directly to more than a million African American movie lovers created a powerful, if not emotional, impact on the core target audience 5 days prior to the movie's release.

- *Objectives:* To generate a buzz within the African American community just days leading into the release of *Baby Boy.*
- *Strategy:* To appeal to the core of the target audience to see the film, preferably during the first week, and to create word-of-mouth endorsements within the African American community.
- *Tactics:* Created an email message from screenwriter John Singleton and sent it to more than 1.3 million African Americans from BlackPlanet.com's opt-in list. Banner ads supported the release on numerous sites that also target African Americans.
- *Analysis:* Demonstrates that some companies, such as Sony Pictures, are beginning to rethink marketing from the inside out. Sony's strategy called for building out from a core list of 1.3 million Africans Americans, then adding online banner ads at Web sites that targeted African Americans. By starting with direct marketing through email and moving out toward mass marketing through newspapers and other mass-marketing vehicles, Sony demonstrated a growing sophistication in the use of segmented email to create powerful results.

Lighter Manufacturer Zippo Turned to Acquisition Email for Product Launch. Zippo Manufacturing introduced a special edition lighter with email acquisition campaigns targeted to serious collectors. Email went out to over 100,000 double opt-in names that Zippo rented for the campaign to drive prospects and customers to *www.zippo.com*. The collectible pays tribute to Hollywood as well as to Zippo's longstanding heritage as the lighter of choice in more than 800 movies over the last 70 years. The launch was also supported by targeted banner ad placement on movie enthusiast sites. Zippo has embraced the concept of identifying customers by name, address, email, and other important personal information, realizing that understanding the specific interests of customers is an important and powerful element of marketing in the 21st century, and the Web and email now enable a quick, inexpensive, targeted means of communicating with loyal customers.

- *Objectives:* To generate sales for its Hollywood Leading Light line of collectible lighters. To capture email addresses and permission from prospects and customers.
- *Strategy:* Target consumers who are movie buffs and collectors of memorabilia. Trade off of Zippo's heritage as the lighter of choice for Hollywood by displaying images of some of the silver screen's most famous stars, such as Elvis Presley, James Dean, and Marilyn Monroe.
- *Tactics:* Used opt-in email to reach over 100,000 known collectors. Promotion was also supported by banner ads on the highly trafficked movie site Internet Movie Database, which is owned by Amazon.com. Zippo designed a Stars of Hollywood sweepstakes on its site for the purpose of collecting names, email addresses, and permission.
- *Analysis:* A good example of how a company can begin to aggressively grow its permission-granted email list in a segmented way, allowing for more targeted and more effective future campaigns. The use of third-party opt-in email to drive qualified leads into the Zippo funnel makes a great deal of sense and will help the lighter manufacturer rapidly develop its own database. The development of its database will ultimately allow Zippo to generate very targeted email campaigns promoting its line of lighters to consumers as well as to businesses as

corporate gifts. Not surpisingly, Zippo's longstanding heritage as an important movie prop helped drive the strategy to adopt a Hollywood theme in this promotion.

AFFILIATE MARKETING

Affiliate marketing is a very effective way of steering qualified prospects to your Web site, particularly if you run an e-commerce site. By linking with other sites that attract the same profile as your target audience, prospects can click through to your site. If that visit results in a sale, the affiliate providing the lead receives a percentage of the sale, usually 5 to 15 percent. Amazon is the heavyweight champ of affiliate marketing, with more than 500,000 affiliate links that drive significant and qualified leads to the super reseller.

The concept of channeling relevant traffic from another site that provides no competitive e-commerce option can deliver extremely low acquisition costs on a per-customer basis, especially if there are many enthusiast sites on the Web that focus on activities that involve the type of products or services that you sell.

Following are examples of how leading marketers are using affiliate marketing programs to drive prospects into the funnel.

Barnes & Noble.com Drives Relevant Prospects with Affiliate Marketing. Online book retailer Barnes & Noble.com teamed up with affiliate marketing manager Be Free in 1997 to help find and drive relevant traffic to the online bookseller's e-commerce Web site at *www.bn.com*. Since that time, Barnes & Noble.com has successfully linked with more than 500,000 online marketing partners and has generated a significant amount of revenue through its affiliate marketing program—all at the lowest cost of customer acquisition of any online program it has initiated. The program involves a diverse group of marketing partners utilizing a number of different partnership business models, including traditional revenue-sharing arrangements with small to mid-size Web sites, innovative sponsorships, and performance-based deals with large portals such as Yahoo! Shopping and high-traffic vertical sites such as MSNBC.

■ *Objectives:* To locate and drive as many relevant book-buying prospects at the lowest possible cost per acquisition (CPA).

■ *Strategy:* To engage affiliate program manager Be Free to recruit and initiate online marketing partnerships with as many relevant, highly trafficked sites as possible.

■ *Tactics:* Linked with marketing partner sites based on a revenue-sharing model that worked best for both parties. Also utilized comprehensive reporting and tracking capabilities in order to be able to analyze all partnerships through to sale. Utilized daily reports that detailed which partners actually drove prospects, and more importantly, which ones resulted in conversion to sales.

■ *Analysis:* A good example of an e-commerce business that sells products that appeal to a very wide range of people—from young to old, male to female, high household income to low household income. This characteristic makes it easier for a business such as a bookseller to link to hundreds of thousands of sites than it would be, for example, for the manufacturer of printing presses. However, the common denominator in the affiliate marketing game is not necessarily the number of sites but more the quality of the leads that a site generates. The ability to quickly and dynamically change merchandising initiatives across the entire network in an industry that literally introduces dozens of new products every day is an invaluable marketing tool. This element allows a marketer to always appear fresh and new in the eyes of prospects and returning customers. This feature also helps to make the partnership work better for both Barnes & Noble.com and the partner site—a key element in sustaining relationships with productive partner sites.

Ashford.com Looks to Affiliate Marketing to Help Drive Gift-Givers.

Ashford.com is one of the world's leading e-commerce destinations offering luxury goods to individual and corporate clients. Ashford started its affiliate marketing program in 1999 and has been successful in recruiting more than 10,000 partner sites with the help of affiliate program manager Be Free. Ashford is able to quickly identify the top performing affiliate sites and work closely with them to enhance the productivity of the partnership, resulting in higher click-through and conversion rates. Comprehensive reporting has allowed Ashford to renegotiate even better deals with its marketing partners on a year-by-year basis.

- *Objectives:* To identify and drive as many individual and corporate gift-givers as possible to *www.ashford.com.*
- *Strategy:* To work with affiliate program manager Be Free to help identify and engage sites that have a higher-than-average likelihood of attracting individual and corporate gift-givers.
- *Tactics:* Used reporting and tracking capabilities to quickly identify the best-performing sites and focused on those sources as it would its best customers who buy direct.
- *Analysis:* With a more limited universe of potential affiliate partners, Ashford has adopted a highly focused service strategy as it relates to handling partners in its affiliate marketing program. Ashford executives agree that a happy affiliate marketing partner—one that is making money—translates into a moneymaking relationship for Ashford as well. To underscore this point, Ashford settles up with its partners on a monthly basis, which helps to create the best type of outbound customer touch available—receiving cash. This B2B marketing approach sometimes requires a dedicated individual or staff, depending on the size of the partner universe. But the additional cost is most often easily justified because of the increased attention and service, which usually translates into a more motivated and productive partner.

SEARCH ENGINE OPTIMIZATION

Largely viewed in the early days of the Web as the way to make or break an online business, search engine optimization is just one of the many important elements that marketers need to understand in order to manage a successful online effort.

The search engine ranking and registration process, based on keyword searches at the major search engines, has always been a rather mysterious game. Many companies have felt left out in the dark, as though everyone else knows more than they do about how the search engines work. There is a science to it, and some of the world's leading marketers are improving the results generated from searches with software that maximizes the unique content on their sites.

At the same time, the inevitable shift to paid search is becoming a popular means of driving qualified traffic to a Web site. Advertisers are now paying for the traffic that is delivered to their sites from search engines, many on a per-click basis. For example, GoTo.com works with nearly 50,000 advertisers that pay an average of $0.19 per click for leads. Following are examples of how leading marketers are using search engine optimization strategies to drive prospects into the funnel.

L.L. Bean Improved Keyword Searches on Major Search Engines. Unhappy with the results generated from keyword searches on the major search engines, outdoor gear and apparel manufacturer L. L. Bean greatly increased the chances of prospects and customers generating an L. L. Bean reference when typing in keywords that are based on the descriptions of products carried at *www.llbean.com.* Working with online marketing firm Inceptor, L. L. Bean took advantage of Inceptor's Excedia software, which helps generate more leads based on product-specific searches that can ultimately drive prospects and customers directly to a product page.

- *Objectives:* To increase prequalified traffic to the company's e-commerce site by increasing the incidence of L. L. Bean-related references based on the keyword searches at any of the major search engines. To eliminate clicks in the process of searching and purchasing.
- *Strategy:* To more closely link the enormous database of product descriptions and Web site copy with keyword searches on the major search engines.

- *Tactics:* Utilized Inceptor's Excedia software to generate more relevant leads tied to keywords that consumers use to find sources for products. More accurately matched those keyword searches to specific landing pages that are a click or two away from checkout, expediting the sales closing process.

- *Analysis:* This is a good example of how technology can help increase site traffic, and more importantly, improve the relevance and quality of the traffic and the likelihood of sales conversion. Any company that sells the number of SKUs that an L.L. Bean does can probably improve the search engine results for the products represented on its site with software that allows the company to better understand how consumers search for the types of products that it sells. Understanding consumers is one of the many Web marketing initiatives that helps improve the odds of driving the most relevant prospects to a site. In the 21st century, relevance rules.

Public Storage Tied Banner Ads to Keyword Searches. In an effort to target people who are moving or storing their belongings, storage company Public Storage teamed with Yahoo! to deliver button-style and banner ads when users searched on certain keywords. The ads were also triggered in certain targeted areas of the site, such as the Real Estate and Jobs sections. The Glendale, California-based Public Storage used these ads to target people who were relocating or storing and were searching for help online from moving and storage resources. A Public Storage banner ad or button promoting the keyword-related service was served up along with results from the search when users entered any of the following words: public storage, moving, movers, moving services, storage, self storage, self moving, truck rental, move, or relocation. Users could click through the ad for each specific service on a specially created DHTML banner or button. The action would link users directly to a product-specific Web page on the company's fully transactional e-commerce site *www.totalmoving.com*, which helps users plan all the elements of a move, including packing, moving, and storing.

- *Objectives:* To generate sales from prequalified prospects for any or all of the company's moving and storage-related services. To reduce customer acquisition costs by routing prospective customers through its highly informational and fully transactional Web site rather than through its call center, where costs are higher.
- *Strategy:* To identify and drive prequalified prospects to the company's fully transactional e-commerce site and promote a special online-only offer for reservations made online.
- *Tactics:* Identified and reserved specific keywords from search engines for the purpose of insuring that a Public Service banner or button ad would appear along with the top listings generated by the search.
- *Analysis:* Here's an example of a traditional offline company that wants to maximize its marketing by targeting and prequalifying prospective customers. Keyword search initiatives can work well to help deliver quality leads, especially for companies in the service sector and for companies with higher customer values. Public Storage offers its customers a one-stop shopping experience, both online and through its call center, for several moving and storing-related products. This keyword initiative helps to position Public Storage as a source for all move-related services, including storage and moving services, truck rental, and packing and moving supplies.

PUBLIC RELATIONS

A very effective and sometimes overlooked feed-the-funnel initiative, public relations can be a powerful weapon in a marketer's arsenal. Most effective around a launch or special event, a good PR campaign can really light up a site. A mere mention on the *Today Show* or in the *Wall Street Journal* can easily generate never-before-seen levels of short-term traffic and can sometimes even crash a site. Following are examples of how leading marketers are using public relations strategies to drive prospects into the funnel:

Taco Bell Uses the Web to Help Launch New Taco Chip. At the same time that America was engaged in a love affair with high-tech IPOs, Taco Bell was seeking a high-profile means of introducing a new type of nacho chip that is actually fried in-store. Taco Bell, a division of Irvine, California-based Tricon Global Restaurants, turned to Edelman Public Relations to help develop a program to promote the new product launch. Edelman created a make believe IPO in order to stoke the interest of American consumers and drive media coverage of the product launch. The clever program included the development of a Web site that promoted the introduction of a new, revolutionary chip. The heavy technology look of the site led visitors to believe that the new chip was a microchip. Ultimately, the new taco chip was introduced at the end of the trading day on Wall Street when the chips became available at Taco Bells nationwide.

- *Objectives:* To generate media and consumer awareness for Taco Bell's new nacho chip—a product for which it is difficult to generate real news value. To spark interest of media and consumers, and build anticipation without revealing the true nature of the campaign until the final moment. To create a fun campaign, in keeping with brand image, and break through the clutter of new product introductions.
- *Strategy:* Use the Web and email to generate an underground buzz about an upcoming IPO for a company that developed a revolutionary new "chip".
- *Tactics:* Created the fake Web site at *www.newchip.com* one week before the event. Ran full-page ads in *Wall Street Journal, San Francisco Chronicle,* and *USA Today* one day before the IPO to drive people to the Web site. The initial site was created to attract investors and give the appearance of an actual technology site at the height of the IPO frenzy. Messages were posted on Internet newsgroups and message boards directly relating to public stock offerings surrounding this new chip. An email titled Most Affordable IPO in U.S. History was sent to 50,000-targeted consumers, with a

message to watch for an announcement on May 2 at the New York Stock Exchange. On May 2, the Taco Bell Chihuahua rang the opening bell at the New York Stock Exchange, announcing the new chip. As soon as the closing bell at the Exchange was rung, *www.new-chip .com* morphed to reflect the post-reveal with information about the new nacho chip at Taco Bell.

■ *Analysis:* The campaign was widely received by the media and consumers as clever, innovative, and humorous. Over 31,000 visits to the Web site prior to and after the ringing of the NYSE bell were generated. The direct e-mail campaign generated a response rate of 10 percent, and over 2,000 visitors signed up to receive more information in the first 3 days of the campaign. As the only traffic driver to the site for the first 4 days of the campaign, the viral marketing campaign generated underground awareness among the target audience—1,000 viral email sign-ups were recorded prior to the product reveal. Week-long media coverage generated more than 43 million impressions, with just 2 days of direct media relations contact.

Bayer Corporation Integrates Offline and Online Marketing to Build Brand Equity. Bayer Corporation's Animal Health unit used public relations to create and maintain visibility of Advantage (imidacloprid) Topical Solution—the company's fast-acting flea control product for cats and dogs. Working with Edelman Public Relations Worldwide, the team developed a Web site, *www .nofleas.com,* to help build awareness and brand equity. The site serves as an information source for the new product and is designed to appeal to consumers who are increasingly turning to the Web for information that is most important and relevant to them. Public relations and advertising efforts directed consumers to the Web site as a call to action.

■ *Objectives:* To increase awareness of the Advantage brand and highlight product attributes. To stimulate sales by driving traffic to veterinarians' offices to request Advantage for flea control.

- *Strategy:* To generate news coverage via aggressive publicity in key flea markets. To create and maintain high visibility through a series of exciting events and activities, and to create a new Web site positioned as the number one source for flea control information. Position the veterinarian as the number one animal health resource.

- *Tactics:* Highlighted product attribute in the URL name—NoFleas.com—suggesting that by using Advantage, dogs and cats would have no fleas. Designed the Web site to include product-specific information, such as Product Overview and Frequently Asked Questions. The site was also designed as a fun destination with interactive elements, such as Singing Pets and Speak Out!, to encourage repeat visits. Promoted key Web site elements such as Flea Mail reminders and a Flea Index that promoted the level of flea activity through national and local news. Used celebrity "spokespets" and veterinarians for local and national interviews. Leveraged the popular Advantage Search for North America's Best Singing Pet contest by allowing Web site visitors to listen to audio of finalists and to vote for their favorite. Promoted online contest in media as a call to action. Placed *www.nofleas.com* URL on all materials distributed to consumers and media and in Advantage television commercials.

- *Analysis:* More than 500 million consumers were reached through 40 hours of TV airtime and 1,500 print stories that directed pet owners to *www.nofleas.com* for information on keeping their cats and dogs flea-free. The public relations efforts helped make Advantage the greatest product success story in Bayer Animal Health history, with Web site traffic steadily increasing, and Advantage leading its category in product awareness. More than 750,000 unique visitors surfed the site, with 18 percent establishing a permission-granted relationship with Bayer by registering for an e-newsletter or by writing to Bayer via the Speak Out feature.

BUSINESS-TO-BUSINESS

The objectives of businesses that sell to consumers are the same as for those that sell to other businesses—get buyers and sellers together in an environment that helps close the sale. Whether it's online or offline, moving customers toward closure is what sales is all about. The Web has given B2B companies of all sizes—from John Deere to the local civil engineering firm—the opportunity to create a consistent communication program with the most likely prospects.

In many cases, B2B companies have a finite number of prospects, making a customer share strategy almost essential. Some companies know every one of their prospects, while others have simply too many to cover with a sales force. Whether your business has 50 prospects or 500,000, or whether your annual sales are $1 million or $10 billion, customer share marketing can help you inexpensively influence your buyers.

During the early years of the Web, many large companies took advantage of the Web as an efficient and effective procurement tool. B2B marketers are now applying the same relevant direct marketing skills that they gained in developing direct mail communications to develop Web-based communications programs with prospects and customers. The Web, in combination with permission-granted email, offers a very unique and intimate means of communicating one-to-one with the decision-makers in an organization. Following are examples of how leading B2B marketers are using the Web to acquire customers.

Monster.com Created Olympic Sweeps to Acquire and Retain. Maynard, Massachusetts-based Monster.com, the leading online career site, created an online sweepstakes tied to its sponsorship of the 2002 U.S. Olympic Team that will compete in the Winter Olympics in Salt Lake City, Utah. The "Go for the Gold" sweepstakes is aimed at its target audience—individuals at companies who are responsible for identifying and hiring employees. This B2B promotion helps Monster.com grow its permission-granted email list of prospects and customers by offering the opportunity to win trips to the 2002 Winter Olympics for those who register.

- *Objectives:* To acquire new customers, increasing its base of paid memberships to the site by employers who have an ongoing need to recruit and fill open positions. To collect additional information from existing customers in order to better understand the current needs of those responsible for hiring decisions in a very tight employment market.
- *Strategy:* To drive current customers as well as prospective customers to its promotional Web site at *www.olympictrip.monster.com* with the prospect of winning an all-expenses-paid trip to the 2002 Winter Olympics in Salt Lake City.
- *Tactics:* Sent in-house permission-granted email to the over 40,000 existing paid members. Third-party opt-in email was also utilized, and the promotion was supported by a print advertising schedule that ran in a limited number of trade magazines.
- *Analysis:* A great example of a promotion that has both acquisition and retention elements, designed to acquire new paying customers and at the same attract more business from existing customers. The company was able to leverage its involvement with the 2002 U.S. Olympic Team to create messages that will help feed the funnel as well as work the list. A good example of how a U.S.-based company can align with the United States Olympic Committee to promote its services within the United States as a sponsor of America's Team.

Affiliate Marketing Program Manager Be Free Markets Itself to Businesses. Even companies that are in the business of helping other businesses promote themselves need to promote their own services to prospective customers. Affiliate marketing program manager Be Free used online and offline direct marketing tactics exclusively to promote its services to marketing managers at more than 35,000 mid-size and large businesses nationwide. Be Free sent more than 25,000 third-party opt-in emails and over 10,000 direct mail pieces to the marketing sides of businesses that could take advantage of an affiliate marketing program to drive relevant traffic to their respective Web sites. The efforts represented the most significant B2B acquisition effort for the Marlborough, Massachusetts-based Be Free, with all recipients made up of prospects outside of the Be Free database.

- *Objectives:* To generate high-quality new business leads and to create a higher awareness of the Be Free brand.
- *Strategy:* Create a direct marketing campaign reaching marketing managers on a one-to-one basis. Appeal to recipients who themselves are trying to acquire new leads at the lowest possible cost. Position Be Free's expertise as a leading affiliate marketing program manager as a solution to help businesses lower their acquisition costs.
- *Tactics:* Created a direct mail piece as well as an acquisition email, and sent to more than 35,000 mid- to large-size companies nationwide. Both efforts were equipped with easy-to-use response mechanisms—a BRC (Business Reply Card) for the direct mail piece and links to the Be Free Web site in the emails.
- *Analysis:* Another example of how companies in the B2B sector have a head start on most traditional (non-direct mail) businesses in embracing the one-to-one marketing model. Direct mail has always been important for businesses that sell to other businesses, as have one-to-one, face-to-face selling at trade shows and on sales calls. But the unique characteristics of the Web and email help to make B2B marketing more efficient, and in many cases more effective, by speeding up production, speeding up delivery time, and speeding up response time—all at a dramatically reduced cost by eliminating the need for paper and postage.

WORKING THE LIST

All marketers are interested in finding ways to make their marketing dollars work harder. But too often, we restrict our thinking to the acquisition of new customers instead of developing new ways to sell more to customers that are already loyal to us. We look to new customers for growth rather than to the customers who have been loyal to us for years. Marketers have historically prospected for increased sales outside of the family of existing customers by selling more products to more people around the world.

Acquiring permission to communicate with prospects and customers through one-to-one, permission-granted programs is the first step in creating dedicated and efficient customer share initiatives that are designed to convert prospects into customers and customers into customers for life. The development of your list will never end. It certainly will evolve over time, as people change their email address, move out of state, buy more products from you, get married or divorced, have children, graduate from college, and even pass away. Managed properly, your list will represent a dynamic snapshot of your core customer base in real time. Your permission-granted list should never be old, out-of-date, or obsolete. It will become the lifeblood of your business in the not-too-distant future.

Working the list is also a perpetual job, and not a project or campaign that comes and goes. Think of it as successfully managing the community of people who are the source of all your revenue today. Communicating with this ever-changing group, taking care to send helpful messages to your best customers, is an important job and one that must never be outsourced.

4

PART

RETAINING CUSTOMERS AND GROWING CUSTOMER SHARE

For the first time in history, marketers of all sizes and shapes are now able to create one-to-one marketing initiatives that are an effective and affordable complement to their mass-marketing initiatives.

Learn how the world's leading marketers are using the Web and their permission-granted databases to create customer share marketing programs that not only help to retain customers, but also help to increase the amount of business they earn from those customers.

WORKING THE LIST: HOW TO RETAIN CUSTOMERS AND GROW CUSTOMER SHARE

By mid 1849, the easy gold was gone—but the 49ers kept coming. There was still gold in the riverbeds, but it was getting harder and harder to find. A typical miner spent 10 hours a day knee-deep in ice cold water, digging, sifting, washing. It was backbreaking labor that yielded less and less.

From the PBS series *The Gold Rush* written by Mike Trinklein

While helping to construct a new mill for John Sutter just east of Sacramento in January 1848, James Marshall discovered some glittering flakes in the streambed of the American River. Little did he know that he would set off an unprecedented migration that helped give birth to a state and changed the psyche of the American people.

Like most easy moneymakers, the California Gold Rush was extremely short-lived. Even though each year it became harder to find gold, the prospectors kept coming and kept trying. By 1854, 300,000 people—or nearly 10 percent of the population of the United States—had migrated to California with dreams of gold. Most of them, however, never realized those dreams.

GOLD RUSH, THE SEQUEL

One hundred years later and 3,000 miles east of Sutter's Mill on the banks of the East River in New York City, another gold rush was brewing. This time the gold came from mining the hard-earned dollars from consumers for a parade of new products—from mouthwash to frozen dinners. Prospecting took the form of running ads out to the masses, driving them to retail mines where they helped themselves to the seemingly unlimited supply of brands that were designed to solve any kind of everyday problem, from the "heartbreak of psoriasis" to "ring around the collar."

But just like the great California Gold Rush of 1849, the great New York Gold Rush of 1949 didn't last forever. By the 1980s, the easy gold was gone. The ability to cajole an increasingly jaded American public into buying products and services with dancing doughnuts and singing spaghetti was getting harder and harder.

BUILDING BRAND EQUITY

Many of the greatest brands in the history of consumer products were built in the last fifty years of the 20th century, primarily through television, print, and radio. The most recognizable brands of all time were largely built by using the reach and efficiency of mass media to convince consumers to "obey our thirsts" (Sprite), "have it our way" (McDonald's), and not to "squeeze the Charmin" (Procter & Gamble). The talent pitching these products ranged from the sublime to the ridiculous—from real people such as Senator Robert Dole, Britney Spears, and Terry Bradshaw to fictional characters such as Mr. Whipple, the Maytag Repairman, and Eva Savalot.

Marketers continue to wrestle with the challenge of getting the attention of one of the busiest generations in history, and as they do so, they ask themselves this question:

> How do we grow, or at least maintain, our brand equity in the minds of the baby boom generation, (born from 1946–1964) as well as their children, when they are watching less network television than their parents, listening to less radio than their parents, and reading fewer newspapers and magazines than their parents?

Advertisers debate about the role of the Web as an advertising medium. Is it a sales vehicle or a branding vehicle? This is a classic example of an old economy practice trying to make an as-is transition to the Web. Just because we built brands almost exclusively with traditional advertising for 50 years, doesn't mean that we will for the next 50 years.

Branding is not a one-dimensional activity. Branding in the information economy means much more than just running lots of big beautiful ads. Every customer touch creates an opportunity to either enhance or erode the brand. By this definition, every customer touch has a role in the branding process—the process of conditioning prospects and customers to feel good about a brand.

DRAWING ON BRAND EQUITY

If you've ever taken a second mortgage on your home, you know about drawing on equity that's been built over time. The objective of building equity around a product or service is to heighten the trust and good feeling between product and customer. Brand advertising also helps to condition customers to default to that brand when the need to buy or replace arises as well as to entertain sales offers from the brand or from the brand's line extensions. Historically, this is how advertisers draw on brand equity or cash in on the energy that their investment has built in the minds of customers.

American Express learned a long time ago that by simply displaying the year that a card member first signed up on the front of the card made people feel a part of something very special—the privilege of membership. This psychological customer stroke is the basis of customer rewards programs such as the frequent flyer programs offered by the major airlines.

Advertisers now have an opportunity to use the Web and permission-granted email not only as a way to continue to build favor with their brands, but also as a way to draw on the equity that their brands have built with customers over a long period of time. Advertisers now have an opportunity to communicate in an extraordinarily efficient way by using messages that are requested, relevant, and respectful.

WORKING THE LIST: USING YOUR PERMISSION-GRANTED DATABASE

Your feed-the-funnel, or acquisition, initiatives help identify and capture your best prospects and customers as part of your permission-granted database—an important and necessary asset for marketing in the information economy and beyond. On the other hand, your work-the-list, or retention, initiatives are designed to keep the customers you've acquired, selling them more of what you have to sell.

Working the list focuses on those marketing initiatives that are dedicated to retention. It's that part of your marketing budget that invests in one-to-one communication with the individuals who are most likely to reward you with incremental business. Working the list is about creating relevant sales strategies that result in successfully upselling or cross-selling your products and services to your customers, growing your company's share of that customer's business.

Your permission-granted database is unique to your business, since all prospects and customers in your database have identified themselves as interested in what you do or sell. Market share initiatives identify groups of individuals by demographics and assume that because they are 29- to 49-year-old females, they should have an interest. Not so with customer share initiatives.

The permission-granted database captures and manages the individuals at the very core of your support universe. It manages—nearly in real time—the never-ending ebb and flow of prospects and customers in and out of your database. This relatively new marketing dynamic also creates a new responsibility for companies that before did not identify their prospect and customer universe by name. Like the magazine circulation director, companies engaged in customer share marketing have the ability to—at any given moment—call up an accurate list of identified loyalists and communicate directly with them through permission-granted email.

WHAT TO SAY AND HOW TO SAY IT

Customer share marketing messages should not sound like annual reports or even like most traditional advertising. Think of these messages as letters to a friend. The tone is friendly, the content helpful and informative, and the message should tell the recipients something that they don't already know. When the message is purely commercial, such as announcing a special offer or a promotion, the tone can sometimes sound desperate. Customer share marketing, on the other hand, is more of a soft sell.

There should be a subtlety to the perspective of your messages, not unlike the lifestyle versus product orientation of many ads today. If you're Orvis or L.L. Bean, you're talking to people who love the outdoors. If you're Kellogg's or General Mills, you're talking to people who care about their health.

Certainly, you want to sell products to buyers, but when crafting customer share marketing messages, picture your prospects as people with varied interests and specific preferences, not just as prospective buyers browsing an aisle.

SELLING WINE BEFORE ITS TIME

A robust database should allow you to create as many relevant buckets for your data as possible. For example, a greater-Boston wine merchant could consider the following data fields when building a database that would ultimately be used for outbound permission-granted messages for the purpose of driving prospects and customers into a local brick-and-mortar retail location:

Name	Ed Perkins
Street Address	123 Tuesday Lane
City/State/Zip	Radley, MA 02026
Telephone	781-555-5555
DOB	02/19/1945
Email Address	ed@customershare.com
White Wine Preference (primary)	Chardonnay
Vineyard Preference	Pahlmeyer
White Wine Preference (secondary)	Pinot Gris
Vineyard Preference	Byron
Red Wine Preference (primary)	Chianti
Vineyard Preference	Fontodi
Red Wine Preference (secondary)	Cabernet Sauvignon
Vineyard Preference	Beringer

With these relatively simple data points, a savvy wine merchant could easily develop an outbound, permission-granted marketing program consisting of regularly scheduled email or e-newsletter efforts to prospects and customers. Whatever form the content takes, don't forget the 3 Rs of customer share marketing. Make sure that your messages are:

- *Requested.* Send only to customers who have directly asked for information. In this case, permission to send information has been granted directly by Mr. Perkins to the wine merchant.
- *Relevant.* Messages should deliver information from the customer's perspective, in this case, about the wines that Mr. Perkins enjoys the most—Chardonnay, Pahlmeyer, Pinot Gris, Byron, Chianti, Fontodi, Cabernet Sauvignon, and Beringer.
- *Respectful.* Don't try to sell him every type of wine in the store just because you may have overstocked some selections. Additionally, Mr. Perkins always has the option of opting out.

E-newsletters are a very popular way to communicate with permission-granted lists, but sometimes can only satisfy the recipient's needs by chance, since most e-newsletters are company-centric—written from the perspective of what the company wants to sell, not necessarily what the customer wants to buy. But if, as in this case, multiple personal preferences relative to product selection can be identified, then there are other, more personalized ways to communicate one-to-one.

An alternative publishing schedule to sending a monthly e-newsletter, which can only randomly fulfill Mr. Perkins' preferences, might be a monthly email program that alerts Mr. Perkins when:

- Any new shipment of Chardonnay is in
- The Pahlmeyer Chardonnay shipment is in
- Any new shipment of Pinot Gris is in
- The Byron Pinot Gris shipment is in
- Any new shipment of Chianti is in
- The Fontodi Chianti shipment is in
- Any new shipment of Cabernet Sauvignon is in
- The Beringer Cabernet Sauvignon shipment is in

- Birthday greetings
- Holiday greetings
- Wine-tastings invitations
- Customer Rewards Program based on Mr. Perkins' annual purchases

E-newsletters can be a very valuable tool and sometimes are the only practical means of consistently communicating with prospects and customers. A good example is Tide's e-newsletter, *Mary's Fabric Care Corner,* that provides useful fabric care tips. It would probably not be necessary to create more granular versions of Mary's e-newsletter, such as a Grass Stain or Blood Stain e-newsletters, since those laundry care issues are relevant to most people who wash clothes. Therefore, broader content is perfectly fine. However, whenever practically possible, use the unique intelligence to send one-to-one messages instead of one-to-many mass-marketing messages. If you've gathered the customer intelligence, put it to good use by communicating one-to-one with customers on the topics that most interest them.

These customer share marketing strategies can help you earn the credibility and respect of the people who support your business today, and in the process, help you turn prospects into customers and customers into customers for life.

THE 3 Rs IN PRACTICE

The bottom half or "Work The List" portion of Figure 12.1 details the activities that drive retention and, most importantly, customer share initiatives. After a variety of sources feed the customer database in the middle of Figure 12.1, outbound permission-granted relationship development begins with three customer share objectives: (1) Turning prospects into customers, (2) customers into repeat customers, and (3) repeat customers into customers for life.

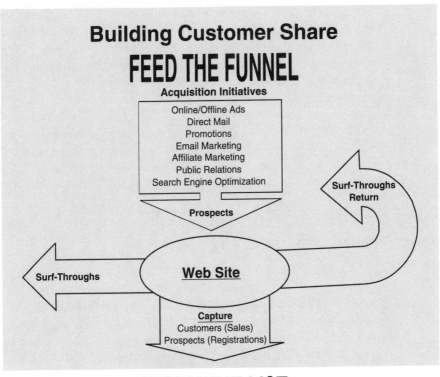

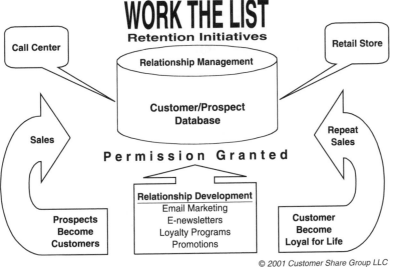

© 2001 Customer Share Group LLC

FIGURE 12.1
Feed the funnel, work the list.

Surgically precise communication that is relevant to prospects and customers provides the most effective means of breaking through all of the commercial clutter of 21st century life. Customer share marketing provides three rather unique communication characteristics that can influence a customer to take action:

1. Communication based on *relevance to the customer*
2. Communication based on *permission from the customer*
3. Communication based on *respect for the customer*

TEN REASONS TO BUILD AND WORK YOUR OWN LIST

All companies can practice customer share marketing. From H & R Block to the corner wine shop, every business has something to say to its customers. More importantly, every business has customers who want to hear what they want to hear. Whether you are a B2C business and your customers are consumers or you're a B2B business and your customers are other businesses, customers expect you to treat them like human beings. They want what they want, not necessarily what you want. They want it when they want it, not necessarily when you want to sell it to them. Of course, you are able to influence these habits and attitudes, but it's up to you to create the atmosphere. It's up to you to make your customers feel special.

There are many reasons why it makes sense for you to adopt a customer share marketing orientation for the products and services that you sell. Here are the top ten:

1. *One-to-one conversation.* Customer share marketing cuts through the noise with one-to-one conversations that are quiet and focused and get the attention of your customer.
2. *Requested.* Customer share marketing messages are invited by the prospect or customer and therefore are

not viewed as interruptions or hostile marketing. These types of messages are also welcomed by the recipient—like receiving email from a friend.

3. *Relevant.* Customer share marketing messages are relevant and are written from the customer's perspective, not the company's perspective—someone, for example, who needs to get stains out of his or her kid's clothes as opposed to a faceless buyer of Tide. Not only are these messages relevant, but they are also helpful in solving the customers' problems—cleaner clothes, faster and easier.

4. *Respectful.* Customer share marketing treats customers like human beings. It first asks for permission. It doesn't force irrelevant messages out to people who may or may not be interested simply because the marketer has something to sell. It also obliges promptly if a customer wants to be taken off the list.

5. *Faster execution and response time.* Customer share marketing programs can be created and executed in a matter of days instead of weeks or months. Response time is 48 hours compared to 3 weeks for direct mail.

6. *Measurable.* Customer share marketing programs are measurable marketing activities. Sending messages electronically to individually addressed prospects and customers allows you to quickly measure who read your messages and who acted on your messages.

7. *More profitable.* Customer share marketing helps you sell more to customers you already have, greatly reducing the cost per sale and delivering more profitable transactions.

8. *Combats churn.* Customer share marketing helps to combat churn—the here today, gone tomorrow revenue associated with uncommitted customers who flit from product to product, usually based on price.

9. *Opportunity to cross-sell and upsell.* Customer share marketing conditions your prospects and customers to consider relevant offers on one or more of

your products in an effort to increase household share.

10. *Zero CPM.* Customer share marketing is extraordinarily affordable; since you build and send to your own permission-granted list, the cost for every thousand customers reached is $0. Though there is no cost associated with the names in customer share marketing, there are other costs associated with the development of customer share marketing programs: (1) building a strategy and a plan, (2) hardware and software to manage the permission-granted database, and (3) list management and hygiene, including the delivery of messages.

Redirecting even a small percentage of your overall marketing budget—let's say 10 percent—into customer share marketing initiatives can dramatically impact both your top and bottom lines over time. You don't necessarily have to spend more money to make your marketing dollars work harder. Customer share marketing gives you a relatively inexpensive way to complement your mass-marketing efforts with one-to-one marketing efforts.

HOW THE WORLD'S LEADING MARKETERS WORK THE LIST

In Chapter 13 "Retaining Customers and Growing Customer Share," you will see how some of the most successful marketers in the world are putting their marketing dollars to work by developing customer share marketing strategies that help retain customers and grow customer share.

Learn how established companies and brands with loyal customers are integrating mass marketing with one-to-one marketing initiatives that increase the amount of business they earn from loyal customers.

13 RETAINING CUSTOMERS AND GROWING CUSTOMER SHARE: BEST PRACTICES

Within a very short period of time, some of the world's leading mass marketers have become some of the world's leading one-to-one marketers. The Web and email have enabled marketers to begin direct conversations with one prospect and customer at a time, complementing the broadcast messages that marketers have been sending through television, radio, and print vehicles for decades.

Campbell Soup now sends more than 3 million permission-granted emails a week, and that number is growing at a rate of between 4 and 6 percent a month. Campbell's is now beginning to effectively work the list. Its feed-the-funnel initiatives, which help the company acquire customers and permission, have begun to reach a critical mass—even when a 1 percent response can create meaningful incremental revenue.

Some marketers have viewed the traditional art of advertising as the primary marketing workhorse responsible for building a brand, generating sales for a brand, and deepening customer relationships. But for the same reason that it is difficult to carry on a memorable conversation during a heavy metal rock concert, marketers must now adopt a more focused, direct, one-to-one conversation with their best prospects and customers in order to cut through the noise of 21st century advertising.

Mass marketers as a group have largely scoffed at the idea of using email as a serious marketing weapon, and at the thought that it could ever become a significant profit contributor. But it doesn't require much of a conversion rate to generate meaningful incremental revenue if you diligently grow your list and deliver only messages that are requested, relevant, and respectful.

For example, if your conversion rate on an emailing to 50,000 permission-granted prospects and customers is 5 percent and offers a $20 product, a single emailing would yield $50,000 in revenue. Viewed as an isolated event, the effort may hardly seem worth it, even though it should certainly yield a profit. But viewed over 1 year, or 5 years, or the lifetime of a customer, the numbers begin to add up.

If the same company that sent 50,000 emails grows its inhouse list to 5 million names, the same 5 percent conversion rate offering a $20 product would yield a tidy $5,000,000 in incremental revenue at a remarkably low cost. It's not difficult, especially if you have a large universe of prospects and customers, to envision the upside.

Over time, as you actively grow your inhouse permission-granted email list, your outbound email efforts will evolve beyond a nice customer service gesture. With patience, your email efforts will evolve into meaningful revenue generators, especially if you adhere to the 3 Rs of customer share marketing. If you get greedy and break from the 3-R-discipline, you will get burned, and getting burned in the online world could mean that millions of prospective customers learn about your practices overnight.

Remember that the purpose of working the list is to enhance and deepen customer relationships so that when you present real sales opportunities to your loyalists, there is a much higher likelihood that the offer will be considered. Because of the relatively low cost of emailing to your own permission-granted list, not every effort needs to be an overt effort to sell product. Resist the temptation of having every message ask for the order.

ONE-TO-ONE CONVERSATIONS WITH A TRUSTED FRIEND

Marketing one-to-one is a centuries-old notion that is returning to vogue in the 21st century. Identifying customers by name, email address, and a handful of characteristics relating to their preferences is increasingly becoming a strategic necessity for businesses all over the world.

This chapter provides a look at how leading marketers are communicating with prospects and customers who have granted them permission to do so. Though the practice of one-to-one, permission-granted marketing is just in its infancy, it's beginning to pick up steam as a relevant and effective complement to mass marketing.

Businesses that move quickly to develop a one-to-one marketing competency with their best prospects and customers can create a competitive advantage in the marketplace. Most times, these efforts will occur without the competition even knowing about it, since your conversations will be one-to-one, and not broadcast over NBC.

As you develop your own customer share marketing programs, keep in mind that you are having a conversation with one friend at a time. Think of how you communicate with your best friends. How bored would you become if they never allowed you to talk, and if, when they talked, it was all about them? The conversation can be civil with no need to yell. There's also no need to talk with them every day. Just because a company might have new CDs to sell doesn't necessarily mean anything to the recipients of an email.

Twentieth century marketers acquired anonymous customers en masse and sold them one product at a time. Twenty-first century marketers will retain known customers one at a time and sell them all of their products.

CUSTOMER SHARE MARKETING: PROACTIVE RETENTION

There are two important elements of customer share marketing that marketers need to think through from the recipients' perspective:

1. *Content:* What do you say? What do they want to hear? What is relevant to them? How do you say it? What is the style or tone? Is it a serious business tone or a homey over-the-backyard-fence tone?
2. *Frequency:* How frequently do you communicate? How often do they want to hear it? Is weekly too frequent and quarterly too infrequent?

Only you can determine what's appropriate for your customers and if it's inappropriate, your customers will tell you. Just because the Web and email afford you the opportunity to send email every day doesn't mean you should. Resist the urge to apply mass-marketing techniques to a type of marketing that requires finesse and moderation rather than frequent brute strength. Talk with customers about what they want to talk about and, even then, resist the urge to bludgeon them with messages just because you can.

Though the term *retention* has been part of the business lexicon for quite some time, many leading marketers are just now beginning to shape proactive retention initiatives. Instead of constantly pushing out further and further, seeking new business from first-time customers, marketers are beginning to craft customer share marketing initiatives that focus on the customers they've worked so hard to find, convince, and sell.

Customer share marketing is every bit as organized, planned, and proactive as market share marketing, with goals, objectives, budgets, schedules, specific campaigns, and most importantly, results that can be measured.

THE DIFFICULTY IN MEASURING CUSTOMER SHARE MARKETING ROI

The ROI metric primarily measures the cost associated with and the revenue generated from specific short-term marketing efforts. It is very difficult to use ROI metrics to measure customer share marketing efforts since (1) permission-granted prospects and customers are acquired over time, not just for individual marketing events, (2) the ever-growing list of names is used in marketing efforts indefinitely, with no cost for the use of the name, and (3) all outbound messages are not always overtly commercial, but used to deepen customer relationships.

Marketers should not be overly concerned with the ROI for customer share marketing efforts. Certainly, there are costs associated with creating and distributing even email messages. But since the cost of the names is $0, it makes it difficult to measure. In some ways, measuring the ROI on customer share marketing initiatives would be like measuring the ROI on a company's telephone usage, capturing the role that the telephone played in the closing of a sale. This is very hard, if not impossible, to do.

How THE WORLD'S LEADING MARKETERS WORK THE LIST

Increasingly, the leading marketers around the world are creating targeted, measurable, and relatively inexpensive conversations with prospects and customers who have requested more information about the types of products and services that they sell. Whether marketers have 50 or 5 billion customers, and whether they sell to consumers or businesses, all marketers have one thing in common—they have something to say to the people who can buy what they sell.

Marketers now have the capability to create one-to-one contextual selling opportunities with customers who have requested them. Learn from some of the most recognizable brands how they are enhancing their customer relationships by complementing their market share marketing initiatives with specific customer share marketing initiatives. Pay close attention to how these marketers use content and frequency to create effective communication, delivering more sales from loyal customers:

RETENTION EMAIL MARKETING

Regular outbound communication to permission-granted prospects and customers through simple text-based email is a very effective means of communicating one-to-one. Remember that you are building a relationship over time with people who have requested information from you. Though rich media is a very effective tool in getting prospects and customers to click through, don't feel as though you must deliver rich-media messages in retention efforts. A simple text message that is relevant to the recipient can be very effective.

Simple text messages also allow you to be a little more flexible in terms of delivering even more customized, customer-specific messages as opposed to send a single e-newsletter to an entire list. Simple text emails to those customers on a wine merchant's list who prefer Chardonnay, for example, require not just a flexible database, but flexible content as well.

Following are examples of how leading marketers are using retention email strategies to grow customer share.

Nordstrom Keeps Customers Informed with Email Marketing. One of the truly great companies with world-class customer service is using email marketing to update customers about the season's new items, latest trends, and events and special offers, online and in-store. Nordstrom, a long-time brick-and-mortar retailer and cataloger, frequently sends out several versions of customer email, including HTML, rich text, and text, as well as in an AOL format. The emails are designed to inform customers and make it easy to click through to check out featured selections on the site, such as women's apparel, men's apparel, shoes, jewelry and accessories, gifts, and sales items.

- *Objectives:* To drive incremental traffic and sales to *www.nordstrom.com*. To provide special offers to Nordstrom's permission-granted email list.
- *Strategy:* To create a series of relevant email promotions, such as the launch of a new tee shirt shop just in time for summer or a July/August sale that celebrates the company's anniversary with a pre-season fall sale.
- *Tactics:* Used the immediacy of email to drive customers and potential customers to the company's Web site. Sent multiple versions of emails to the inhouse permission-granted email list, directing members to *www .nordstrom.com* or to their local Nordstrom store.
- *Analysis:* This is an outstanding use of the Web and email that takes advantage of the speed to produce, speed to deliver, speed to respond qualities of marketing online to narrow the window on promotions. It allows the marketer to accomplish one or more in-season promotions that would not have been practical or cost-effective prior to the Web. The time and cost to produce, deliver, and most importantly, respond has been greatly reduced by the Web and email, and can result in more relevant messages. The Web and email allow marketers to promote products and services for the current season as well as the next season. Nordstrom continues to show that it knows how to treat customers and create a consistently pleasant, customer-centric experience both offline and online.

Capitol Records Uses Viral Email to Drive Record Sales. Capitol Records is using the power of customer share marketing to drive sales of new CD releases. Using viral emailing techniques, Los Angeles-based Capitol helped drive early sales of *Amnesiac* from alternative rock group Radiohead. The email campaign was distributed to nearly 250,000 permission-granted music fans prior to the CD's release and offered a sneak preview of songs on the CD. The effort helped immediately push the CD's "Kid A" single straight to the top of Billboard's Hot 100.

- *Objectives:* To drive early sales of the Radiohead CD *Amnesiac.* To grow the permission-granted lists at both Capitol's Web site, *www.hollywoodandvine.com*, and at the band's Web site, *www.radiohead.com*.
- *Strategy:* To generate pre-release buzz and word-of-mouth and viral promotion around the new release within the group's passionate core audience.
- *Tactics:* Used inhouse permission-granted lists from the group as well as the label to reach nearly 250,000 core Radiohead and modern rock fans prior to the CD's release. Used viral emailing tactics to encourage recipients of the email to forward to friends, engaging the core as recruiters identifying new prospects in the target audience.
- *Analysis:* Here is a great example of how the diligent capturing of permission and personal preferences can help both a musical group and a record label provide early energy around a new release. By capturing music preferences from registered users at Capitol's Web site, the label is able to match segments of its database with the genre of any group or individual artist that it represents—from Radiohead to Judy Garland. The use of retention email is perfect for new product releases, especially in the area of entertainment, and in promoting the new release of intellectual properties such as music, movies and books.

General Motors Promoted New Buick SUV through Retention Email. General Motors Corporation used permission-granted email to promote the arrival of the 2002 Buick Rendezvous sport utility vehicle to an inhouse list of nearly 100,000. GM acquired the names through an earlier sweepstakes that promoted the benefits of the new Rendezvous and awarded the sweepstakes winner a brand new 2002 Rendezvous. The email also included a link to a streaming or downloadable video that promoted the benefits of the new model.

- *Objectives:* To generate interest and sales prior to the availability of the new 2002 Buick Rendezvous SUV.
- *Strategy:* To generate qualified leads for the new Rendezvous by creating a promotion that identified interest in the vehicle as well as captured permission from individuals.
- *Tactics:* Created a two-part promotion that (1) generated a qualified permission-granted list of individuals who demonstrated interest in the new Rendezvous, and (2) served the list with email promoting the benefits of the new model, including streaming video that showed the Rendezvous in action. Part one of the promotion involved a Rendezvous-specific sweepstakes with portal partner *www.msn.com* that helped generate the names.
- *Analysis:* General Motors provides an example of a very well thought-through two-part promotion. It also provides a good example of how to feed the funnel and work the list, demonstrating discipline to keep the initiatives separate. For example, once GM built its list, it did not use the permission-granted email effort to solicit new names of friends or family of the recipients. GM did not include any viral component as part of the campaign, choosing instead to take a more conservative approach to building its permission-granted list one name at a time, receiving permission directly from each consumer.

Johnston & Murphy Used Email to Target Women for Father's Day.
Footwear marketer Johnston & Murphy used email to target women for one of the year's key gift-giving holidays for men: Father's Day. Nashville, Tennessee-based Johnston & Murphy, a division of Genesco Inc., generated a series of email drops using both its inhouse permission-granted list and third-party opt-in lists to drive women to its Web site just prior to the mid-June holiday.

- *Objectives:* To drive near-term sales and to help build and broaden the Johnston & Murphy database with relevant appeals to women and to a younger audience.
- *Strategy:* Reach women just prior to Father's Day, particularly women who influence the clothes-buying habits of the men in their lives. Push this target to the Web site, to Johnston & Murphy's 150 brick-and-mortar retail locations, or to more than 3,000 reseller locations across the United States. Capture information and permission at the company's Web site.
- *Tactics:* Emails were sent to its own inhouse permission-granted list as well as to third party opt-in lists starting 3 weeks prior to Father's Day. Permission-granted list of nearly 50,000 was culled from its own catalog and Web sources, while the opt-in lists were rented from YesMail. A link in the emails directed recipients to a special Father's Day section of the Web site, *www.johnstonmurphy.com*, where prospects and customers could browse through an array of Johnston & Murphy products, such as selected footwear, silk shirts, wallets, key chains, money clips, and other offerings appropriate as Father's Day gifts.
- *Analysis:* Johnston & Murphy is perceived as a brand that primarily appeals to an older, male-oriented audience. This initiative provides a good example of how a company can use email to accomplish several goals: (1) Drive near-term sales, (2) grow a permission-granted list, and (3) begin to change a perception of a brand in a very relevant way. These types of online initiatives are practical and relatively inexpensive, and provide an outstanding complement to more conventional mass-marketing efforts to help a company accomplish its overall sales and marketing goals.

Travelocity.com's Weekly Email Serves up Savings for Customers.
Mega-travel site Travelocity.com serves up frequent emails called Fare Watcher that alert many of its more than 30 million members to great deals on air travel. Travelocity brings relevancy to the individual traveler by offering this outstand-

ing tool that keeps track of changes in airfare to cities that the traveler designates. Travelers are alerted by email when the fare between cities drops by an amount also specified by the member. Publicly owned Travelocity.com was the only pure-play Internet company named in *Business Week's Information Technology 100 in 2000*—a listing of the world's best performing companies.

- *Objectives:* To alert members of savings opportunities on travel for the purpose of engaging customers in Travelocity.com while generating incremental sales.
- *Strategy:* To create a consistent and inexpensive communication vehicle that has the capability of including personalized information on travel savings.
- *Tactics:* Created emails that gather all of the latest deals on air travel and delivered them directly to permission-granted prospects and customers. Linked customers from the email to a specific area within the Travelocity.com Web site and to a variety of different destinations within the Web site at *www.travelocity.com* for fares between cities that members indicated were important to them.
- *Analysis:* Travelocity.com is a database-driven travel marketing and transaction company that was launched in 1996. The Fare Watcher feature was launched in 1997 as a means of providing customers with more control by alerting them to offers that are relevant to their needs and desires. In identifying and anticipating the needs of its customers, Travelocity.com has realized significantly higher booking rates for those who receive the Fare Watcher emails—another good example of how relevance rules in 21st century marketing.

The Economist Used Rich Media Email to Announce Redesign. Weekly business publication *The Economist* used RadicalMail to announce the redesign of the publication to both subscribers and prospective subscribers through the use of inhouse and third-party opt-in lists. This type of interactive email allows for video and audio as well as for a deep level of user tracking and post-campaign analysis. The emails included a link to a streaming video version of the magazine's 60-second television ad as well as a viral element that made it easy for recipients to forward the email to a colleague or friend.

- *Objectives:* To raise awareness within the community of current and prospective subscribers that the physical publication has improved its look with an extensive re-design. To attract new subscribers to the business publication. To expand the magazine's permission-granted email database by capturing registrations at *www .economist.com.*

- *Strategy:* To supplement traditional direct mail and direct response television commercials with rich-media email that links to the magazine's 60-second television commercial via streaming video. Spin a trial offer for four free issues through all media as a way to drive trial and capture new subscribers.

- *Tactics:* Sent rich-media emails to over 800,000 permission-granted names and nearly 100,000 third-party opt-in names. Concurrent direct mail campaign and direct response television advertising carried the same trial offer. The rich-media email included a viral element, encouraging recipients to forward the email to a colleague or friend.

- *Analysis: The Economist* presents a good example of how a company can integrate its various marketing efforts into one consistent campaign, including the opportunity to give costly television commercials a second life through rich-media email. The magazine was also able to track and measure a number of actions taken on the part of the recipients of the email, including measuring the (1) number opened, (2) number of viral emails forwarded, (3) number of new subscribers who took advantage of the trial offer, and (4) the duration of each streaming video viewed. *The Economist* was also able to securely generate subscriptions directly in the body of the email through an SSL-encrypted shopping cart.

Northwest Airlines Served up Rich Email to WorldPerks Members.
Northwest Airlines boosted WorldPerks member traffic at
www.nwa.com by promoting its WorldPerks Mall and Fly
Free Faster promotional campaign with rich-media email. Taking advantage of the technology that delivers electronic messages with high-end sound and flash animation, Northwest
successfully attracted permission-granted members back to its
site in large numbers for the launch of its new Mall. The Mall
offers members special deals, including WorldPerks miles, on a
variety of products and services from partners such as Hilton,
Avis, WorldPerks VISA, Ashford, and Custom-Framed Art.

- *Objectives:* To increase member usage of WorldPerks
  Mall products and services, thus generating more World-
  Perks mileage revenue. To increase participation in the
  Fly Free Faster campaign to help build member loyalty
  to Northwest.
- *Strategy:* To build member awareness of the WorldPerks
  Mall and of the participating partners as well as the Fly
  Free Faster promotion. To make it easy for members to
  take immediate action to visit the Mall to make purchases and also to register for Fly Free Faster.
- *Tactics:* Promoted the WorldPerks Mall and the Fly Free
  Faster program through permission-granted email, highlighting a promotion that could earn customers 10,000
  miles for using five partner companies' products or services within a limited time frame. Participating members
  were also entered in a drawing for a chance to win one
  million WorldPerks miles. To add to the excitement, the
  emails were delivered with rich media, including Flash
  animation and sound.
- *Analysis:* This is a good example of a program that allows members benefits beyond the core product offering
  of the company through partner companies that have
  products and services that are relevant and compatible
  with the lifestyles of WorldPerks members. The program
  also rewards members for using partner companies'
  products and services. This is also a good use of rich

media that sometimes can be overused. There's no doubt that the technology gets attention, in this case garnering a 28 percent click-through rate and contributing to a 244 percent increase in week-over-week site traffic. Combining rich media with the launch of a special members-only program is an effective use of the technology. But remember the analogy of the supermarket's electronic door: Though it catches your attention the first few times you go through it, after a while it becomes invisible.

WB Television Network Tapped Rich Media to Hook Young Viewers. The WB Television Network used rich media as a way to promote its shows to new young viewers, combining the technological ease of viral marketing with the power of word-of-mouth recommendations and endorsements from friends. The WB utilized a smart envelope technology from rich media developer Gizmoz that streams text, images, sound, and motion to the envelope that can sit on a consumer's desktop after downloading. The envelope is updated each day when consumers log on, and includes exclusive programming information and a daily sweepstakes.

- *Objectives:* To grow viewership of all shows on the WB Network. To capture permission from both current viewers and prospective viewers for these and other programs on the WB.
- *Strategy:* To enlist the help of the core, passionate viewers of current programs on the WB to expand the audience base of two of its most popular shows.
- *Tactics:* Used the power of word-of-mouth and the ease and excitement of viral marketing through a rich-media application to drive the popularity and viewership of two of the WB's most popular shows. Displayed the smart envelope on the company's Web site at *www .theWB.com* for viewers to download. Also sent the smart envelope to nearly 1 million consumers on the WB's permission-granted email list, using technology that delivers streaming audio and video directly to a

smart envelope that can sit on a consumer's desktop for daily updates and be easily forwarded to a friend, essentially as a peer endorsement.

■ *Analysis:* Peer endorsement for teens and young adults is a powerful weapon. This rich-media technology provides a good example of how a company, the WB, whose product essentially is rich media, used the technology to expand its core viewership from inside the core out. The combination of these elements can generate extraordinarily high open, click-through, and pass-along rates, especially during the early part of a campaign. Click-through rates in the 30 to 40 percent range are not uncommon.

Hunting and Fishing Gear Maker Cabela's Used Niche Email. A long-time cataloger and retailer of hunting and fishing gear, Cabela's is segmenting its permission-granted list into groups that define the specific interests of the enthusiasts. The Sidney, Nebraska-based marketer used email to target individuals who have identified themselves as interested in hunting and fishing. Individuals are also identified by the type of hunting or fishing that they do. For example, Cabela's is able to promote to enthusiasts of trout fishing all about their favorite sport, including the equipment they need to fish for trout. Emails are also linked back to *www.cabelas.com*, where customers can search for more information or order products. Additionally, the emails can be generated by zip code, allowing Cabela's the ability to push customers into its brick-and-mortar retail outlets.

■ *Objectives:* To generate online sales of its hunting and fishing gear or to enable customers to request a physical catalog for ordering.

■ *Strategy:* To segment the permission-granted list by type of fishing and/or hunting activity in order to be able to serve customers with information by email that is more relevant to the activities that they prefer.

■ *Tactics:* Sent permission-granted email as well as the company's e-newsletter, Cabela's Connection, to customers by vertical interest, such as bass fishing or moose hunting, including information about the activity from experts and about the equipment for that particular specialty. The e-newsletter is also used to push customers into Cabela's brick-and-mortar outlets across the United States.

■ *Analysis:* Cabela's provides a good example of how a company can segment its list by customer preference, making communication much more relevant and effective—very similar to the wine merchant who communicates to customers vertically by specific wine preference. This is a very good application of the 3 Rs of customer share marketing by delivering requested, relevant, and respectful messages electronically. Also, Cabela's current permission-granted email database is made up entirely of customers—consumers who have actually made a purchase. The response rate to its permission-granted efforts has been so impressive that the retailer has resisted adding opt-in prospects to the list, proving once again that if managed correctly, an existing, loyal customer base will act on relevant commercial offers. Cabela's is committed to the customer share marketing principles of generating more from less and to a philosophy that focuses on capturing the lifetime value of a customer.

Olympic Team Sponsor Xerox Tapped USOC's Email List. Xerox Corporation took full advantage of its sponsorship of the 2002 U.S. Olympic Team by accessing the United States Olympic Committee's permission-granted email list that it has been building at *www.usolympicteam.com*, primarily through sign-ups for free memberships in its Gold Medal Pass program. Member benefits in the Gold Medal Pass program include the ability to receive updates on any Olympic sport of the member's choosing. This direct marketing program with Xerox marks the first time that the USOC has shared its permission-granted email list with a sponsor. The USOC has aggressive plans to grow and segment its list on a sport-by-sport basis that could lead to limitless possibilities for outbound promotions to friends of the Olympic movement.

■ *Objectives:* To sell Xerox products directly to members of the USOC's Gold Medal Pass program. To merchandise Xerox's sponsorship of the U.S. Olympic Team by providing a value-added program designed to move product. To create a member-only benefit for registrants.

■ *Strategy:* To take advantage of the USOC's permission-granted database by partnering to offer discounts on Xerox products. This strategy allows the USOC to leverage its database as a new asset that truly delivers a value-added benefit.

■ *Tactics:* Sent nearly 25,000 emails from the USOC, touting a special offer from Xerox. Positioned the partnership with Xerox as a way to bring additional exclusive benefits to members of the Gold Medal Pass program, such as savings on Xerox printers and copiers.

■ *Analysis:* This is a good example of how capturing permission can help create real commercial value, and perhaps even a revenue-generating value, for the USOC. It also demonstrates how one entity can capture permission on behalf of sponsors or advertisers and jointly send out email messages as a partnership that should greatly reduce the chance of an unusually high opt-out rate. It seems clear that the USOC's long-term strategy will ultimately be to test the effectiveness of fundraising by email, especially since it is segmenting its list on a sport-by-sport basis. For Xerox, this would be considered the use of a third-party opt-in list and creates a real opportunity for Xerox to not only generate sales but also to acquire permission directly from prospects and customers in building its own permission-granted list.

RedEnvelope Used Online and Offline Direct Marketing for Mother's Day.
Direct marketing cataloger RedEnvelope of San Francisco, California, attacked the Mother's Day holiday on two fronts—offline with a special Mother's Day catalog that was sent to over 2,000,000 prospects and customers and online with a series of emails to over 400,000 permission-granted names on its in-house list. Positioned as the source for special gift-giving year round, RedEnvelope is targeting the most significant gift-giving

holidays for its promotional pushes, investing the lion's share of its marketing dollars around Valentine's Day, Mother's Day, Father's Day, and December holidays. Its promotions are designed to extend the marketing investment on the part of the cataloger by creating a second level of sell in building a permission-granted list for future communications to prospects and customers by email.

- *Objectives:* To acquire new customers and to drive near-term gift-related sales for Mother's Day. To extend the marketing investment of producing and sending physical catalogs by aggressively building a permission-granted list asset by capturing information and permission from prospects and customers who have not yet provided it.
- *Strategy:* To reach prospects and customers through both offline and online vehicles just prior to Mother's Day—one of the year's top gift-giving holidays.
- *Tactics:* Created a Mother's Day-themed catalog and mailed it to over 2,000,000 names and addresses in its database. Concurrently sent a series of three emails to the over 400,000 permission-granted names in the Red-Envelope database just prior to Mother's Day, intended to drive recipients to *www.RedEnvelope.com* for the purpose of driving short-term e-commerce sales.
- *Analysis:* Though paper and postage costs are nonexistent for marketers using email as the basis of their direct marketing campaigns, paper and postage costs are a reality for catalogers such as RedEnvelope. Though it is hard to predict the long-term health and status of physical catalogs—especially when a high percentage of revenue is tied to them—it's clear that a multichannel approach that includes both targeted physical catalogs as well as an e-commerce site is an important strategy for RedEnvelope.

E-NEWSLETTERS

Relevance is critical if you want your customer share marketing messages to be read. Many of us have opened and read spam that just happened to strike an emotional or special-interest chord for us. This is why it is imperative to pay attention to the feedback that you receive from the prospects and customers who receive your e-newsletter. Your e-newsletter content should fill their needs first, not yours. The capability to track and analyze customer patterns in reading your e-newsletters or in other Web interactions certainly exists, and some marketers are using that information to dynamically adjust content for the next issue of the e-newsletter.

Remember, your e-newsletters must truly serve a purpose or fill a need for your audience. When you do sell product in your e-newsletters, serve up the reference in context rather than as overt appeals for sales. People rarely subscribe to offline magazines that are of no interest to them. There is probably still a curiosity and novelty factor relating to the people who grant permission to receive e-newsletters. After all, they are free. But send a consistent stream of company-centric or irrelevant information to a prospect or customer, and ultimately they will stop reading your efforts. Even if they don't opt out and linger as a name on your list, they've likely tuned you out and simply haven't gone through the sometimes cumbersome process of unsubscribing or opting out.

Though e-newsletters are discussed in this book as a retention-marketing tool, they certainly can be—and are—effectively used when sending email to third-party opt-in lists in acquisition email efforts, or as a sample posted on your Web site for surfers to check out.

Following are examples of how leading marketers are using e-newsletters to grow customer share.

American Express Promotes Customer Travel with AmExcursions E-Newsletter. Customers of American Express can opt in to receive a weekly e-newsletter on travel and entertainment deals. AmExcursions delivers information on select vacation specials, last minute travel deals, international travel, cruises, and dining and entertainment specials for American Express customers. The e-newsletter also features an Island of the Month, and offers a special travel package to that island as well as bonus premiums, such as $100 in American Express Travelers Cheques and other perks. The e-newsletter also helps to cross-sell other American Express products, such as its popular Travelers Cheques.

- *Objectives:* To promote incremental use of the American Express card on selected travel, dining, and entertainment specials for card members.
- *Strategy:* Provide a consistent information source that promotes special deals from American Express and its numerous partner companies, such as airlines, hotels, and car rental agencies, and also promotes a host of dining and entertainment specials.
- *Tactics:* Created a weekly e-newsletter, "AmExcursions," that delivers special deals right to customers' inboxes. Took advantage of email combined with the Web to deliver last-minute travel values that were simply not possible to communicate to customers prior to email and the Web.
- *Analysis:* This is another good example of how email combined with the Web can help to move last minute inventory in the travel industry. Filling seats is the name of the game in travel, and American Express has created a weekly vehicle that can be instantly delivered to the most likely prospects for special travel fares and discounts. The e-newsletter also links to other sections of *www.americanexpress.com*, such as American Express Vacations and American Express Travel & Entertainment.

Orvis Shares a Passion for the Outdoors with its Customers by E-Newsletter. One of the country's oldest direct marketers is using e-newsletters to help inform prospects and customers of special sales opportunities, new product developments, and news tailored to their interests. Charles F. Orvis sent out the company's first catalog in 1856, and nearly 150 years later, the company is using the latest technology to communicate with prospects and customers in its second century of selling outdoor gear. Now "Orvis News" arrives from Manchester, Vermont, electronically each month to offer news of interest, new products, and Web-only specials.

- *Objectives:* To inform Orvis prospects and customers and to generate incremental sales from existing customers.
- *Strategy:* To create a consistent outbound customer communications program on topics and products of interest to subscribers.
- *Tactics:* Created a monthly e-newsletter, "Orvis News," that is tailored to the prospect or customer's particular interest. Subscribers can choose from any of the following options to customize their e-newsletter: fishing, wing shooting, men's clothing, women's clothing, country home furnishings, and travel.
- *Analysis:* This is a good example of serving a niche. Orvis attempts to appeal to the subsegments of its audience through options that tie to Orvis's traditional focus, positioning, and product offering. Also, it is a good example of a company that is not trying to be something that it is not. It has very strong brand, especially within the fishing community and is working hard to serve that core constituency. Orvis uses a double opt-in process for registration for its e-newsletter, both through online registration and via telephone sales. This makes the Orvis e-newsletter recipients an extremely qualified purchasing group. Orvis is another good example of a seasonal retailer that now has the capability to communicate with prospects and customers multiple times in season—something that was just impractical and costly offline. Orvis also respects its subscribers and makes it incredibly easy for them to opt out. With two clicks of the mouse, and without even using the keyboard to type in URLs or other information, subscribers can be taken off the list. This level of customer respect is symptomatic of a company that knows how to manage its customer relationships.

Campbell Soup's "Meal-Mail" E-Newsletter Helps Plan Meals, Sell Soup.
Campbell Soup is offering a free e-newsletter to busy consumers that helps them plan meals by the day or by the week. Consumers can receive their copy of "Meal-mail" daily (Mon-

day through Friday) or weekly (Monday) with a recipe of the day attached. Each recipe of the day involves using one or more Campbell Soup products as part of the recipe. Each "Meal-mail" also includes links to *www.campbellsoup.com*, where customers can view other featured recipes or search for specific recipes based on the ingredients that the customer has on hand.

- *Objectives:* To help busy people plan and prepare meals, and at the same time, encourage them to use more Campbell Soup products in the preparation of their daily meals.
- *Strategy:* To develop a consistent, permission-granted email communication to Campbell Soup customers that provides them with regular ideas for quick and easy meals.
- *Tactics:* Created "Meal-mail," an e-newsletter that delivers a recipe for a meal directly to customers on a daily or weekly basis. Customers can also indicate their preference—for example, meatless, healthy, and 20 Minutes or Less—for recipes that suit their eating habits or those of their family.
- *Analysis:* This is an outstanding example of how a company can be both helpful and enterprising at the same time. Drawing on a database of virtually limitless recipe options, Campbell's "Meal-mail" can suggest meals based on the type of Campbell products or the type of other ingredients, such as meat, chicken or pasta, that consumers have on hand. During parts of any given year, Campbell products can be found in up to 90 percent of all U.S. homes. With more than 500,000 consumers signing up for the program in the first 2 years, it's clear that Campbell's has a winning customer share marketing initiative that truly serves the customer. Over time, this type of practical promotion could help Campbell's generate a great deal of goodwill from its loyal and substantive customer base.

"Dove Dimensions" E-Newsletter Delivers Skin Care Tips, Offers. Unilever, the makers of Dove beauty bars, body wash, and antiperspirant, has been delivering skin-care tips for years through the popular "Dove Dimensions" quarterly print newsletter. Now, the skin-care experts have turned to the Web and email to deliver its free e-magazine to thousands of women, who can personalize their e-magazine according to their own skin type and skin-care concerns. "Dove Dimensions" is published quarterly, delivering product reviews and exclusive online offers on Dove products along with skin-care tips such as how to care for your skin during the winter months and how to create your own private spa.

- *Objectives:* To reinforce Dove's position as the skin-care experts with prospects and customers. Deliver incremental sales based on exclusive online offers to loyal users.
- *Strategy:* Move the popular offline newsletter "Dove Dimensions" to the online environment as a more dynamic e-magazine that delivers the same valued tips and advice, but with the ability to deliver links to a variety of related sites.
- *Tactics:* Offered existing "Dove Dimension" subscribers the opportunity to opt for the online version of the newsletter, migrating away from the physical publication in favor of electronic delivery. This move saves the company money on paper and postage and creates an opportunity to involve readers with a more dynamic electronic publication, making it easier for them to take advantage of special offers. Subscribers have the option to customize their own e-magazine based on their own face and body skin types, as well as on specific skin-care concerns, such as acne, wrinkles, or age spots.
- *Analysis:* This is a very good example of a brand that is using the unique characteristics of the Web and email to deliver much more customized and relevant information based on the customer's personal preferences. Dove upgraded its communication with its best customers by

changing from a one-size-fits-all newsletter format to one that speaks to the skin-care concerns of the individual customer. Moving online was also a cost savings initiative for Dove, due to the enormous success of the offline newsletter, which over time helped build a database of over 6 million names. The growing cost of servicing the offline list with a physical newsletter was becoming prohibitive. The migration of offline subscribers to online subscribers has already resulted in generating more than 500,000 online subscriptions with close to a 70 percent reduction in the cost of delivery. The quandary of migrating an offline list to an online list is a real issue for many marketers, especially those that have historically had success promoting products or services through the mail.

Betty Crocker Cooks up E-Newsletters for Customers. For over 75 years, the name Betty Crocker has been synonymous with trusted cooking advice, and now the Minneapolis-based division of General Mills offers that great advice through its monthly e-newsletter. The e-newsletter provides recipes, tips, and special offers from BettyCrocker.com as well as the option to receive special merchandise offers from the Betty Crocker points catalog. The integration of the e-newsletter with the Web site at *www.bettycrocker.com* also helps drive consumers to its merchandise points catalog which gives customers the opportunity to realize significant savings on all items in the online or print versions of the catalog.

- *Objectives:* To provide tips, information, and offers to those individuals who grant permission to do so through the company's Web site. To drive sales in the online merchandise catalogs as well as to encourage incremental offline sales through participation in the overall General Mills points program.
- *Strategy:* To create a helpful outreach communication program with Betty Crocker's best permission-granted prospects and customers.

■ *Tactics:* Offered a variety of e-newsletter options at *www.bettycrocker.com*, including the Betty Crocker .com e-newsletter, Betty Crocker.com special offers, Bisquick Recipe Club, and a General Mills e-newsletter that provides offers and updates on other General Mills brands such as Cheerios, Yoplait, and Pop Secret.

■ *Analysis:* This is a good example of taking an outstanding brand directly to the people, consistent with the way the brand has been positioned for decades. If General Mills customers were able to redeem points over the Web from its popular offline rewards program, the impact could be eye-popping. Considering the robust participation level that companies like Frito-Lay and Coca-Cola have enjoyed by using the Web for registration purposes in recent promotions, a move to the Web could enable a much higher level of participation in the General Mills points program.

Delta Air Lines Creates SkyMiles E-Newsletters for Members. Members of Delta Air Lines SkyMiles frequent flyer program now have the option of receiving a number of travel-related updates via email, from details about Delta Shuttle offers to information on special fares relating to a member's departure city-of-choice. Members are also able to access their accounts online and check their up-to-date mileage balances. Members signing up for this program agree not to receive future account updates via physical mail.

■ *Objectives:* To sell more airline seats and increase loyalty of SkyMiles members, making them more aware of the myriad travel opportunities related to utilizing their SkyMiles balances as well as special fares on flights departing from and returning to their city of choice.

■ *Strategy:* To create more frequent opportunities to communicate with SkyMiles members regarding the benefits of membership, including discounted airfares relevant to an individual member's departure city. To speed up the communication process in terms of getting relevant information into the hands of members who can put the information to good use. To give customers the choice of receiving electronic or paper communications from Delta Air Lines.

■ *Tactics:* Introduced a two-pronged, online communication program, offering the opportunity to sign up for as many as 12 different email products on a variety of travel-related topics as well as the ability to have 24/7 online access to the member's SkyMiles account and mileage balances instead of relying on monthly paper statements.

■ *Analysis:* This is a great example of a program that is designed to take a big step toward communicating travel specials that members can actually use. A Delta special fare from Philadelphia to Atlanta is unlikely to appeal to a member who lives in Boston. Delivering information on special fares based on the city of departure supplied by the member makes a lot of sense. This win-win program not only greatly speeds up the delivery of more relevant information to members based on their preferences, but also allows Delta to begin to eliminate the delivery of largely irrelevant, terribly slow, and increasingly costly information by mail.

CUSTOMER PROMOTIONS

Marketers historically have spent as much as five times as much to acquire a customer as they do to retain one. A small investment in retention goes a long way toward creating a deeper relationship with customers and encouraging them to spend more with you. Companies are increasingly providing unique benefits to loyal customers, which keeps them coming back for more. Investing a little more money in the people who regularly give money to you in exchange for the products and services that you sell just makes sense.

Customer promotions typically come in the form of one-time specials specifically designed for the people who are most loyal to you. These promotions often focus on a season or holiday and motivate customers to take action based on an exclusive benefit offered only to them.

Following are examples of how leading marketers are using customer promotion strategies to grow customer share.

Hallmark.com Delivered Fresh Cut Flowers for Mother's Day Promotion.

Greetings card giant Hallmark created a special promotion for its customers by offering them the opportunity to send fresh cut flowers to their mothers. Customers utilizing the special offer had the chance to include a free CD from Hallmark Music if the flower delivery occurred by the Thursday prior to Mother's Day. Kansas City-based Hallmark, demonstrated the effectiveness of customer share marketing when the message is requested, relevant, and respectful.

- *Objectives:* To generate incremental sales of Hallmark products prior to one of the most significant card-giving holidays of the year, Mother's Day.
- *Strategy:* To provide an incentive to Hallmark's prospects and offer customers the opportunity to do something special for their mothers on Mother's Day.
- *Tactics:* Since cards and flowers are two of the top purchases for mothers on this special occasion, *www .hallmark.com* combined the two to create maximum appeal to prospects and customers on its inhouse permission-granted list. Hallmark added a third option— a free CD to encourage early ordering—that cross-promoted Hallmark's music division all in the same promotion.
- *Analysis:* Long known for its innovative approach to relationship marketing, Hallmark created a very relevant promotion that not only provided real added value, but also tugged at the heartstrings of the prospects and customers on the company's inhouse permission-granted list just prior to Mother's Day. The promotion was not only profitable for Hallmark, but also resulted in a 167 percent increase over the prior year's Mother's Day promotion. Hallmark once again proves that it knows its customer base and also knows how to motivate those

customers to take action. This is an outstanding example of a company that effectively markets with a high level of customer respect, and gets rewarded in the process.

Road Runner Sports' Customer Promo Sells Endangered Shoes. Road Runner Sports, the San Diego-based running shoe retailer, alerted permission-granted members of its Run America Club of the 112 different running shoes that were being discontinued by the manufacturers. According to the email, the list contained some of the best-performing shoes of all time and urged prospects and customers to check them out on its Web site at *www.roadrunnersports.com* before they were gone forever. The offer was an exclusive from Road Runner Sports and gave member runners—some of whom are very finicky about their shoe selection—an opportunity to buy another pair or two of a favorite brand or style.

- *Objectives:* To alert runners that a number of popular running shoes were being discontinued or replaced by the manufacturer. To move inventory that will soon become obsolete.
- *Strategy:* Contact club members, many of whom are serious competitive runners, with a positive, outbound permission-granted email that serves as a positive, customer service-oriented outreach to club members.
- *Tactics:* Sent a brief first-notice email alert to permission-granted members of its Run America Club—according to its Web site, the largest running club in the world. Included email links directly back to a specially created Endangered Shoes list/page at Road Runner Sports' Web site. Made the promotion an online exclusive.
- *Analysis:* This is a great example of how a smart marketer can turn a negative into a positive. Instead of sending out a company-centric email that attempts to unload soon-to-be-obsolete inventory, the company creates a customer-centric email that positions the outbound communication as yet another benefit of

membership. This promotion also demonstrates Road Runner Sports' depth of understanding of serious runners. They know firsthand that many runners fall in love with a style and inevitably that style is discontinued or replaced. An elegant use of the Web and email, Road Runner Sports lives up to its name and marketing competency as a fleet-footed and agile gazelle.

CUSTOMER REWARDS PROGRAMS

Customer rewards programs have been around for a long time. Rewarding customers in relation to the amount of money they spend with you—a *quid pro quo* approach to marketing—provides an incentive for customers to spend more, and at the same time protects the company from supporting marketing programs that fail to generate incremental revenue. Gone are the days of collecting stamp books and trading them in for largely irrelevant gifts at a redemption center. For decades, the major airlines have rewarded customer loyalty with free air travel to a destination selected by the customer. But the Web has made it easier for any company to create short-term and long-term rewards programs, and even easier for customers to take advantage of them.

The Web has also made it possible to reward all kinds of loyal customers, including teens, who are increasingly spending more time online and who represent the next generation of consumers. Teens have also been the beneficiaries of new and creative payment options, such as prepayment plans and online currency, since most under the age of 18 do not have access to traditional credit cards.

Rewards programs will continue to migrate from the traditional industries that have offered them in the past, such as airlines and credit cards companies. The Web enables many more industries to create and manage rewards programs of all kinds that provide relevant incentives to customers who increase their share of business.

Following are examples of how leading marketers are using customer rewards programs to grow customer share.

Blue Loot: All-Online Rewards Program from American Express Blue.
American Express Blue, the credit card option from American
Express that allows customers to pay off their credit balances
over time, is rewarding its loyal customers with Blue Loot, an
online rewards program. Blue cardholders earn one Blue Loot
point for every dollar spent online or offline using the American Express Blue card. Blue cardholders can redeem their
earned Blue Loot points online for a selection of brand name
products—from gift certificates at J. Crew to an RCA portable
CD/Radio Cassette recorder. The program is designed to encourage use of the Blue card over all others in charging products and services both online and offline.

- *Objectives:* To generate increased usage of Blue from
  American Express.
- *Strategy:* To provide additional incentive for Blue cardholders to use the Blue card when charging products
  and services either online and offline.
- *Tactics:* Created an online rewards program that allows
  cardholders to register, manage their accounts, and redeem their Blue Loot points in an online environment.
  American Express partnered with a wide variety of merchants that accept American Express, either online or
  offline, to offer an exciting selection of national brand
  name products.
- *Analysis:* This is another effective customer rewards
  program from American Express. Tailored to a younger
  target audience, the reward incentives in the Blue Loot
  program definitely skew toward the cool side, with an
  emphasis on music, consumer electronics, and recre-
  ation. The Blue Loot program ties nicely with the Blue
  for Music—a separate Web site designed to appeal to
  music lovers in the Blue cardholder universe. Members
  can listen to streaming music at the site and can qualify
  for deep discounts on selected CDs from VirginMega-
  store when using the Blue card. This program works
  hard to encourage customers to increase their share of
  business with Blue.

Sprite Rewards Loyalty with RocketCash. Loyal customers of Sprite were able to turn that loyalty into RocketCash to spend online for products such as CDs, books, and clothing. Sprite, a brand of the Coca-Cola Company, partnered with online currency company RocketCash, and allowed Sprite customers the opportunity to earn cash every time they purchased a Sprite product. Sprite customers simply registered at *www.sprite.com* and created a RocketCash account. Each time a customer purchased a specially marked bottle of Sprite, he or she could enter the unique 15-digit product code from under the bottle cap to earn RocketCash. Each code number was worth between $.20 and $1.00 in RocketCash that could then be used to purchase products from over 100 online merchants, such as *www.jcrew.com*, *www.nordstrom.com*, and *www.cduniverse.com*.

- *Objectives:* To generate incremental sales of Sprite from its loyal customer base.
- *Strategy:* To allow Sprite customers to earn rewards tied to their purchases of Sprite. Create a rewards program that allows participants the ability to select their own rewards, similar to the airline's frequent flyer programs.
- *Tactics:* Partnered with online currency company RocketCash to develop a rewards program for Sprite customers based on their multiple purchases of bottles of Sprite. The use of RocketCash as the means of currency that was both stored and used online encouraged the wide participation of teens, many of whom do not have the ability to purchase online. Also, utilized permission-granted email during the campaign, including a monthly e-newsletter titled RocketFlash that highlighted the prizes that could be earned, encouraging increased participation.
- *Analysis:* This is a good example of rewarding loyal customers with "cash" so they can determine their own rewards. Some online/offline customer promotions can be clumsy, but this program was very simple for participants. Customers could easily manage their accounts in

one location online and actually see their RocketCash balances as they shopped at participating sites. This type of promotion has the flexibility to change the front-end promotion, while keeping the back-end means of accounting in place. This way, consumers don't have to learn a new means of tracking cash or points earned with each new promotion. The front-end promotion can change, the back-end rewards can change, but the administrative rewards program engine in the middle doesn't have to change. Consumers can rollover points earned during previous promotions.

Membership in MarthaStewart.com Comes with E-Newsletters, Deals. Consumers signing up for membership at *www.marthastewart.com* can learn something new just about every day from the woman who has made living well an art form. Upon registration, members immediately receive 10 percent off any purchase made through Martha By Mail, the site's online store. Members also get full access to daily updated content and special Web-only features; notification by email of special promotions, events, and exclusive discounts; automatic entry into the site's monthly sweepstakes; and a choice of receiving any or all of the following e-newsletters: "Cooking," "Gardening," "Crafts," "Home & Keeping," and "Special Partners' Promotions."

- *Objectives:* To capture the identity of prospects and customers who visit the site and to generate incremental sales by immediately encouraging prospects to become customers through an incentive when registering.
- *Strategy:* Create a means to consistently and relevantly communicate with prospects and customers through permission-granted email. Develop a membership program that offers prospects and customers the opportunity to tailor content to their own desires and needs.
- *Tactics:* Provided a simple and easy-to-use discount for immediate use in the online store to prompt new memberships and increase sales. Develop e-newsletters across a variety of subjects for the purpose of delivering

relevant information and for building vertical buckets that segment consumers by preference, such as gardening, cooking, and decorating.

■ *Analysis:* This is a great example of how the Web can enable a company to subsegment an audience of enthusiasts based on personal likes, then communicate to them in an environment that is tailored to those preferences. Though all are members of *MarthaStewart.com,* each member's interaction with the company is slightly different, making the experience more meaningful for each user. This is a good example of how to work the list, and with 1.9 million members and counting, the list is yielding more and more each day. There are also plans to ultimately deliver a more customized Web site experience based on consumer preferences.

CROSS-SELLING AND UPSELLING

There truly is an art to cross-selling and upselling, and your chances of success are greatly enhanced if you (1) create a core of loyal customers over time, (2) present relevant cross-sell and upsell opportunities in context, and (3) provide a benefit to the customer for up-buying or cross-buying.

There are some automated technologies that serve up related product suggestions when a customer buys online. But at this point, the most effective means of cross-selling and upselling involves human intervention either by telephone through a call center, through live chat on a Web site, or with a sales representative at a bricks-and-mortar location. It is difficult for technology, for example, to lead a conversation that might wander off course before arriving at an unpredictable sales destination. Human intervention is critical, especially by knowledgeable customer representatives who can relevantly lead the conversation to the benefit of both customer and company.

Following are examples of how leading marketers are using cross-selling and upselling strategies to grow customer share.

SAM'S CLUB Increasing Customer Share With Online Ordering. Membership warehouse retailer SAM'S CLUB is increasing its online visits by allowing customers nationwide to order online and pick up the order at one of more than 480 local warehouses. A division of Bentonville, Arkansas-based Wal-Mart Stores, SAM'S CLUB allows its more than 42 million cardholders to use its Click 'n' Pull feature to order from more than 2,500 products at *www.samsclub.com*. The service requires a minimum order of $250. Members can pick up their orders at their local SAM'S CLUB within a 24-hour period.

- *Objectives:* To offer additional value and convenience to the more than 42 million SAM'S CLUB members.
- *Strategy:* To target members who have a need to buy in volume, but are too busy to browse the warehouse. To create a convenient yet profitable way for members to use the Web to place orders.
- *Tactics:* Created the Click 'n' Pull feature on the company's Web site that enables members to place orders from the over 2,500 products that are part of their local club's real-time physical inventory. The order is received locally and is picked and packed within a 24-hour period. Members receive an email from the club when their order is ready to be picked up.
- *Analysis:* This is an outstanding example of how a brick-and-mortar location can use the Web to sell more to its current members. This is also an example of an e-commerce application that results in the transaction taking place in the physical store, even though it is placed over the Web. Requiring the orders to be at least $250 also demonstrates the money-making savvy that helps drive the company. With over 42 million existing customers, even modest participation in the program— for example, 1 percent of the existing member base— would result in 420,000 orders of at least $250 each, or an additional $105,000,000 to SAM'S CLUB without an enormous amount of investment. Though a permission-granted email database of 42 million customers is unrealistic for most companies to build, this example hints

at the power of such a list to deliver meaningful incremental revenue. This type of program was just not possible, from an administrative and cost standpoint, prior to the introduction of the Web and email.

Albertson's Enables E-Shopping in Greater Seattle Area. Supermarket chain Albertson's offers its customers an opportunity to shop and place orders online at more than 30 locations in the Seattle area. Orders that are placed by midnight can be picked up after 12 noon the next day—seven days a week. Boise, Idaho-based Albertson's also offers home or office delivery throughout the greater Seattle and Tacoma market. Currently, home delivery is free on all orders of $60 or more. The initiative is expected to help increase the amount of business from existing Albertson's customers who can essentially browse the shelves online at their convenience, 24 hours a day, seven days a week.

- *Objectives:* To make it easier for customers to shop from home without having to visit a retail location. To encourage incremental sales by essentially putting the supermarket in the home through the Web. To add a service that is increasingly consistent with customers' habits and lifestyles.
- *Strategy:* To create another option for busy consumers through an online shopping experience that reduces the need for customers to visit a brick-and-mortar Albertson's location.
- *Tactics:* Enabled an e-commerce version of the Albertson's brick-and-mortar offering on the Web at *www .albertsons.com.* Enabled all greater-Seattle area locations to offer next day pick-up by customers with no service fee on orders over $60. Generated revenue from a $5.95 service fee for pick-up orders under $60. Additionally, enabled a small number of these stores to provide home delivery, free on orders of $60 or more and $5.95 on orders under $60.
- *Analysis:* Prior to the Web, it was simply too difficult to offer this type of service for customers of supermarkets

like Albertson's. If this test proves successful, look for Albertson's to expand the service to other locations. Another example of how an established offline retailer with an established customer base can cleverly use the Web to (1) add enhanced customer convenience and service to the existing shopping experience, and (2) encourage and enable incremental sales from the loyal customer base.

BUSINESS-TO-BUSINESS

The objectives of B2B retention marketing are no different than those of B2C applications. The same guidelines apply: Send requested, relevant, and respectful messages to businesses that buy from you help to insure a higher percentage of email open rates, click-through rates, and conversion rates. Though the stakes are typically higher in a B2B application, the marketing psychology and tactics are the same—to influence individuals who may need or desire your product or service to purchase it from you.

Following are examples of how leading B2B marketers are using customer share strategies to sell more to their existing business customers.

IBM Uses Emails to Influence Business Customers. Computer and software giant IBM is using both simple text and rich-media email to communicate with its business customers in an effort to educate them on the benefits of its products, such as its new e-server. In one campaign, entitled What's In the Box, about 6,500 IBM Gold Service customers received a rich-media email that also offered an incentive to complete a questionnaire. Customers on IBM's permission-granted list are able to customize their own Web site on an IBM server, making it easier for them to manage their relationship and purchases with Big Blue. When IBM sends customer email, it can include links in the email that connect directly to the customer's Web site at IBM, creating a seamless and elegant means of managing the selling as well as the buying.

- *Objectives:* To drive customers to their own personalized Web site at www.ibm.com/gold/companyname. To increase sales of IBM's e-servers by generating qualified in-person, follow-up sales calls for IBM's sales force.

- *Strategy:* To reach a relatively small number of business executives who are highly influential in the process of selecting and purchasing products such as those in IBM's e-server series.

- *Tactics:* Focused on the company's inhouse, permission-granted list and drove prospects and customers to the company's Web site, *www.ibm.com*, through links in the emails. IBM also used a technology that allows recipients to forward the email to colleagues, making it appear as though the sender was the colleague, and not IBM. This viral technique essentially enlists the help of IBM's current customers to identify and recruit new prospects or key influencers. The database is updated weekly to insure that the most accurate list of permission-granted prospects and customers receive the latest email offering.

- *Analysis:* This work-the-list customer share marketing example from Big Blue allows the company to segment its various universes of prospects and customers into a customer contact database that can be easily managed and easily served with messages that are requested, relevant, and respectful. IBM's email campaigns demonstrate that even the largest of companies can effectively complement its market share marketing tactics with customer share marketing tactics that help educate, upsell, and cross-sell to the loyal customers that it already has.

Ferro Corporation Uses E-Newsletter to Communicate with B2B Customers. Thermoplastic elastomer (TPE) manufacturer Ferro Corporation has determined that a periodic e-newsletter is an effective way to communicate directly to its prospects, customers, sales representatives, and distributors worldwide. Ferro Corporation is a major international producer of performance materials for industry, with operations in 20 countries. Realizing the benefit of direct, one-to-one, permission-granted communication, the Cleveland, Ohio-based Ferro sees the e-newsletter as an effective way to educate both current and prospective customers—some that have never even been visited by a Ferro sales representative.

- *Objectives:* To reduce the sales cycle of its TPEs to the automotive and architectural industries. To expand its reach in promoting to smaller prospective customers that were too expensive to cover through more traditional means, including a direct sales force. To reduce the cost and improve the effectiveness of its marketing efforts to its relatively small universe of prospects and customers.

- *Strategy:* To consistently educate prospects and customers on advancements in the development of rubber-related products, especially its Alcryn MPR product that is used in the automotive and home-building industries. To demonstrate through case studies how other manufacturers are using Ferro rubber compounds in the products that they manufacture.

- *Tactics:* To send e-newsletters directly to 1,500 prospects and customers. To inform recipients of advancements in rubber compounds used in the products that its prospects and customers manufacture. Rent opt-in names from trade publications for future emailings.

- *Analysis:* Ferro provides a good example of how a company with fewer than 2,000 prospective customers can zero in on prospects and deliver its pitch one-to-one. This type of communication on narrow topics, though entirely self-serving to the advertiser, creates an alternative means of promotion to running ads in vertical trade publications. It represents a promotional application that probably would have been too slow and too expensive prior to the Web and email. Also, for companies that exhibit at industry trade shows, the registration of highly targeted prospects through contests, drawings, and other promotions can be a very effective way to trap names, email addresses, and permission.

MARKETING IN THE NEXT ECONOMY

Over the first decade of the 21st century, marketers will struggle to develop the appropriate mix of vehicles that deliver the best return on investment as they learn to integrate the Web and email with traditional advertising vehicles. At least two generations of American marketers never had to deal with understanding the nuances and benefits of a brand new medium that brought with it the need to embrace and understand a new way to communicate with prospects and customers. From 1950 to 1990, the marketing mix for advertisers was pretty much fixed, and it was more a matter of how a marketer used print, radio, television, direct mail, and direct sales forces to generate sales. But, the introduction of the Web in the early 1990s added new complexities associated with marketing disciplines that most marketers were simply unprepared to manage. The understanding and adoption of the science of one-to-one marketing will not be limited to only certain types of companies in the future. The practice of customer share marketing will be a marketing imperative for all successful companies in the next economy.

5

MARKETING IN THE NEXT ECONOMY

■ **CHAPTER 14**   Maximizing the Power of Mass and Direct Marketing

As the overall marketing landscape continues to shift, marketers will continue to be challenged to develop new and effective ways of communicating to multiple generations of consumers, all with very different social habits and attitudes:

- *Baby Boomers,* born between 1946 and 1964, will begin retiring starting in 2011. This generation never knew a world without television.
- *Generation X-ers,* born between 1964 and 1980, the oldest of whom are approaching middle age. This generation never knew a world without the computer.
- *Generation Y-ers,* born between 1980 and 1999, the oldest of whom are entering the workforce. This generation never knew a world without MTV, VCRs, email, and, for the most part, the Web.

What about the offspring of Gen Y-ers? What will Gen Z-ers, many of who will be alive when the United States turns 300 years old, experience that no other generation before them ever has?

How will marketers in the next economy reach this and future generations of consumers who are becoming more and more elusive?

14 MAXIMIZING THE POWER OF MASS AND DIRECT MARKETING

As you are reading this book, it is highly likely that we are in the midst of shifting from one type of economy to another. It seems as though we went from the old economy to the new economy to the information economy overnight. If you are marketing in the economy *du jour,* you are probably successfully treading water as a me-too marketer—following marketing trends instead of leading them.

The truly visionary marketers are always operating in the "next economy"—beyond whatever is currently the vogue economy. The primary element necessary to operate in the next economy is, and always will be, the appropriate use of new customer intelligence. Without it, you will follow. With it, others will follow you onto the customer share battlefield.

In his 2000 letter to Wells Fargo shareowners, president and CEO Dick Kovacevich underscored the importance of leading a business in the next economy with a customer share focus:

> It costs us five times as much to add new customers as it does to keep those we already have. Every 2 percent of customers we keep is equal to cutting costs 10 percent. To grow revenue in double digits every year, we must sell at least one more product to every customer every year. Our customers buy three times more products from our competitors than from us. Our customers will reward us with more of their business when we give them better service.

As Kovacevich suggests, the time for giving lip service to improve management of customer relationships is over. Now is the time to move proactively to keep and grow the amount of business from our most loyal customers, while learning the habits and attitudes of future generations of customers.

REACHING THE HARD-TO-REACH

According to a recent survey of the first college graduates from Gen Y by the Customer Share Group LLC, these newly minted consumers spend nearly twice as much of their free time with noncommercial information and entertainment forms as with commercial forms. The big winners: listening to music and watching movies. The big losers: newspapers and magazines.

The jury is still out on how the habits and attitudes of those in Gen Y will evolve as they enter the workforce, establish a routine, and approach their 30s. But one thing is certain: No other generation in history has grown up with more choices than this one. Their choices for food, clothing, information, entertainment, communication, education, employment, investing, and more seem limitless, but their ability to sort through the tidal wave of marketing messages designed to influence their choices is most definitely limited.

The real challenge for marketers will be first to reach this new generation and then to speak their language. Currently, this generation's members prefer to spend their free time listening to music, watching movies, reading and sending email, chatting and Instant Messaging, talking on the telephone, playing electronic games, and even reading books—all in places where the advertiser is not. Advertisers and their agencies have two choices: (1) Hope that as each successive class of Gen Y-ers graduates from college and migrates into the workforce, their current habits with respect to noncommercial information and entertainment forms will change, or (2) Begin to find effective ways of communicating with them where they spend their time today.

BACK TO THE FUTURE

As technology continues to improve the means and quality of delivering all digitized forms of communication, marketers will continue to learn more and more effective means of applying that technology to more efficiently communicate commercial messages and to better manage customer relationships. The focus for marketers of products and services must now rapidly shift to initiating effective ways of deepening their relationships with prospects and customers.

In many ways, the maturation process of the Web resembles the development of television in the 1940s and 1950s. Like the Web, broadcast television went through an early technology phase that enabled the distribution of signals. But it didn't take long for the enabling technology to give way to the development and distribution of news, sports, and entertainment programming as the driving force behind the medium and the gateway to advertising revenue.

As the emphasis shifted from enabling technology to content development, television took off and became one of the most profitable businesses of the 20th century. Unlike television, though, nobody owns the Internet. Engineers built this channel for the purpose of two-way communication. In contrast, when television was developed, it was designed for the purpose of one-way communication and was basically controlled and owned by three companies—NBC, CBS, and ABC—and its content was determined by a handful of people. Now the Web can be programmed by anyone with a computer and access to the Internet.

Like television, the Web will help businesses grow and thrive. But this time, it won't be advertising alone that contributes to the success of the businesses utilizing the online space. Revenue generated from consumers through e-commerce transactions, subscriptions, memberships, and fees will increasingly become important contributors to the online revenue mix. But those sources represent only the consumer revenue that is captured online. The Web will also play an important role as a facilitator of significant and measurable offline sales.

FACILITATING OFFLINE SALES

So much of the focus in the early days of the Web was on building profitable businesses online rather than using the Web as a marketing tool to drive incremental sales into any and *all* sales channels. This was in large part because the spotlight focused on the significant number of new companies, many of them e-commerce resellers, that had no sales or customers whatsoever at the outset. The overwhelming investment directed their way from both public and private sources commanded the spotlight—and rightly so. However, the spotlight is now squarely focused on the ability of marketers to effectively use the Web to impact sales—online and offline.

It's unlikely that in our lifetime we will ever see online B2C sales even remotely approach offline B2C sales. But for a number of industries and individual businesses, much of the revenue the Web and email enable will never be credited to the Web because it won't be transacted online. These are the marketers who are using the Web as a *facilitator* of sales—driving customers to the Web either to learn more about a product or service (cars and real estate) or for the chance to win prizes or earn points toward the redemption of customer-selected merchandise online. These types of promotions are designed to create repeat sales, usually within a limited timeframe.

From multibillion dollar packaged goods companies to the local wine shop, the Web provides a relatively inexpensive and simple means of motivating customers to take action. For Sprite, that might mean entering a unique product code from under a bottle cap to receive RocketCash that can be used to buy products online. For the local wine shop, it might mean sending an email to customers who have expressed a preference for Chardonnay to let them know that the 1998 Pahlmeyer is in and offering a 15 percent discount on a case. Both of these examples represent powerful, game-changing marketing strategies that the *innovators* are already applying.

When traditional brick-and-mortar companies, such as Frito-Lay, break a retail sales record for a holiday week due in large part to the company's ability to use the Web to encourage repeat purchases, an important marketing shift has occurred, not just for major packaged-goods companies, but for every company that has something to say to the people who buy their products and services.

For companies that use the Web promotionally—big companies and small—it's about cleverly using the Web to generate more business offline from loyal customers. Going forward, it's difficult to imagine any significant marketing campaign that will not involve the Web and permission-granted email.

Look for more companies to deliver electronic coupons via email that can be used at local retail stores. Companies such as Campbell Soup will be able to deliver a recipe that suggests the use of its Cream of Mushroom soup, and at the bottom of the email will be a UPC code that can be printed out and scanned at the local supermarket for a discount on the purchase of Campbell's Cream of Mushroom soup.

A NEW COMPANY ASSET

Companies such as Hallmark, Campbell Soup, and Wyndham Hotels are using the Web and email to nurture the relationships they already have with customers, selling them more cards, more soup, and more hotel rooms—with most of those sales occurring offline. Certainly, online sales are the lifeblood of many companies, but when the book on the early history of the Web is written 25 years from now, it will chronicle how companies and brands with established and loyal customer bases greatly benefited from the medium.

The true impact of the Web as a sales facilitator may ultimately be difficult to measure, not just because of multichannel sales, but because companies involved in customer share marketing are progressively increasing their future marketing might with every passing day and promotion. The one-to-one marketing power of companies engaged in customer share marketing can exponentially grow from one campaign to the next. With each successive promotion, the ability to energize a core constituency via permission-granted email for the next promotion grows. It's not uncommon for nationally branded advertisers to capture over a million new names, email addresses, and permissions during a single promotional campaign. In the process, companies increase the marketing usefulness and value of a relatively new company asset—the permission-granted database.

In the magazine, newspaper, and catalog industries, the database of customers has always been the asset, and is often the most important factor in determining company valuation. The future success of all companies ultimately comes down to how well they manage their customers. Some might say that's always been the case, and that's true. But the difference today is that consumers have heightened expectations of the way they are handled by companies, especially companies with which they have been doing business.

MEETING CUSTOMER EXPECTATIONS

Most often, companies react to problems that are brought to their attention. The overwhelming majority of the major challenges in business revolve around the failure to fulfill on the promise that marketing makes about a product or service. Brand erosion events, such as late deliveries, constantly sending company-centric email, or the failure to respond to inbound email, are just some examples of breaching a promise and failing to meet customer expectations. The failure of companies to proactively match customers' heightened expectations will lead to a silent erosion of brand and customers. In such instances, customers leave and never return, and the company never realizes that it has effectively caused the opposite of customer retention—customer defection. Such a business cancer quietly and slowly damages a company over time, and the cause of the erosion is usually not obvious to management.

The days of company as master and customer as slave are over, and the clock is ticking for those companies that aren't seriously responding to the heightened expectations of the customers that they have invested time and money to acquire. There is some evidence that suggests that the pendulum is beginning to swing back toward improving all customer touch points. Boasting a healthy growth rate over the forecast period, the worldwide customer relationship management (CRM) services market is expected to total over $148 billion by 2005, demonstrating a 5-year Compound Annual Growth Rate (CAGR) of 25.2 percent. This growth rate remains well above that of the overall IT services market, which shows a 2000–2005 CAGR of 12 percent (IDC, Worldwide CRM Services Market Forecast and Analysis, 2000–2005, May 2001). These statistics suggest that we are in the midst of a shift in spending and that the management and handling of customers will play an ever-increasing role in the success or failure of all businesses.

It has taken more than a few years and more than a few failures for marketers to begin to realize two important things about the Web as it exists today:

1. *The users of the Web control it.* They go where they want when they want, often gathering in communities with others who have similar interests. Their use of the Web is most often to fulfill a task, such as checking a fact, planning a trip, or buying a sweater.

2. *It's difficult to get the attention of users through online advertising.* Because the user's interaction with ads on

the Web can be measured, online advertising has been scrutinized like no other advertising in history, and it's that scrutiny that has raised the specter against all forms of advertising. At the outset, advertising's role as a significant revenue stream for some Web sites and an effective means of promoting marketer's products and services was greatly overestimated.

The advent of the Web largely blindsided advertisers, coming out of nowhere as possibly the greatest sales and marketing tool ever—all neatly delivered on a silver platter without any involvement from advertisers, agencies, or media companies. Now, advertisers need to act on the hard lessons learned during the Web's formative years, embracing permission-granted email as an efficient, effective, and logical complement to mass-marketing efforts.

ACQUIRING SHARE, RETAINING SHARE, AND GROWING SHARE

As marketers' experience with the Web matures, they will progressively move along the Web marketing continuum, shown in Figure 14.1, becoming more and more comfortable and adept at communicating with prospects and customers on a one-to-one basis.

On one end of the continuum, some marketers will be stuck in the mud—the *turtles* that are largely content to be using the Web for customer service outreach. On the other end of the continuum, marketers such as Frito-Lay have wings on their feet— the *gazelles* that are beginning to break new marketing ground while delivering impressive and measurable results.

All businesses that have Web sites fall into one of the categories shown in Figure 14.1. Moving from left to right, the Web marketing ability, agility, and speed of businesses increases with each phase, with the most advanced and accomplished Web marketers on the extreme right in Phase V.

PHASE I ACQUIRE SHARE	PHASE II ACQUIRE SHARE	PHASE III ACQUIRE SHARE	PHASE IV RETAIN SHARE	PHASE V GROW SHARE
TURTLE	HIPPO	GORILLA	ZEBRA	GAZELLE

OLD ECONOMY MARKETING   NEXT ECONOMY MARKETING

© 2001 Customer Share Group LLC

FIGURE 14.1
The Customer Share Marketing Continuum.

Where is your company on the customer share marketing continuum?

1. *Turtle:* Moving slowly to adapt to the new technology on the outside, but inside, wishing it would go away so they can return to business as usual. At least now they can tell the Board, "It's official—we have a Web site."

2. *Hippo:* Moving faster than a turtle, but still lacking marketing agility. They communicate with their prospects and customers through online and offline advertising and URL tagging that essentially says "Come visit us at *www.wehavethingstosellyounow.com.*"

3. *Gorilla:* Moving faster than the hippo, but still pretty company-centric. Even though they're sending out email to their prospects and customers, they haven't adapted to looking at their business from their customers' perspective. They're essentially saying, "Give us your email address and we'll send you something that's important to *us.*"

4. *Zebra:* Moving faster now, they've made the shift to more of a customer-centric marketing perspective. They are engaging their customers, learning who they are and what interests them. They are essentially saying to their target audience: "Share your preferences with us and we'll send you something that's important to *you.*"

5. *Gazelle:* They are the fastest animal online. But more than that, they move with elegant grace, finessing

their customer relationships across all touch points. Their intelligent customer-centric use of the Web is helping them impact sales. If they are engaged in e-commerce, they may even be using CRM analytics to better understand their customers' online habits. But whatever they do, they share no customer information with any other company, and they communicate with messages that are requested, relevant, and respectful. They are essentially saying to prospects and customers: If you request information from us, we will send it to you. If we send it to you, it will be relevant to you. We will always respect you as an intelligent human being who has unique—not cookie cutter—habits, attitudes, needs, and desires, and who supports us through your loyal patronage.

There currently aren't many *gazelles* on the Web, but with each passing day, smart marketers are progressing from left to right and some will ultimately get there. It's a matter of time and belief that the Web delivers a new marketing dimension and dynamic that advertisers and agencies need to embrace as meaningful to the overall marketing of a product or service.

Old Economy Marketing versus Next Economy Marketing

Old economy marketing started inside the company and focused on what and when the company wanted to sell what it had to sell. Messages then moved out to the world, predominantly through mass-marketing initiatives that were primarily designed to acquire market share. Next economy marketing starts outside the company, with customers, to learn who they are, literally and figuratively. That intelligence can then be used to craft relevant, one-to-one messages that are delivered directly to prospects and customers with permission.

Marketers can no longer live exclusively in the mass-marketing space. The Web has forced every company to become direct marketers. The *gazelles* have embraced the Web as a tool that enables them to grow customer share through permission-granted email, while the *turtles* complain about all the emails they have to deal with from so many customers. Customer share marketing using permission-granted email is more than just a nice thing to do for customers. It's an effective marketing tool that can greatly impact sales over time—at a fraction of the cost of other forms of marketing. Though delivering world class Customer Share Management (CSM) requires investment, the return is more than worth it.

MOVING BEYOND GOODWILL

Frito-Lay has effectively moved beyond retention, beyond providing simple snack ideas that generate goodwill from customers. It has moved on to generating incremental revenue from customers. It has moved beyond sending emails simply because it's an inexpensive, nice thing to do for customers. It proactively uses the Web as a sales facilitator at the center of a strategy that goes beyond just retaining customers.

Frito-Lay has moved through the five progressive stages of customer share marketing and is actively growing customer share. The folks at Frito-Lay are *gazelles,* fully engaged in customer share marketing and effectively using the Web and working the list to generate incremental sales.

10 MARKETING TRENDS TO WATCH, MORE OR LESS

Looking ahead, as the next economy gains traction, we will undoubtedly see more of some things and less of others in the world of marketing products and services to prospects and customers: From a macro standpoint, over the next 5 years we should see

1. *Fewer resellers.* It will become increasingly difficult to make money, online or offline, selling someone else's product because of limited margins, and the high cost of inventorying hundreds, if not thousands, of products, not to mention the cost of managing—even through sophisticated e-procurement—countless supplier and vendor relationships.

2. *More manufacturers selling their own products.* More companies, such as Timberland, will successfully manage channel conflicts as they engage in e-commerce, marketing directly to customers, selling directly to customers, and distributing directly to customers.

3. *More manufacturers partnering to sell online.* Look for an increase in the number of manufacturers that partner with other manufacturers to sell online. Partnerships such as BMG and Universal's joint online music store will help to overcome the possibility of restricting choice for customers when the selection is limited to one marketer.

4. *Fewer direct mail catalogs.* Look for the number of catalogs to be reduced. It's becoming too expensive to produce and send physical catalogs. As paper and postage costs continue to increase, the number of physical catalogs from established catalogers will decrease, with many of the lost sales migrating to online catalogs.

5. *More marketers will market with permission.* Marketers will increasingly realize that it's just more effective to nurture and grow their own list of permission-granted prospects and customers, and that as the list grows, outbound marketing efforts will increasingly become more and more of a meaningful sales contributor.

6. *More privacy protection.* Unfortunately, it will take more legislation to help curb the blatant use of

unsolicited commercial email and other forms of invasive threats to privacy. Practices such as email harvesting, where sophisticated software can sweep a Web site and capture publicly displayed email addresses for spamming purposes, needs to stop. Also, look for the heightened focus on privacy that the Web has generated to impact and adjust marketing strategies in other channels, such as outbound telemarketing upsells. It should become easier for consumers to opt out of such solicitations that, ironically, are largely initiated by companies with which the consumer is already doing business, such as credit card companies or long-distance services. Unwanted telephone solicitations from companies that have not acquired the permission from the customer to do so will increasingly not be tolerated.

7. *More marketers practicing customer share marketing.* Marketers will increasingly realize that investment in retention efforts results in selling more to the customers they already have. Over time, it will become obvious to marketers that investing more time in managing the customers they already have will pay huge dividends down the road.

8. *More use of captured customer intelligence through eCRM.* Look for an increase in the ability to capture and analyze customer information electronically. The key here, though, will be in how the intelligence is used to market to customers. In the wrong hands, the exploitative use of sensitive data will backfire and erode brand. Smart marketers will find ways to navigate these largely uncharted waters by respecting the customer first, then applying the new insights to outbound marketing efforts or even real-time efforts that could enhance sales. But again, selling in the future will be much more about relevance to the customer, and much less about the desperate selling of products and services to people who don't need or want them. It will still be difficult for software to automate the gathering of all types of helpful customer intelligence.

Look for some companies to use the Web to conduct their own research, perhaps even through focus groups with customers, not just to garner a deeper understanding of what a customer did or did not do, but also why they did or did not do it.

9. *The dramatic evolution of electronic messages.* Over the coming years we will see continued improvements in the quality and capacity in the distribution of all things digital. Film shorts, such as those developed by BMW, will become commonplace as we inch closer to the inevitable sale (or lease) and distribution of all intellectual property over the Web. This represents a sea change opportunity for owners of intellectual property to exponentially increase sales—especially producers of music, and ultimately, first-run movies. This shift will not occur without its fair share of litigation as well as improved technological safeguards to help prevent the illegal distribution of the product.

10. *More invasive advertising.* Unfortunately, advertisers will join with technologists to continue to develop invasive ways of placing commercial messages where consumers will increasingly be spending their time. Look for a backlash when advertisers try to muscle in on consumers' private conversations, such as Instant Messages and online chats. Also, advertisers will increasingly embrace the music and movie industries as a way to market their products, such as through sponsored tours and product placements in movies, both during shooting and in the aftermarket, and by superimposing logos and products onto films distributed at such outlets as Blockbuster Video.

Overall, look for established brands to make dramatic gains, both in their sophisticated use of the medium and in creating meaningful and measurable sales increases. The Web will play an increasingly important role in the launch of brand-line extensions, such as Crest toothpaste's launch of its Whitening Strips, which were presold through Drugstore.com prior to their retail availability in 2001.

MARKETING IN THE NEXT ECONOMY

One of the most significant challenges facing marketers in the next economy will be getting the attention of Generation Y—not to mention their offspring. Already, many in Gen Y have chosen noncommercial entertainment forms as their leisure-time activities of choice over more traditional advertising-supported media. Newspapers, magazines, television, and radio are often passed over in favor of movies, music, electronic-games, cell phones, email, Instant Messaging, and online chats by this multitasking generation of consumers that may engage in two or more of these activities at the same time.

These are the consumers of the future, and the challenge will be in reaching them with any consistent frequency when they are spending less time with commercial forms of information and entertainment. Marketers must now take a hard look at using permission-granted email as one of the most effective means of reaching tomorrow's consumers.

ONE MORE TIME

At a marketing conference recently, someone asked me what I thought would be the key elements for successful marketing in the information economy. I thought for a moment, then replied, "Make certain that you complement your mass-marketing initiatives with one-to-one initiatives that are *requested, relevant,* and *respectful.*"

If you're counting, that's the 87th time I've chanted that mantra in this book. I must think it's important. Of course, that's just my opinion. I'd love to hear yours.

You can email me at the Customer Share Group, *tosenton@customershare.com*. We're open 24/7, and we always respond promptly to our emails.

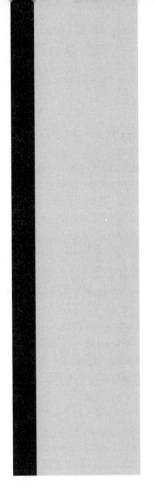

INDEX

8 reasons why you should read the Financial Times for 4 weeks RISK-FREE!

To help you stay current with significant
developments in the world economy ...
and to assist you to make informed business
decisions — the Financial Times brings you:

❶ Fast, meaningful overviews of international affairs ... plus daily briefings on major world news.

❷ Perceptive coverage of economic, business, financial and political developments with special focus on emerging markets.

❸ More international business news than any other publication.

❹ Sophisticated financial analysis and commentary on world market activity plus stock quotes from over 30 countries.

❺ Reports on international companies and a section on global investing.

❻ Specialized pages on management, marketing, advertising and technological innovations from all parts of the world.

❼ Highly valued single-topic special reports (over 200 annually) on countries, industries, investment opportunities, technology and more.

❽ The Saturday Weekend FT section — a globetrotter's guide to leisure-time activities around the world: the arts, fine dining, travel, sports and more.

For Special Offer See Over

FT FINANCIAL TIMES
World business newspaper

The *Financial Times* delivers
a world of business news.

Use the Risk-Free Trial Voucher below!

To stay ahead in today's business world you need to be well-informed on a daily basis. And not just on the national level. You need a news source that closely monitors the entire world of business, and then delivers it in a concise, quick-read format.

With the *Financial Times* you get the major stories from every region of the world. Reports found nowhere else. You get business, management, politics, economics, technology and more.

Now you can try the *Financial Times* for 4 weeks, absolutely risk free. And better yet, if you wish to continue receiving the *Financial Times* you'll get great savings off the regular subscription rate. Just use the voucher below.

4 Week Risk-Free Trial Voucher

Yes! Please send me the *Financial Times* for 4 weeks (Monday through Saturday) Risk-Free, and details of special subscription rates in my country.

Name_____

Company_____

Address_____ ❏ Business or ❏ Home Address

Apt./Suite/Floor _____City _____State/Province_____

Zip/Postal Code_____Country _____

Phone (optional) _____E-mail (optional)_____

Limited time offer good for new subscribers in FT delivery areas only.

To order contact Financial Times Customer Service in your area (mention offer SAB01A).

The Americas: Tel 800-628-8088 Fax 845-566-8220 E-mail: uscirculation@ft.com

Europe: Tel 44 20 7873 4200 Fax 44 20 7873 3428 E-mail: fte.subs@ft.com

Japan: Tel 0120 341-468 Fax 0120 593-146 E-mail: circulation.fttokyo@ft.com

Korea: E-mail: sungho.yang@ft.com

S.E. Asia: Tel 852 2905 5555 Fax 852 2905 5590 E-mail: subseasia@ft.com

FT FINANCIAL TIMES
World business newspaper

www.ft.com

Where to find tomorrow's best business and technology ideas. TODAY.

- Ideas for defining tomorrow's competitive strategies — and executing them.

- Ideas that reflect a profound understanding of today's global business realities.

- Ideas that will help you achieve unprecedented customer and enterprise value.

- Ideas that illuminate the powerful new connections between business and technology.

ONE PUBLISHER.

Financial Times Prentice Hall.

FINANCIAL TIMES
Prentice Hall

WORLD BUSINESS PUBLISHER

AND 3 GREAT WEB SITES:

ft-ph.com

Fast access to all Financial Times Prentice Hall business books currently available.

InformIt.com

Your link to today's top business and technology experts: new content, practical solutions, and the world's best online training.

Business-minds.com

Where the thought leaders of the business world gather to share key ideas, techniques, resources — and inspiration.